GLEN CANYON DAMMED

GLEN CANYON DAMMED

Inventing Lake Powell and the Canyon Country

Jared Farmer

THE UNIVERSITY OF ARIZONA PRESS

TUCSON

First printing

The University of Arizona Press

© 1999 The Arizona Board of Regents

All rights reserved

∞ This book is printed on acid-free, archival-quality paper.

Manufactured in the United States of America

04 03 02 01 00 99 6 5 4 3 2 1

Farmer, Jared, 1974–

Glen Canyon dammed: inventing Lake Powell and the canyon
country/Jared Farmer.

p. cm.

Includes index.

ISBN 0-8165-1992-7 (alk. paper)

ISBN 0-8165-1887-4 (pbk.: alk. paper)

1. Powell, Lake, Region (Utah and Ariz.)—History. 2. Glen
Canyon (Utah and Ariz.)—History. 3. Glen Canyon Dam
(Ariz.)—History. I. Title.

F832.G5 F37 1999   99-6099

627´.8´097913—dc21   CIP

British Library Cataloguing-in-Publication Data
A catalogue record for this book is available from the British
Library.

Publication of this book is made possible in part by the pro-
ceeds of a permanent endowment created with the assistance of
a Challenge Grant from the National Endowment for the Humanities, a federal agency.

To those who would call Utah home

CONTENTS

ILLUSTRATIONS

PREFACE

Glen Canyon is more than just a lake.

—National Park Service leaflet for children

The camera sweeps across slickrock, then falls into a canyon where a desert river runs. There's a man in the water, standing. He's shouting: "Repent! Repent!" The camera zooms in. It's John the Baptist in the Colorado River. "Come near," he says, "and listen to the voice of one crying in the wilderness. Every valley shall be filled, and every mountain and hill shall be brought low, and the rough ways smoothed." It's 1962.

George Stevens, director of *The Greatest Story Ever Told*, wanted a backdrop with biblical feel. He found the perfect location: Glen Canyon in southern Utah. "Not scenery like that of the Holy Land," remarked Charlton Heston, who played the Baptist, "but more as the Holy Land should be, still with the fingerprints of God on it."[1] Only this was temporary grace. Just downstream from the banks of the Jordan, men in hard hats spread thick, glistening concrete on the crest of 710-foot Glen Canyon Dam. It was the greatest story ever made, by the reckoning of the U.S. Bureau of Reclamation, and it was going to be the last. No one would be baptized in this river again. Not after 1963.

Today in southern Utah, you can't really miss the fingerprints of man: paved roads, dirt roads, tracks, and trails. You might shrug off these things; so far—if only so far—this desert of stone absorbs them. You can't, however, try as you might, get around Lake Powell, Glen Canyon's successor, the second largest reservoir in America. It's vastly out of place. Here you are, driving through a sunbaked sandstone hoodooland. Outside the car, beyond the reach of the air conditioner, the wind blows hot and dry. About the time you start craving a drink, you crest a hill, blink, and swear. Does the Sea of Cortez extend this far? No, must be a mirage. No, again, must be Lake Powell.

"Campsite reached by boat through watery canyons, Lake Powell, 8/20/83."
(Photograph by Mark Klett.)

If it were ugly, a wasteland nobody wanted to see, my story would be unambiguously tragic. But in fact, some three million people per year come to Glen Canyon National Recreation Area, and it's easy to see why. Deep blue water, soaring red cliffs. Almost two hundred miles of exceptional waterskiing, not to mention the scores of canyon tributaries to fish and explore. If, like so many Americans, you like lolling in the sun on a boat in a lake within a wild scenic wonderland, well, this is the place. Visitors search for a word that describes Lake Powell; more often than not, they settle on "paradise."

But Glen Canyon Dam wasn't built to provide recreation. It had two original purposes: storing water and making money. It's the "cash register" for the Colorado River Storage Project (CRSP), a system of dams and waterworks authorized by Congress in 1956. This billion-dollar project promised to convert the river's Upper Basin—Colorado, Wyoming, Utah, New Mexico—into a land of prosperity. That promise was realized in a small way at a large price. Hundreds of miles of desert streams, biological lifelines, died by drowning. Native fish populations perished or critically declined. An entire riverine ecosystem transformed due to the up- and downstream effects of dams. Consider the river that flows through Grand Canyon: it's not the real thing. It's the programmed discharge from Glen Canyon Dam. This new Colorado—cold and clear like a mountain stream—has destroyed old habitats and created new ones. The environmental impact of Lake Powell permeates far beyond its slickrock shore.

Then there's the emotional impact. What is paradise for some is Paradise Lost for others. Edward Abbey floated down the Glen in 1959, a once-in-a-lifetime experience that haunted him till death. His novel *The Monkey Wrench Gang* is an extended fantasy on blowing up the dam. In 1981, when the founding members of Earth First! (the "real" Monkey Wrench Gang) went public, they chose the dam at Glen Canyon for their stage. From the lip of the monolith, they unfurled a three-hundred-foot ribbon of black polyethylene tapered at the bottom to resemble a crack. A media stunt, to be sure, but one with deep symbolism. "In the view of conservationists," John McPhee once observed,

> there is something special about dams, something—as conservation problems go—that is disproportionately and metaphysically sinister. The outermost circle of the Devil's world seems to be a moat filled mainly with DDT. Next to it is a moat of burning gasoline. Within that is a ring of pinheads each covered with a million people—and so on past phalanxed bulldozers and bicuspid chain saws into the absolute center of Hell on earth, where stands a dam.
> . . . Possibly the reaction to dams is so violent because rivers are the ultimate metaphors of existence, and dams destroy rivers. Humiliating nature, a dam is evil—placed and solid.[2]

And were there an associated ranking of evil, Glen Canyon Dam would stand near the top. At the "cracking" of the "damn," Edward Abbey made a speech: "Surely no man-made structure in modern American history has been hated so much, by so many, for so long, with such good reason." The reason? Glen Canyon was heartbreakingly splendid—the most beautiful place on earth, some say—and the centerpiece of the most rugged, remote country in the Lower Forty-Eight. That alone, however, doesn't explain the deep religious feeling people have for the Glen. It's so important because it's gone. In death, it has joined the realm of sacred myth: the time before The Flood. Someday, the faithful know, the river will be resurrected

Glen Canyon dam site before blasting began, 1956. (Photograph by Fred S. Finch.)

in its original state of perfection. With moving sincerity, Eliot Porter and others have referred to the Glen as "Lost Eden." Since the "holocaust" of 1963, the canyon has inspired paeans, laments, and diatribes, a remarkable body of literature—the literature of the lost.[3]

Historians, meanwhile, write about the canyon generally in one of three ways. First, there's the local story, which explains who lived by the river, who worked by the river, who floated downstream using what kind of boat, from antiquity to the present. (For an overview, see the "Outline History of Glen Canyon before the Dam" following the main text.) You don't have to be a river runner to enjoy this kind of history. Great rivers attract great personalities, and the Colorado in Glen Canyon was no different.

The second story steps back to consider the canyon's meaning to the American conservation movement. Up until the 1950s, everyone took the Bureau of Reclamation at its word. Dams meant progress. But finally the Bureau crossed the line: as part of the draft CRSP, the federal agency proposed a pair of dams within Dinosaur National Monument. A national coalition formed in opposition. With unparalleled zeal and organization, conservationists lobbied Congress, and eventually, to everyone's surprise, they won. Minus the controversial dams, the legislation for the CRSP passed easily; construction soon began on Glen Canyon Dam. At the time, the preservation of a national monument (and, by implication, the entire park system) overshadowed the loss of some faraway place in southern Utah. By 1963, however, the perspective of conservationists had changed. Out of curiosity, then urgency, thousands had gone to see what was going under, and they couldn't believe their eyes. Glen Canyon Dam became the anti-symbol of the emerging environmental movement, the epitome of human arrogance and destructiveness. It provided the next generation of activists with a warning: know what you're compromising; better yet, don't compromise at all. By winning at Dinosaur, conservationists strengthened their political position. By realizing their loss at Glen Canyon, they strengthened their resolve.[4]

The third story concerns federal reclamation. At the far end of the timeline stands Hoover Dam (1935), a concrete monument with an optimistic message: *The desert can be redeemed.* At the near end stands Glen Canyon Dam (1963), a concrete instrument with an ambiguous message: *The desert can be changed, but at what price?* The Bureau of Reclamation built dams before and after these giants on the Colorado, but its glory days fall between, when the agency had unlimited funding and unlimited purpose. Its motto said it all: "Our Rivers: Total Use for Greater Wealth." Under the direction of the Bureau (or its political competitor, the Army Corps of Engineers), the great rivers of the West—the Columbia, the Missouri, the Colorado, the Rio Grande—became engineered water. Economically, some of the government's big dams made sense. More did not. Ecologically, not a one held water.

Glen Canyon wasn't supposed to be the swan song of the Big Dam Era; the Bureau had more plans. But the era closed. Congress had better pork to fund, and the public, influenced by the wilderness movement of the 1960s, took an increasingly skeptical look at the relationship between dams and progress. Regulations enacted in the 1970s provided activists with legal monkeywrenching means. After Glen Canyon, every big dam would be delayed, if not defeated.

The sequel to this third story traces the gradual evolution of the Bureau of Reclamation from an empire builder to a water conservation agency. In the early 1990s, coming almost full circle, the Department of the Interior (the Bureau's parent agency) proposed to decommission two dams in Washington for salmon run restoration. Congressional funding has been

Workers place concrete on two of the forty-eight blocks composing Glen Canyon Dam, 1963. (Photograph by A. E. Turner.)

slow to arrive, yet scientists and activists can't help thinking ahead: some-day it may be politically feasible to take out medium-sized dams on the Snake River, or even six-hundred-foot Flaming Gorge Dam on the Green River, a CRSP project. In 1996, hoping to force the issue, the Sierra Club began a quixotic campaign to drain the big one, Lake Powell. Dan Beard, former Reclamation chief under Bill Clinton, has called the plan "breath-taking." Others, including some environmentalists, scoff. Glen Canyon Dam is too big, too important to mess with. So people say. Yet even here, the religion of reclamation has quietly been dismantled. The watershed mo-ment came on 26 March 1996, when Interior Secretary Bruce Babbitt pushed a ceremonial control button that began a weeklong maximum wa-ter release. In terms of power production, this artificial flood was money down the tubes. But it didn't matter; the water was let go for a different reason, simple and subversive: the attempted restoration of habitat in down-stream Grand Canyon. In other words, a dam was being used to redeem itself.[5]

These three stories are worthwhile, and they've been told. I take a dif-ferent tack. Frankly, no matter how you tell it, Glen Canyon is gone. That's what gets me. I'm captivated by the loss. Though I see a perpetrator (in a word, politics) and a victim (a place), I dwell most on the affected second parties, those people forced to confront the loss, or, as with my generation, entrusted to remember.

My generational bias is strong. As bad as I feel about Glen Canyon, I cannot sing a dirge. I never knew the place; I came to a world without it. Seeing Lake Powell as a fact of life, I have to ask, What's the use in hating it? I'd rather make peace with the place, though heaven knows it's hard. For some, impossible. Those who knew and loved the Glen have concrete rea-sons for bitterness. I honor these remaining people of the river, and under-stand if they question my purpose. For if I had known the canyon . . .

My fantasy: I'm floating down the river, drifting with the current. Glen Canyon runs about 170 miles, the longest stretch of smooth water on the Colorado's journey through the Colorado Plateau. Every canyon has per-sonality; this one is intimate, animate. My thoughts turn to John Wesley Powell, the first to run the river (in 1869), and the first to make the standard inventory of wonders: rounded cliffs, tapestried walls, hanging gardens. "From which of these features shall we select a name?" he asked. "We de-cide to call it Glen Canyon."[6] Powell understood: this canyon is most re-markable for its side canyons, one after another. Some of these glens meet quick and exquisite dead ends: a pool lined with ferns, or the dry, sculpted chute of a waterfall waiting for rain. Others stray for miles, turning at times so dark and narrow they feel alien. Places like Twilight Canyon, Dungeon Canyon, Labyrinth Canyon. Right now I'm walking up Forbidding, which in fact belies its name. I carry my shoes so I can wet my toes in the streamlet. I stop by a pool, lie on my back, listen to the frogs and wrens. Later, when the canyon forks, I go left, through a section of narrows and perpetual shade. A cool breeze blows. Ahead the canyon widens, deepens, and when I look up I see a rainbow hanging three hundred feet above my head. A rainbow made of rock. Rainbow Bridge.

Before 1963, this was the one mandatory side trip on a Glen Canyon river run; the hike took most of one day. With the dam, the trip remains mandatory, but otherwise nearly everything has changed. Boaters now cruise up the flooded gorge and park within sight of the span. One thing has not changed: it's an amazing place. People often speak of Rainbow Bridge National Monument as one of the Seven Natural Wonders of the World. In fact, it's not on the list—but those who know, know better. Because the history of Rainbow Bridge is wed to Glen Canyon/Lake Powell, it figures largely in this book. More to the point, the bridge occupies an intermediary world between canyon and reservoir, past and present, nostalgia and vision.

If, like a raven, you could rise into the blue, you would see Bridge Canyon as one of a thousand cuts in a mass of red-orange sandstone. This land grows rocks instead of trees. "When speaking of these rocks, we must not conceive of piles of boulders, or heaps of fragments," wrote Powell, "but a whole land of naked rock, with giant forms carved on it: cathedral shaped buttes, towering hundreds or thousands of feet; cliffs that cannot be scaled, and cañon walls that shrink the river into insignificance."[7] This is the canyon country. Though found primarily within southern Utah, this subregion ignores state lines by jutting into western Colorado and northern Arizona. The forested High Plateaus form a definite boundary on the west, as do the stark Book Cliffs on the north. Less obvious is the remainder. Make a line from Grand Junction, Colorado, to Kayenta, Arizona, and from Kayenta to St. George, Utah, for the approximate eastern and southern perimeters. Inside you'll find a maze of canyons and a profusion of slickrock, the area's defining characteristic.

Rise higher into the air—higher than any bird can fly—and you'll discern that the canyon country fits within a larger physiographic region. The

Colorado Plateau, as it's known, centers on southeastern Utah and covers parts of the other Four Corners states. Millions of years ago, this land rose ten to fifteen thousand feet as a block—a gargantuan plateau. Today's fractured topography constitutes the erosional remnants of that ancient uplift, the material that hasn't yet been flushed down the canyons to the river to the sea. The combination of massive sedimentary rock and minimal vegetative cover makes the geologic record of the Colorado Plateau plain to see, and spectacular. This region includes such world-famous attractions as Grand Canyon, Zion, and Monument Valley. In 1985, the United Nations received a petition from Scott Matheson, then governor of Utah, to admit the entire 130,000-square-mile plateau as a World Heritage Site. Nothing came of it, yet the region contains the highest concentration of nature preserves on the planet.

Compared to the entire Colorado Plateau—or any western state—the canyon country looks small. But don't be fooled by maps. This country hides its space: each canyon serves as a micro-world, secluded and singular. If you ironed out the region's wrinkles—canyon after cliff after canyon, plus the scattered island mountains—you'd be left with a plain as wide as Texas.

Deceptive: you wouldn't think people could live here, but for at least eleven thousand years they've tried. The Anasazi lasted the longest—about one millennium. Practically every canyon system shelters relics of these agriculturalists. At their peak, the Anasazi numbered in the tens of thousands. After their out-migration circa A.D. 1300, human use of the region was restricted to small, seminomadic groups of Southern Utes, Southern Paiutes, and later Navajos. Patchy colonization by Mormons occurred in the final third of the nineteenth century. Today, some forty thousand people—Anglos, Utes, Navajos, and others—make their homes in southeastern Utah, an area of 27,400 square miles. That's a population density of 1.5 persons per square mile over an area the size of Massachusetts, Vermont, and New Hampshire (where eight million people live). More remarkably, most of the forty thousand cluster at the edges of the canyon country. The rockbound interior has been forsaken.

People have a hard time describing the canyonlands. It's hard, even for the practiced writer, to avoid the language of brochures: VAST, TIMELESS, BREATHTAKING, MYSTERIOUS. Typically, people end up reciting names of localities—Cathedral Valley, Robber's Roost, and on and on—to suggest the character of the country. More suggestive, if less appreciated, are the

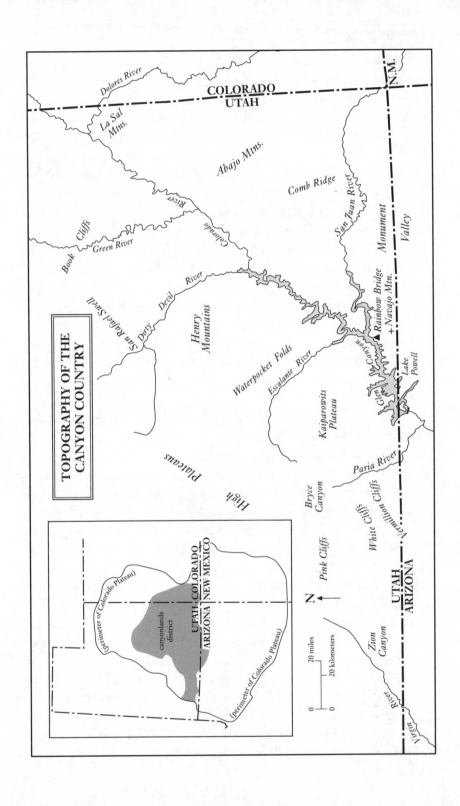

TOPOGRAPHY OF THE CANYON COUNTRY

diverse *regional* names: attempts to capture the essence of the land in a phrase. I'll share some from my files.

Names denote distinctive geomorphic features: *Rim Rock Country, Slickrock Country, Cliffland of the Southwest, Castle Country, Bridgeland.* Or they describe the region's palette: *Land of the Crimson Cliffs, Land of the Painted Cliffs, Rainbow Land, Rainbow Canyon Country, Flaming Canyons, Red Rock Country, Red Ledge Province, Color Country.* Names call attention to the myriad gullies and gorges: *Upside-Down Country, The Inverted Mountains, Canyonlands, Canyon Wonderland, Canyon Country.* They refer to the scale and remoteness of the landscape: *Land of Space and Dreams, Back of Beyond.* Certain monikers evoke the region's "exotic" inhabitants, real or imagined: *Anasazi Land, Arabian Nights Land of America.* Likewise, place names have been translated, adapted, or corrupted from Native American languages: *Land of the Sleeping Rainbow, Land of Room Enough and Time Enough, Standing Up Country, Stone House Land, Rock Rover's Land.* Still more refer to the regional constellation of national parks and monuments: *Painted Parks, Golden Circle, Grand Circle, Great Circle, Magic Circle.* A few designations are state-specific: *Utah's No Man's Land, Utah's Sun Country,* and the oft-heard (and remarkably elastic) *Southern Utah.* Two famous authors have been honored with names: *Zane Grey Country, Abbey's Country.* Finally, toponyms suggest the consecrated—*God's Land, Land of Mystery, Enchanted Wilderness*—and the unholy: *Land that God Forgot.*

For the twenty-first century, I would like to propose a new name: *Unforgotten Land.* Though few actually live here, millions come to visit from all across the globe. Their annual total grows, with no end in sight. People fill the parks, then spill into the backcountry. When Edward Abbey was a ranger in Arches National Monument (now a national park) in the late 1950s, solitude was cheap. His classic memoir, *Desert Solitaire: A Season in the Wilderness* (1968), starts with a provocative description of Moab, Utah: "This is the most beautiful place on earth." Words like that are now clichéd or shamelessly commercial. "Top 10 Unknown Places!" blares another glossy cover.

The modern discovery of the canyon country can be measured in ink. Stop by Back of Beyond Books in Moab and see for yourself. In addition to the complete works of Edward Abbey, the store carries dozens of hiking guides, climbing guides, biking guides, jeeping guides. Most have copyright dates after 1990. Check the other shelves and you'll find an array of "nature books" in German, French, and Japanese. In English, the choices multiply. Seems like every nonfiction writer in the West must pilgrimage to southern Utah. How come? "For once," explains Charles Bowden, "we are not dealing with the world we lost—the virgin forests of the East, the prairies of the Midwest, the short grass and tall grass Great Plains, the vast savannas of California's central valley, well, just about anywhere else in this nation—but with a world that still persists."[8]

For how much longer? That's the question, right?

Every moment in time is a threshold—thus the wonder and terror of life. The canyon country, like everything and everyone, has an undecided future, but that future will depend on its past. In recent history, this land has gone through two general stages of environmental and economic change. One started in the late nineteenth century, when Mormon settlers established towns on the periphery and cattle herds in the interior. In all but the southeast, nomadic use by Native Americans came to an end. With World War II came the next stage, industrialization: uranium mines, coal-fired power plants, paved state highways, I-70, and, especially, Glen Canyon Dam. Concurrently, through the creation of national parks, the canyon country entered public consciousness as a scenic treasure. Out of this, a third, overlapping stage has all but emerged. Its likeliest designation seems to be "industrial tourism" (Abbey's term)—as if modern mass tourism could be anything else.

Trails are being beaten into desert crusts and backcountry canyons. Archaeological sites passed over by looters are being crushed by admirers. Sacred sites are being publicized. National parks are being overwhelmed. Adjacent towns are being colonized, or gentrified, or both. As individual changes go, these may seem small next to five million cubic yards of concrete choking a river. Cumulatively, however, and over the long run, tourism has the power to transform this land as much as Glen Canyon Dam. The potential becomes more impressive—alarming—if you connect future visitation with the future population of surrounding states. "The interior West is no longer a faraway land," writes William Kittredge from Montana. "Our great emptiness is filling with people, and we are experiencing a time of profound transition, which can be thought of as the second colonization."[9] In the last two decades of the twentieth century, this region has grown faster than any other in America. Most of the growth stems from the service and high-tech economies, which have long since surpassed (financially if not politically) the industrial economy of the interior West. The region's major cities—Denver, Albuquerque, Phoenix, Las Vegas, Boise,

Glen Canyon Dam.

Salt Lake—have splayed into metropolises. In the next half century, the population of Utah's Wasatch Front will double and then some. Five million people, predictions say. Of course, as a city grows, so does its edge effect. Already, Utah's scenic hinterland has become coveted real estate. Between 1990 and 1995, western counties with designated wilderness—an item on the checklist for "most liveable" status—absorbed new residents at twice the rate of other counties. Some of these émigrés are yuppies with modems; some are boomers on early retirement—the very first wave. Those not buying at least come to play; outdoor recreation has become the outback's mainstay. Urban, rural, wild: every part of the region is confronting change.

Looking ahead, it's hard to see a future for western wilderness as we know it. By the same token, now is as good a time as any to reimagine the West and the western story in which wilderness usually appears. You know— that old story of people discovering a promised land and exploiting it without any regard for those already there, or those yet to come. Have things really changed? The new service economy, particularly tourism (never mind its sparkling veneer), may pick up the plunder where the old, colonial extractive industries left off. New western immigrants have, it seems, already bought the rights to the umpteenth sequel to *How the West Was Lost*.

I'm hardly the first to make this observation. At the close of the twentieth century, a swell of regionalist writers have self-consciously (perhaps presumptuously) set out to create a new story—a new, deeper "sense of place"—for westerners. "It's easy to be a writer in the West these days," admits Rick Bass. "All writers in the West are spending their days scribbling furiously like mad monks from dawn to dusk and beyond, trying to keep up with the loss, trying to transcribe the rampant falling-apart, trying to weave back with stories the explosive unraveling."[10] It's a paradox: the writers of the New West draw their lifeblood from the very narrative they hope to kill.

I know the feeling. I don't want to write about loss, but how can I not? How can I ignore what I see? Forget the West; for me, it's hard enough to adjust to Utah's new face. Like most Utahns, I hail from the Wasatch Front in the northern tier of my state. Specifically, I grew up in a town-cum-sprawl called Provo. In 1997, Provo's mayor paraded the new state census and the city's new rank as second most populous. He gibed at the frontrunner: "Salt Lake is hardly growing." "Hardly" meant a 7.9 percent growth rate over the first half of the 1990s, compared to Provo's 21.3. "If that margin kept up over a long period of time," the mayor continued, "I could see Provo catching Salt Lake."[11] Exactly. That's my fear. Already, I've watched the invasion of the superstores and minimarts. I've watched the last few orchards felled for the fruits of "planning": homogeneous subdivisions with names like "Deer Haven." It's rare to see deer or snakes or even grasshoppers in my neighborhood anymore. Though I still call it home,

I'm sometimes possessed to forsake the place. I check my runaway compass; it always points the same direction—south.

My discovery of the southland came late, at least by Provo standards. I was in junior high, in a gloom. I'd slough my classes and retreat to the library (where the librarians, bless their souls, kept me a secret). For no obvious reason, I gravitated to the nature section, where I found a book called *Desert Solitaire*. After reading Abbey, I had no choice: I had to see the canyons. I asked my dad to take me to Capitol Reef National Park; he thought it was a good idea. On that camping trip, life made sense again, or at least it didn't hurt. I was too busy experiencing things: the taste of juniper berries in my mouth, the feel of slickrock on my hands. Everything was new and everything was better. I thought I'd found my true home. Each subsequent trip—this became a habit—brought the same euphoria. I lived for it. If I couldn't spend the weekend in the desert, I camped out at the library, surveying books and old maps. Sadly, this preliminary research convinced me I'd arrived too late. The country was in twilight; I'd awakened only to see the afterglow. The big wild places were gone. The most glorious place, Glen Canyon, languished underwater.

Even more discouraging, I could sense the continuing loss. For example, in the decade following my introduction to Capitol Reef, the character of the park changed. Between 1985 and 1995, the number of annual visitors doubled, from approximately 358,000 to 706,000. In response, the National Park Service black-topped the red-dirt Scenic Drive. In and around the park's gateway community, Torrey, developers put up new motels, RV courts, gas stations, gift shops, restaurants. Tacky ranch-style second homes made their appearance—and threatened to multiply. Within the park, canyons I remembered for their solitude seemed crowded.

My love for Capitol Reef hasn't left me, but I have a sinking feeling that this is just the beginning. I worry about tourism. The way I see it, at least three sets of questions demand public debate: (1) Can tourism alone support the economy of the canyon country? Even if it could, is that what people want? Can traditional rural industries such as ranching survive and coexist? Can new, noninvasive forms of industry take root? (2) Environmentally and socially, how disruptive is tourism here? How can we best mitigate the impacts? (3) Is an enterprise based on transience good for people's relationships with each other and with the land? When and how is it good to be a visitor in the canyon country?

I will touch on the first two sets of questions, but only in passing. Mostly I consider the third, treating Glen Canyon as a historical case study in visitation. I want to know: Why have people come to the river and the reservoir? What have they found? What have they taken away? And what have they lost?

This book revisits some losses of the past—the loss of Glen Canyon, the loss of southern Utah's isolation, and a little of my own loss of innocence. When it comes to losing places, I feel I know something, if only by virtue of being from Utah. I've always thought it'd be great someday to be an Old Geezer, sitting in my chair, shaking my head: "Remember when this state was the best place to live? Well, I do!" It worries me, however, that by my late teens I was feeling nostalgic for the way Utah was when I was born. There's no satisfaction being a premature geezer.

Loss of place is common in America, whether it be a backyard forest cut down for condos or an old-growth forest cut down for timber. Of course, one person's loss may be another's gain, or perhaps merely a fact of life. Landscape change can be evaluated in any number of terms. Ecologically and archaeologically, for example, the flooding of Glen Canyon was a disaster. By different criteria, such as aesthetics or recreation, the issue becomes ambiguous. We're faced with a common conundrum: if landscapes always change (and they do), where's the line between good and bad? When does change become loss? To make this determination, people often compare the present to an idealized past. Among environmentalists, it's usually described as "wilderness"; among westerners, it's "the way things were back then." By believing in the ideal, people have something to fight for; they have the moral ground on which to defend the places they love—places worth defending. At the same time, however, romanticizing the past tends to obscure how every landscape is contingent on history and culture. It likewise obscures the possibility that loss may be balanced by gain, as well as the opportunity for restoration.

People have done a lopsided job in addressing the transformation of Glen Canyon, and the American West in general. "What perspective to take?" asks historian Patricia Limerick. "There seem to be two choices, neither of them offering much in the way of tranquility or wisdom: the perspective of complacency and congratulations or the perspective of regret and distress."[12] There are those who exalt Lake Powell as creation, and those who damn it as destruction. The former generally acknowledge no loss, thus denying Glen Canyon any meaningful history; the latter generally commemorate the canyon as a wilderness Eden (another kind of historical denial), and argue that the best way to absolve the loss—short of draining the reservoir—is to protect as much adjacent land as possible as designated wilderness.

I'm somewhere in the middle—or somewhere else entirely. As much as I support the wilderness movement, I'm troubled by its singular focus. What about the mountains that have already been mined, the canyons that have already been flooded? What about all the non-wilderness areas in the West where people live and work, the places they call home? Can westerners cherish what they have as much as the memory of what they've lost?

I want to believe they can. Accordingly, I offer a corrective to the weariest Glen Canyon–Lake Powell dualism: once perfection, now pollution. I want to complicate the picture, showing that the canyon may not have been everything we imagine, and that the reservoir could be more than we've let ourselves admit. In other words, I want to suggest that before we can recover Glen Canyon—if that's indeed what we want—we will have to remember it more completely. And before we can ever crack the dam wide open, we will have to appreciate Lake Powell for what it is—both good and evil, gain and loss.

For this endeavor I find encouragement from an unlikely source: the late Barry Goldwater, longtime Arizona senator, longtime champion of dams, yet also a sensitive photographer of the Southwest and an alumnus of Glen Canyon. Goldwater made a "delightful journey" down the river in 1940. In 1976, looking back, he said,

> Of all the votes I have cast in the 20-odd years I have been in [the Senate], if there is one that stands out above all that I would change if I had the chance, it was a vote I cast to construct Glen Canyon Dam on the Colorado River. [. . .] While Glen Canyon [Dam] has created the most beautiful lake in the world and has brought millions of dollars into my state and the state of Utah, nevertheless, I think of that river as it was when I was a boy. And that is the way I would like to see it again.[13]

Nostalgia? Yes. But there's wisdom here, too.

The Colorado River at Klondike Bar, Glen Canyon, 1962. (Photograph by Philip Hyde.)

PART 1

THE ROAD TO DISCOVERY

ROAD MAP

Robert Marshall, forester, supertramp, and financial force behind the newly created Wilderness Society, had a job for Althea Dobbins of Washington, D.C.: Study all the road maps for the continental United States and look for the big blank spots, the places without tracks. Three months later, in 1936, Dobbins finished her anti–road map and gave it to Marshall, who penned a companion essay. His published text, "Largest Roadless Areas in America," focused on Dobbins's research. In the draft, however, titled "Last Outposts of the Frontier," Marshall took time to discuss the relationship between roads and wilderness. "While wildness cannot be absolutely measured," he wrote, "there is one definite quantitative measure which has an interesting bearing on wildness. This is the acreage of different areas in the United States without any roads." By far the largest acreage—a black blob on Dobbins's map—surrounded Glen Canyon in southern Utah. The "Colorado River roadless section" came to 8.9 million acres, about double the size of the next largest section in the Lower Forty-Eight. (The state of New Jersey, for comparison, takes up 5.6 million acres.) "Of course, the word 'road' is a vague term," Marshall admitted. "One sees old Mormon wagon roads in Utah, and old tote roads in the Adirondacks which seem to have made little change in the character of the country. However, it was our feeling that there was a great difference between some old wagon road and a road over which the passage of mechanized transportation was possible."[1]

Thus, according to one of America's early wilderness advocates, wilderness was someplace cars couldn't go. But where *wouldn't* cars go? In 1989, near the end of the automobile century, Dave Foreman and Howie Wolke, founding members of Earth First!, published a detailed follow-up to Marshall's little-known inventory. "One is struck by what we have lost," they wrote. The best (or worst) example came from Utah, where the largest roadless area was now merely twentieth largest in the continental United States. At 850,000 acres, it amounted to 4 percent of the size of metropolitan Los Angeles. Foreman and Wolke could take a bit of consolation in the fact that southern Utah's roadless lands were effectively bigger than their raw acreage, owing to the tumultuous topography. "Despite the best efforts of the Mormon settlers and the uranium miners, and despite the Bureau of Reclamation ('Wreck-the-Nation') which drowned Glen Canyon in the early 1960s, Utah has some of the wildest, most remote land in the lower 48 states."[2]

In 1976, the Bureau of Land Management (BLM), the agency that manages 42 percent of Utah and the majority of its roadless acreage, received instructions from Congress to inventory its national holdings for areas suitable for designation under the Wilderness Act (1964). To help identify wilderness, the BLM developed three "key factors." One was an "outstanding opportunity" for solitude and/or a "primitive and unconfined type of recreation." The second factor was "naturalness," and the third was size; under normal circumstances, a potential wilderness area had to encompass at least 5,000 contiguous acres of roadless country (compared to Robert Marshall's 500,000-acre minimum). But what exactly does roadless mean? At first, the BLM used as a working definition "the absence of roads which have been improved and maintained by mechanical means to insure relatively regular and continuous use." Hoping to clear up the ambiguous language within this definition, the BLM later added several subdefinitions but conceded that "there will *still* be a wide range of opinions as to what constitutes a 'road.'" Ditto for "naturalness."[3]

With so much subjectivity built into the inventory process, the BLM relied heavily on public opinion—and its unpopular cousin, politics. In Utah, angry environmentalists accused the federal agency of political corruption. How else could they explain the BLM's final wilderness recommendation: 1.9 million acres should be designated out of 3.2 million that qualified. Rebutting these numbers, the Utah Wilderness Coalition, based in Salt Lake City, conducted its own field inventory. The published result, *Wilderness at the Edge: A Citizen Proposal to Protect Utah's Canyons and Deserts* (1990), concluded that the BLM had 5.7 million acres of roadless land in Utah—most of it in the canyon country—and that exactly 5.7 million acres qualified to be wilderness. In 1998, after a citizens' reinventory that paid more attention to Utah's West Desert, that figure was raised to 8.5 million.

Meanwhile, most county officials in southern Utah pushed for zero wilderness. They resented both urban environmentalists and Washington bureaucrats for telling them what their land was for. Yet it is the federal government that legally controls this land, and if Congress and the president choose to designate wilderness, they can. Rural Utahns know this all too well, and when their resentment becomes belligerence, they build roads. On the Fourth of July, 1980, the commissioners of Grand County watched as a flag-bearing bulldozer reopened a dilapidated survey road in Negro Bill Canyon, a Wilderness Study Area. More recently, wilderness opponents and states' rights advocates have championed a Civil War–era law, R.S. 2477, which granted state and local governments the right to construct "highways" over unreserved public lands. Though R.S. 2477 was repealed in 1976, preexisting roads may still be claimed. The problem again is definition. Do historic cattle and wagon trails count as roads? How about the abandoned tracks of prospectors? In 1996, when Interior Secretary Bruce Babbitt tried to initiate a partial reinventory of potential BLM wilderness in Utah, several counties turned their graders loose on "roads" that hadn't been used in years. "Routine maintenance," they said—readily admitting, however, that the wilderness review was on their minds.[4]

Today, Robert Marshall would hardly recognize his Glen Canyon roadless area. The core has been flooded; the periphery has been divided by roads. The former change—the damming of the Glen—may appear to be exceptional, but from the right perspective it becomes one (large) event in a long, connected history of people making changes to the canyon country. Within this history, twentieth-century road work figures most prominently. For both residents of and visitors to the canyonlands, access, or the lack of it, means everything. Automobile roads tie together the major issues in contemporary southern Utah—environmentalism, tourism, and economic development. Meandering in and around Glen Canyon, these roads convey an important message: when people try to realize their visions of the land, the result is not often what they expect.

HOLE IN THE ROCK

A highway sign greets westbound drivers on Utah State Highway 24 near Capitol Reef National Park. The sign is blue, meaning it relates to recreation: "Scenic views next 14 miles." It's a message for tourists, of course. And for tourists, it's easy to agree: this land was meant to be viewed, to be enjoyed. It's easy to forget that tourism—a specific form of consumer enjoyment—is relatively new to southern Utah. Its ascendance, an outcome of the automobile age, has occurred while traditional local industries—ranching, and to a lesser extent farming, logging, and mining—have declined. The pace of this economic change has been impressive: it took but one century to go from "trackless wilderness" to "scenic byway." The first Euro-American settlers, the Mormons, probably could not have foreseen it.

Soon after locating to the Salt Lake Valley in 1847, the Mormon church began its geographic expansion. Brigham Young, the prophet, envisioned a string of settlements from the Rocky Mountains to the Pacific Ocean. By the 1850s, this "Mormon Corridor" had reached the southwestern tip of the present state of Utah, an area called Dixie for its warm climate. From Salt Lake to Dixie, the road was rough but straightforward: it followed the continuous line of mountains and plateaus that form the backbone of the state. To the east and beyond, however, travel proved more difficult, and Mormon settlement followed a different pattern: towns generally started through the initiative of individuals rather than the church.

One famous exception is Bluff, Utah, the result of the San Juan Mission. In 1879, dozens of families from southwestern Utah, mostly Iron County, received a "call" from church authorities to settle an as-yet-unidentified location near the San Juan River in southeastern Utah. This remote country was still a refuge for Utes, Paiutes, and Navajos. Through colonization, the Mormon church hoped to befriend (better yet, convert) the Indians while shoring up the Mormon empire in the Intermountain West. The San Juan River lay nearly due east of Iron County, but the only established routes required huge detours to the north (via the Old Spanish Trail) or to the south (through Navajo territory). Relying on faith and misinformation, the 230 members of the San Juan Mission chose instead the "direct" route—through the heart of the canyonlands. They had already passed the final town, Escalante, when a scouting party returned with the bad news: the *best* way to reach the Colorado River in Glen Canyon was through a *crack*—too narrow for a wagon, not much wider than a man. This crack led to a near-vertical drop of forty-five feet, beneath which was a second drop-off and finally a gully that dropped about a thousand feet in three-quarters of a mile. And the land across the river was, unbelievably, even more godforsaken. "You want us to tell you what kind of a country this is, but I don't know how," Elizabeth Decker wrote her parents. "It's the roughest country you or anybody else ever seen; it's nothing in the

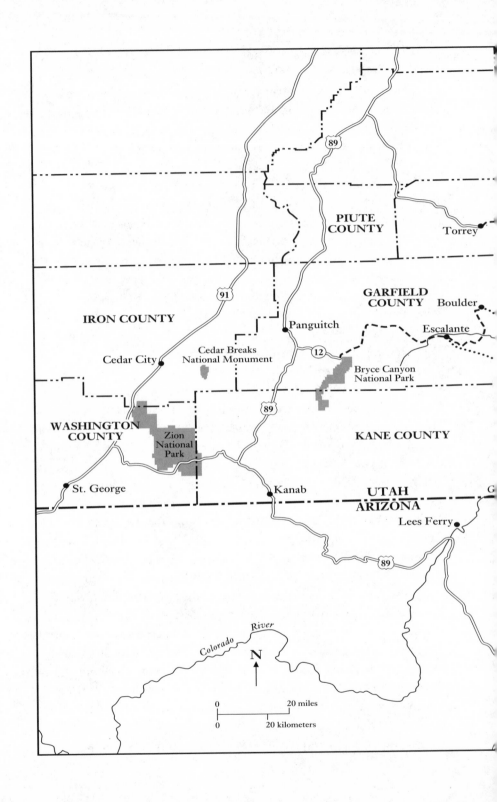

PIUTE
COUNTY

Torrey

91

GARFIELD
COUNTY   Boulder

IRON COUNTY

Panguitch   Escalante

Cedar Breaks
National Monument   12

Cedar City   Bryce Canyon
                                              National Park

89

WASHINGTON
COUNTY   Zion   KANE COUNTY
              National
              Park

St. George   Kanab   UTAH   G
                                     ARIZONA

                                              Lees Ferry

                                     89

Colorado River

N

0   20 miles

0   20 kilometers

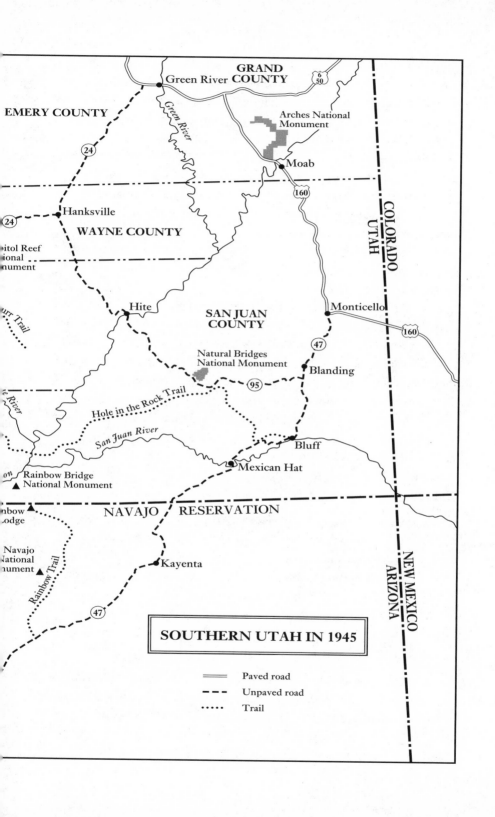

SOUTHERN UTAH IN 1945

Paved road
Unpaved road
Trail

world but rocks and holes, hills and hollows. The mountains are just one solid rock as smooth as an apple. Dixie is a good road to the side of this."[5]

Confronted with such an appalling spectacle, anyone else would have turned around. But not these Mormons. They said some prayers, cast a vote (unanimous), and sent back a request for some blasting powder. In the meantime, they assaulted the crack with picks and hammers. They called it Hole in the Rock. "I don't think I ever seen a lot of men go to work with more of a will to do something than that crowd did," remembered one. "We were all young men; the way we did make dirt and rock fly was a caution." But the hardest job—the initial cliff—remained. When the powder arrived, volunteers were lowered over the precipice on ropes, where, dangling in the subfreezing January air, they chiseled holes and placed the charges by hand. It took weeks.[6]

To avoid the second drop-off and to conserve the precious black powder, Benjamin Perkins, a former coal miner from Great Britain, developed the audacious idea of a hanging road. To begin, workers picked a shelf into the rock wall wide enough for the inside wheels of a wagon. Below this, they drilled a parallel line of holes, ten inches deep, two and a half inches wide, and one and a half feet apart. Then, having scoured the area for oaks, they planted stakes in the holes, laid poles across them, and filled the gaps with brush and debris. Thus this twenty-five-foot section of road ("Uncle Ben's Dugway") was literally tacked onto the cliff.

Below the dugway, the road was straightforward: straight down. As Decker wrote from the trail:

> Coming down the hole in the rock to get to the river was ten times as bad [as crossing the river]. If you ever come this way it will scare you to death to look down it. . . . The first wagon I saw go down they put the brake on and rough locked the hind wheels and had a big rope fastened to the wagon and about ten men holding back on it and then they went down like they would smash everything. I'll never forget that day. When we was walking down Willie [her son] looked back and cried and asked me how we would get back home.

Remarkably, every wagon made it down and across in one piece. After crossing the Colorado River piecemeal on an oar-powered ferry barge, the party went on, day after day, blasting, clearing, singing. "No pioneer company ever built a wagon road through wilder, rougher, more inhospitable country," a historian later wrote. This fact wasn't lost on the Hole in the

View of Hole in the Rock, 1967. Note Lake Powell at bottom. (Photograph by Mel Davis.)

Rock expedition. They sensed they were making history; they believed they were doing the Lord's work. But the trek took its toll. When they arrived at the San Juan River in April 1880, the pioneers were months behind schedule, and tired beyond reason. Only eighteen miles of blessed flatland separated them from the intended site, yet they stopped in their tracks and started the town of Bluff.[7]

Most canyon-country settlements, like Bluff, date to the period after Brigham Young; the "Great Colonizer" died in 1877. These towns came relatively late because no one since the Anasazi had managed—or even tried—to settle this land. More Mormon settlements failed for environmental reasons on the Colorado Plateau than in any other region. In the towns that survived the droughts and the floods, pioneer descendants took great pride that their ancestors made homes where other Mormons, people famous for their gumption, would have given up. Not surprisingly, the descendants of the San Juan Mission typically assumed top positions in the social hierarchy of San Juan County. For many people in southeastern Utah, the story of Hole in the Rock served the same function as the story of the Mormon exodus to the West. It was an inspiration and a reference point. They could survive because their ancestors had survived the worst.[8]

Life in a town like Bluff or Hanksville or Escalante meant isolation and occasional privation. People often worked multiple odd jobs and survived stretches without work. Most ran a few cattle on the side. Wealth was not the point. As a rule, small-town Mormons only wanted enough to keep their children in their homeland, to keep alive the connections of family, community, labor, and land. They thought of money in terms of resources— animals, crops, timber. Yet one of their greatest sources of potential wealth would prove to be intangible: scenic beauty.

FIX THE ROADS, THE TOURISTS ARE COMING!

In the most basic economic terms, nature tourism requires a consumer (the tourist), a commodity (scenery), and a transportation link between them. In America, that link was originally the railroad. By the 1880s, railroad companies were offering western scenic trips to the middle class, for whom hiking and tent camping were becoming popular activities. It took the automobile, however, to fully "democratize" (commodify) outdoor recreation. In 1910, Americans owned 458,000 cars; that figure jumped to 23 million in the next two decades. In response, the federal government and private entrepreneurs rushed to provide roads and roadside improvements. In many parts of the country, tourism entered a new era of spectacular growth. But in southern Utah, the infrastructure for tourism was nonexistent at the advent of the automobile age. Due to the region's remoteness from centers of population and capital, outdoor recreation had to play catch-up. Moreover, local residents had to learn to market the beauty around them. Their primer was Zion National Park.[9]

Zion Canyon of the Virgin River is located at the edge of the Colorado Plateau near Utah's Dixie. Zion belongs to the Grand Staircase, a geologic district that overlaps the canyon country geographic district. True to its name, the Grand Staircase consists of a series of cliffs and terraces that descend from the 11,000-foot Markagunt Plateau to the Colorado River in Grand Canyon. Marvelous gashes such as Zion expose the slickrock that underlies the terraces, but the Grand Staircase as a whole lacks the sweep of naked stone that defines the core section of the canyon country in southeastern Utah. Comparatively speaking, the Grand Staircase is easy to get across, almost hospitable.

Though explorers repeatedly passed near Zion Canyon, none apparently entered before Nephi Johnson, a Mormon scout, in 1858. By this time, Mormons had begun to settle the lowlands of the Virgin River and were looking to expand their fields of cotton. With the help of a local Paiute, Johnson made a reconnaissance of the upper valley of the Virgin, then continued upstream to Zion. He returned with favorable news about the upper valley, and work soon began on a road. Johnson's Twist, as it was called, eventually led to the mouth of the big canyon, where two towns, Springdale and Shunesburg, sprang up in the 1860s. Later on, a few Mormon families moved into the canyon proper to farm and ranch. They called the place Little Zion.

Among the first non-Mormon visitors was Major John Wesley Powell. In 1872, on a break from his second expedition down the Colorado River, Powell descended sinuous Parunuweap Canyon (of the East Fork of the Virgin River) to its junction with Mukuntuweap Canyon, the Paiute name for Little Zion. Curiously, Powell said little about the place in his report. It was left to Clarence Dutton, a subsequent member of the Powell Survey, to paint a description. In 1882, sounding more like a promoter than a geologist, he wrote, "In coming time [Zion] will, I believe, take rank with a very small number of spectacles each of which will, in its own way, be regarded as the most exquisite of its kind which the world discloses." Dutton was corroborated in 1904, when another associate of Major Powell, the popular explorer and writer Frederick Dellenbaugh, wrote a lead article for the celebrated *Scribner's Magazine*. Through full-page photographs and detailed prose, readers learned about a "valley practically unknown to the outer world, yet rivaling in beauty and grandeur even the Yosemite, the Yellowstone, and perhaps the Grand Canyon." Dellenbaugh also made some oil paintings which went on display at Utah's booth at the World's Exhibition in St. Louis. Zion was hitting the big time.[10]

The owner of the land, the federal government, suddenly took more interest. It ordered a survey. In 1908, surveyor Leo Snow of St. George submitted his report with the opinion, "This canyon should be set aside as a national park." Just weeks later, the acting secretary of the interior drafted a proclamation for the president, and on 31 July 1909, under the power of the Antiquities Act, William Howard Taft created Mukuntuweap National Monument.[11]

In the short term, the designation had no effect but to exclude the land from mining and homesteading. Ignorant of the long-term changes in store, Mormon settlers continued to grow cantaloupes and graze cattle in the canyon. "The Zion area was not set aside as a Monument because of any local agitation," remembered one area resident. "Local people were entirely unconscious of the scenic possibilities of the area." That's different, it should be said, from being unconscious to beauty. Local Mormons didn't call the place Little Zion for nothing. They just couldn't conceive of making money out of rocks. Up north in the capital city, however, people were talking. Since the completion of the Salt Lake–Los Angeles railroad in 1905, prominent Utahns had pushed the idea of mass tourism. In fact, the slogan "See America First," made famous in the 1920s, originated at a tourism conference in Salt Lake City in 1906. The conference host, the Commercial Club of Salt Lake, had begun to sponsor "expeditions" to locate and advertise scenic spots in southern Utah and northern Arizona. In 1911, club member Wesley King went to Mukuntuweap for an appraisal. He and his wife returned from the buggy trip "speechless with wonderment" but aching from the ruts and bumps. "Washington and Iron counties have great natural resources and wonderful possibilities which will blossom into realities only when the transportation problem has been solved," King wrote.[12]

The good-roads movement gained an influential sponsor in 1913, when the governor, William Spry, visited Zion. The following year, some local support finally materialized with the establishment of the Grand Canyon Highway Association. Another boost came from Washington, where Utah Senator Reed Smoot secured a fifteen-thousand-dollar appropriation for a Zion Canyon access road in 1916. Smoot's timing was perfect: during the same session, Congress provided the first federal funding for automobile roads and created the National Park Service. Soon after, the new agency's acting director, Horace Albright, made a visit to Mukuntuweap via the brand-new automobile road. He decided right then that the monument, if not its multisyllabic name, was worthy of national park status. Since a park deserved something better than a dirt road, Albright approached Utah's new governor, Simon Bamberger, who purportedly replied, "I build no more roads to rocks!"[13] Nonetheless, Albright got his other wish: Mukuntuweap National Monument graduated to Zion National Park in 1919. Soon people were raving about Utah's "Yosemite in Oils."

For state tourism boosters, here was another lesson in the advantages of working with the federal government. Not only could you get free money, you could get free publicity. National parks and monuments meant instant recognition—and subsequent tourist dividends. So why stop with Zion? In 1919, trying to take advantage of the moment, the state legislature sent a joint memorial to Washington proposing "Temple of the Gods National Monument." Today, everyone knows it as Bryce Canyon.

Technically, Bryce isn't a canyon at all but a series of steep-walled amphitheaters forming the eastern escarpment of the Paunsaugunt Plateau. Hosts of colorful sculptures inhabit each amphitheater. Bryce comprises one section of the Pink Cliffs, the summit of the Grand Staircase. The White Cliffs, Zion's layer, runs two steps below. In history, like geology, Bryce Canyon parallels Zion Canyon, following this general chronology: intermittent use by Native Americans; accolades from a few forgotten nineteenth-century government surveyors; utilization by Mormons (to quote the famous words of Ebenezer Bryce, "a hell of a place to lose a cow"); "discovery" by outsiders driving automobiles; publicity in magazines and newspapers; and then attention from movers and shakers in Salt Lake and Washington. Here again, few locals initially worked to develop the scenic resources. Lack of interest? Perhaps—but also lack of time. According to one local history, "Our grandparents were thrilled with [Bryce Canyon's] beauty and often referred to it as beautiful 'Potato Valley Mountains.' . . . But they could do little about it. They were too busy trying to make a livelihood for their families. There were no roads, just poor trails, their wagons and wagon wheels were worn out, their horses or ox teams were poor and unable to make any trips, save for the bare necessities." In 1916, Ruby and Minnie Syrett homesteaded a few miles from the rim of Bryce Canyon. "Apparently, the Syretts lived at the Bryce ranch for six weeks before a [neighboring] rancher, Claude Sudweeks, introduced them to the rim: 'They were speechless, just stood and looked. When they could talk, they could only whisper.'"[14]

In time, as more people became aware of the Pink Cliffs, the Syretts found themselves accommodating guests. Taking advantage of the unexpected, the family built the Tourists' Rest lodge. After achieving some success, the Syretts sold the operation to the Union Pacific Railroad in 1923, the year Bryce Canyon became Bryce Canyon National Monument. To manage the lodge and similar facilities at Zion and the North Rim of Grand Canyon, the railroad formed a subsidiary, the Utah Parks Company. A new spur line led to Cedar City, Utah, home of the company-owned El Escalante Hotel. From there, buses left daily for a "Celestial Circuit" of the "Painted Parks," descriptive phrases used in a series of national advertising campaigns. Without question, Union Pacific did more than anyone else to promote tourism in southwestern Utah in the 1920s and 1930s. Second place went to the federal government. During the same era, the feds paid for two important additions to the region's transportation infrastructure: Navajo Bridge (across the Colorado River in northern Arizona) and the Zion–Mount Carmel Tunnel. Upon their completion in 1929 and 1930, respectively, Utah was connected to Arizona, and Bryce to Zion.

During 1943–45, the Utah Parks Company shut down for World War II. It reopened to a different world: "The automobile was king. Soon both train service to Cedar City and connecting bus service to the parks were abandoned."[15] In fact, as early as 1926, cars had surpassed all other forms of traffic to Zion, Bryce, and Grand Canyon. Here the infrastructure for mass tourism was mostly in place by 1930, but then the Depression and the war intervened. Afterward, for better or for worse, southwestern Utah would become a famous scenic drive-in.

While it's useful to look at tourism in southwestern Utah as a precursor to tourism in southeastern Utah, there's a crucial difference: remoteness. Merely compare Zion, Utah's second park unit, with its first, Natural Bridges National Monument. Both were far from the centers of civilization but not by the same factor. People *lived* in Zion Canyon, after all. In contrast, White Canyon, home of three stone bridges, lay thirty air-miles from the nearest town, Blanding, with warped terrain between. Though well known among archaeologists and pothunters by the 1890s, this region didn't show up on tourist maps until the "Colossal Bridges of Utah" received their first national publicity in 1904 (some twenty years after their "discovery"). Soon after, the Commercial Club of Salt Lake sent a pack train expedition to White Canyon. In 1907, a report of the trip appeared in the *National Geographic;* the magazine called on the government to preserve the area as a park, "so that roads may be opened and these greatest of the world's natural bridges can be made accessible."[16]

Somebody in the government was listening, for Teddy Roosevelt created Natural Bridges National Monument the next year. Not until 1916, however, with the creation of the National Park Service, did the monument receive any administrative supervision. The agency determined that one custodian—something less than a park ranger—would more than fill the needs of this remote monument. Luckily, there was a waiting candidate, Zeke Johnson; in fact, he petitioned insistently for the job.

Zeke Johnson was born in southwestern Utah in 1869, the son of Joel Johnson, one of Joseph Smith's early converts. Originally from Massachusetts, Joel made the trek to Utah, entered into polygamy, and helped settle Parowan. He and his immense family later moved to Kanab, where he died an octogenarian in 1882. Four wives, 29 children, 127 grandchildren, and 54 great-grandchildren survived him. The youngest child was not yet one. Joel's third wife, Margaret, Zeke's mother, was left "practically destitute" with seven children. Out of necessity, Zeke became the wage earner. All of thirteen, he ran the mail route from Kanab to Dixie via Zion Canyon and later worked as a cowboy.[17]

Zeke married at nineteen and tried an array of occupations, including gold mining on the San Juan River near Bluff. After his marriage fell apart, he courted a Bluff girl, Annetta Nielson, the daughter of Hole in the Rock pioneers. Annetta re-converted Zeke, a lapsed Mormon, and they married in the Salt Lake Temple in 1900. Soon after, as a measure of his devotion, he spent two very lonely years as a missionary in the Pacific Northwest. Upon his return in 1905, he and Annetta moved to Blanding, where Zeke resumed his work for the Bluff Co-op, a Mormon ranch operation. During his years chasing cattle, Johnson memorized the lay of the land, gaining knowledge that permitted him to enter his next occupation: guiding. Johnson's business card read, "I take you where you want to go." His own favorite place was the natural bridges of White Canyon, which he first saw in 1908. "I was just thrilled," he recalled, "and resolved that I would be their protector." For the next two decades, Zeke personally led the majority of visitors to these natural wonders, otherwise known as "Zeke Johnson's bridges."[18]

After his inevitable appointment as custodian, Johnson singlehandedly built hiking trails between the bridges. He even applied his small government stipend toward trail work. It was a labor of love. He never missed a chance to promote San Juan County, his home, and especially the monument, which he yearned to make accessible to automobiles. He agreed wholeheartedly with the slogan of the Bluff Commercial Club: "Fix the roads—the tourists are coming!" He would have built a road by himself; he had the determination, if not the resources.

In 1920, volunteers from Blanding, with the cooperation of the Forest Service, began upgrading the access trail to the monument, which skirted the intervening canyons by crossing the highlands of Elk Ridge. Unfortunately, before the construction was finished, the money ran out. "Now if Uncle Sam would come across with a little [money] we could soon drive to the Bridges in a car," Johnson hinted in a letter to the Park Service in 1924. "Oh, our time will come some day." In fact, Zeke didn't have to wait long—thanks to the state, not the feds. Oil exploration on Elk Ridge motivated the state to appropriate ten thousand dollars to complete the road. The national monument's first automobile arrived in 1928. Soon after, a touring magazine pronounced the new road "epochal" for opening to the public "matchless examples of nature's architecture."[19]

Zeke Johnson's initial elation at the development soon turned to confusion: "I am wondering what can be done with me. Since the auto road has been built out to the monument I have no way of making a dollar out there. I got a concession for handling saddle horses on the monument but feed is scarce and prices too high for tourists so they all prefer to walk." The road's steep descent into the monument came to be known as "Johnson's Last Half-Mile." It threatened to be literally true: who needed a guide now that you could drive a car? By 1931, Zeke was sounding desperate. For the past eleven years, he had made his best money guiding Charles Bernheimer, a New York businessman, around southern Utah and northern Arizona, but this year he wasn't coming. Consequently, Zeke would have to forego his time at the monument in order to earn some money in town. He pleaded with the National Park Service for financial help. Without it, he wrote, "I will be obliged to give up in despair, but it makes me blue blue blue to think of it for I have lived and struggled these many years with the hope that some day I could see [the bridges] in their glory." The Park Service in Washington felt sympathy but no responsibility. "As times change, so do conditions change for an old-timer like Zeke," one official wrote. Roads, like so many forms of progress, left some folks in the dust. Nonetheless, the agency offered a modicum of help by upgrading Johnson's position to temporary ranger. By splitting his working time between Salt Lake City, Blanding, and the bridges, Zeke managed to make ends meet. Until 1942, he worked seasonally at the national monument.[20]

Tourism increased modestly over Johnson's long tenure, but it never hit the jackpot. Part of the problem was fixed in 1947, when the dead-end road to the monument was connected to a new road and river ferry to the north (the road now state highway 95). The vast Colorado River roadless section admired by Robert Marshall had been cut in two. Now a car could be taken from Capitol Reef National Monument in Wayne County to Natural Bridges and beyond. At the dedication of the road and ferry, Zeke Johnson naturally appeared as a VIP.

Just as San Juan County had Zeke—someone who selflessly and tirelessly worked to promote the beauties of his home region—Wayne County had Joe Hickman and E. P. Pectol. Taking inspiration from Zion National Park, these brothers-in-law formed a two-man booster club in 1921. Hickman and Pectol believed that the red cliffs of "Wayne Wonderland" were just as beautiful as Zion and deserved to be recognized. In 1924, Hickman won a seat in the legislature, and he took his cause to Salt Lake City. The result: the Board of State Park Commissioners was established with the purpose of identifying and creating parks. Hickman clearly meant Wayne Wonderland to be first on the board's list. In July 1925, he and other county leaders staged a local celebration for "Wayne Wonderland State Park." There was a rodeo, a dance, and a Sabbath-day assembly in the town of Fruita (now the location of the Capitol Reef National Park visitor center). Many speakers, including the governor, looked forward to the day when the state, and ultimately the National Park Service, would assume responsibility for the scenic country adjacent to Fruita. With federal designation would come good roads, something the state couldn't easily pay for on its own.[21]

Sadly, Hickman died in a boating accident just two days after the festivities. Despite the loss, Pectol carried on. A natural leader—for fifteen years he served as the local Mormon bishop—he helped organize an umbrella group to address southern Utah's persistent economic problems, made even worse by the Depression. The charter meeting of the Associated Civic Clubs of Southern Utah (ACCSU) took place in Richfield in 1930. Ten counties were represented. "The purpose of the associated clubs," reported the local paper, "will be to foster, encourage and provide by every honorable means the growth and development of the communities of southern Utah, . . . to give publicity to the scenic and commercial resources of southern Utah, and to exploit systematically the products of southern Utah for exporting and consumption."[22]

The ACCSU considered road improvement one of its primary goals and supported national park status for Wayne Wonderland in large part because it promised to stimulate interest in an east–west highway linking Mesa Verde National Park to Zion, Bryce, and Grand Canyon. The result, proponents believed, would be a "golden circle" of accessible scenic areas in the Four Corners states. Tourism seemed guaranteed. It was time, the members of the ACCSU believed, to make this beautiful, harsh land pay. So far, despite the best efforts of the Mormon pioneers and their descendants, the canyonlands had yielded little. Maybe this was God's Country, but from an economic perspective it seemed like The Land that God Forgot. By emphasizing the former, however, tourism boosters believed they could help alleviate the latter. This spirit of entrepreneurship was well expressed by J. E. Broaddus, a Salt Lake photographer who, working with Ephraim Pectol, produced a promotional slide show about Wayne Wonderland. "Utah people have failed to realize," he said, "that they have a great industry in the promotion of their scenic attractions and have also failed to see that they have a greater variety of scenery than any state in the Union."[23]

The National Park Service held a similar opinion about the people of Utah. Unfortunately, federal officials, like most outsiders, rarely acknowledged the efforts of local boosters like Broaddus and Pectol. They preferred, it seemed, to categorically belittle locals for blindness. With high paternalism, Robert Sterling Yard, an early publicist for the Park Service, once wrote, "People had to 'come in' before [Bryce Canyon] was appreciated. And so it will be with . . . the entire great region of the High Plateaus, where people have not yet come in. Other national parks no doubt there await discovery."[24]

Several years later, the agency found a big one: Glen Canyon of the Colorado River. Following the bold, sometimes imperious leadership of Interior Secretary Harold Ickes, the Park Service staked its claim to the canyon in 1936, the same year Robert Marshall published his roadless area inventory. The proposed Escalante National Monument would have covered 6,968 square miles, twice the size of Yellowstone National Park, or about 8 percent of Utah. "Naturally and logically," wrote a Park Service official, "the question arises as to why this great area of outstanding scenic resources has not become known to the public generally. The simple and direct answer may be synthesized in a simple word—inaccessibility." Indeed, the boundaries of the megamonument generally agreed with Marshall's Colorado River roadless section. The Park Service surely would have broken the roadlessness with many scenic drives, but, as one supporter wrote, "Even after roads have been built into this magnificent section, it will be generations before its hidden recesses have been fully explored—and therein lies its fascination."[25]

This unsurveyed region contained one "town" (Hite, population ten—give or take nine), and an estimated 27,000 cattle and 218,000 sheep. The owners of these animals lived in outlying settlements such as Moab, Monticello, Loa, and Escalante. In the 1930s, grazing constituted the single great economic use of the monument area, especially before the Taylor Grazing Act of 1934 (which initiated federal regulation under the Grazing Service, predecessor of the BLM). Under normal Park Service regulations, however, all grazing would have been eliminated. Disgracefully, only *after* its proposal went public did the Park Service, under pressure from the state of Utah, seek out the opinions of local ranchers. Eighty-seven appeared at a public hearing in Price, Utah, in June 1936. David Madsen, a low-level Park Service employee and a lifelong Utahn, had the unenviable task of explaining the motivations of his superiors in Washington. In the meeting he tried to sympathize with the ranchers and expressed his hope that provisions could be made for the continuation of grazing rights. However, he suggested that the highest economic use of the land was not ranching but recreation.

Charles Redd, one of state's most respected stockmen, stood up and made the opening reply. The people of southern Utah "do, and have for a long time, recognized the value and importance, the unusualness of the scenery we have here," he said. However, "the exploitation of these natural wonders is not inconsistent with the full and free use of the range by livestock." To the assembled ranchers, an attack on their labor was also an attack on their land. Where some people saw only beautiful wild country, Redd and his peers saw wild, beautiful country made better by three generations of Mormons. Though they understood that the American people technically owned the land, they didn't necessarily believe the public deserved it. "Now, I am willing for the people who wish recreation to have rights and privileges," said W. A. Guymon of Huntington, "but I don't think that it is fair for them to tell me to move off simply because my land has some kind of an attractive object that the people think should be given to them. Let them pay the price." Better yet, let them get their money's worth at Utah's existing recreation areas. In a resolution drafted after the meeting, the ranchers called attention to Natural Bridges National Monument (1908) and Arches National Monument (1929). "The Park Service to date has expended nothing to make them accessible to the traveling public; and we strongly maintain that the monuments already created should be developed before vast additional areas are withdrawn for recreational purposes to the expense of our basic industry."[26]

Reacting to opposition from ranchers and politicians in Utah, the Park Service trimmed its proposed monument to 2,450 square miles in 1938. Still skeptical, the state of Utah pushed for ironclad safeguards on future grazing, mining, and dam building. The Park Service resisted, and the proposal soon degenerated into bickering and miscommunication between the state and federal governments. Eventually, Escalante National Monument lost momentum within the Roosevelt administration and died. Thus Glen Canyon remained the same—without public roads or recognition or protection.[27]

Forgotten amidst the controversy, however, was the creation of a much, much smaller national monument in Wayne County, a monument closer to the ideals of rural Utahns. The big break occurred in 1933, after Ephraim Pectol attained Joe Hickman's old seat in the legislature. From there he shepherded a unanimous resolution to Congress urging the establishment of a Wayne Wonderland park and a regional highway connecting it to the "chain of natural wonders" in the region. Pectol also secured the support of Utah's congressional delegation. In response, the National Park Service authorized a feasibility study, the first of many bureaucratic hurdles. Pectol and the ACCSU continued to lobby and worked to allay the concerns of local ranchers, who didn't share their enthusiasm for tourism. Ultimately, in 1937, President Franklin D. Roosevelt created Capitol Reef National Monument by executive order. (Many in Utah disliked the monument's name; Congressman Abe Murdock tried unsuccessfully to reinstate Wayne Wonderland.) Said Governor Henry H. Blood at the dedication, "Capitol

Reef is but a beginning, roads must follow—and with roads must come development and new areas to be opened up."[28]

It took more waiting, however. In the words of one historian, "Roads were very slow in coming, few trails were built, no campgrounds were set up, no administrative structure was put in place, and no scenic highway was constructed connecting Capitol Reef with the other monuments and parks in southern Utah."[29] The monument didn't even have a budget until 1950. As such, it contributed little to Wayne County's economy. Understandably, locals felt betrayed by the Park Service. For decades, the national monument sat in hibernation, to the chagrin of tourism boosters.

The year after the creation of Capitol Reef National Monument, the *Saturday Evening Post* ran an offbeat editorial about southeastern Utah:

> The obituary of America's Last Frontier has been recited many times since 1890, but it is still there, and likely to be indefinitely. . . . [If] you genuinely wish to Get Away From It All, ask for a Utah road map and go, as Willie Keeler said, where they ain't. . . . The area includes the Robbers Roost country in which Butch Cassidy and his bank robbers hid out in the 90's. It offers exactly the same refuge to the desperado today, but the softer, urban modern criminal would perish quickly there of hunger and thirst. The Mormons have explored it all and rejected most of it, and where the Mormon cannot reclaim the desert, the Gentile is well advised not to try.[30]

Ostensibly, the Wild West survived in Utah—but it wasn't a place the armchair pathfinder would want to go.

This would change, of course. A little over two decades later, the *Post* printed what could be considered a belated retraction. The last frontier had taken the form of a "new frontier" for tourists. "The fabulous wilderness of Southern Utah may be the proving ground for our next experiment in national expansion," the article suggested.[31] The proposed experiment was simple: establish parks, campgrounds, motels, and a connecting system of roads so the American public could easily see this wonderland; then stand back, see what happens.

Southeastern Utah had waited its turn. Even after the recognition of adjacent Zion and Bryce Canyon national parks, few tourists had ventured east into the heart of the canyon country. Then again, why would they, when the road map was mostly blank? In 1941, hoping to fix the situation,

Welcome and warning for motorists, ca. 1940. Monument Valley is in the background.

Governor Herbert B. Maw consolidated several state offices into the Department of Publicity and Industrial Development with the charge of building and improving roads into Utah's scenic areas and otherwise promoting tourism. Yet, despite the efforts of the department and emerging groups like the ACCSU, automobile tourism didn't rev up until midcentury. The spark came from historical forces beyond the control of state and local boosters. A national postwar trend—the increasing mobility of the expanding middle class—coincided with two watershed episodes in the history of the Colorado Plateau: a uranium boom (ca. 1952–58), and the construction of Glen Canyon Dam (1956–63). The canyon country would never be the same.

U-BOOM

The nuclear arms industry altered the map of the American West. The military took over large sections of federally owned arid land—Hanford in Washington, Rocky Flats in Colorado, the Nevada Test Site, and more—for the development and detonation of atomic weapons. But before the government could test the bombs, or even build them, it needed uranium, and in the middle years of the atomic weapons program, most of that deadly ore came from newly developed mines on the Colorado Plateau.

Uranium is the heaviest naturally occurring element on earth. Though widespread in particle form, it rarely comes in concentrate. By a geologic fluke, however, the Four Corners region contains abundant carnotite, one of the two richest uranium-bearing minerals (the other being pitchblende). In addition to uranium, carnotite contains the elements vanadium, used to strengthen steel, and radium, used to treat cancer. French physicists Pierre and Marie Curie isolated radium in 1898, just two years after scientists discovered the radioactive properties of uranium. The subsequent scientific and industrial demand for radioactive elements supported a modest carnotite business in western Colorado and southeastern Utah. The market, however, was anything but stable. As one Utah miner remembered:

> During the early 1900's, the only use for this ore was for its radium content. We producers got built up what was considered in those days a fairly good market for our [carnotite]. Then, all of a sudden they came up with a rich strike of pitch-blende ore in the Belgian Congo, and we all went out of business overnight. Then, eventually, the wonderful properties of Vanadium, as a steel alloy, especially where great tensile strength was required, were recognized. . . . However, late in February 1944, the Government suddenly discovered that it had Vanadium 'running out of its ears'. . . . So, we went out of business again. . . . Then, late in 1944 and early in 1945, the Government needed Uranium badly, in connection with its Atomic Bomb program.[32]

Finally, carnotite had found its best customer. The Atomic Energy Commission (AEC), the bureaucratic successor of the Manhattan Project, wanted to secure a domestic stockpile of uranium. In the opening years of the cold war, 75 percent of the nation's supply came from African mines. To encourage domestic ore development, the agency, the sole legal buyer of uranium in the United States, upped the purchase price 1,000 percent in 1948 and guaranteed it for a minimum of ten years. Uranium production didn't explode until 1950, however, when President Harry S. Truman authorized the development of the hydrogen bomb. Shortly thereafter, the AEC upgraded its uranium procurement program, and the real incentives began.

At an information center at the AEC's regional headquarters in Grand

Junction, Colorado, would-be "uraniumaires" received free guidebooks and maps. The U.S. Geological Survey (USGS) was in high gear, producing the fifteen-minute topographic series—the first detailed map coverage of the canyon country. The USGS also helped the AEC drill nearly six million feet of exploratory holes in the Four Corners states between 1948 and 1956. Prospectors could read about the results in a series of technical papers. Promising drill sites were open for lease to the private sector, but citizens were also encouraged to look for their own mother lode. The AEC offered advice and even loans for exploration work and promised premiums for high-grade ore. Through aggressive mine development, entrepreneurs could also win a variety of bonuses. To ease the transportation of ore, the AEC established eleven buying stations throughout the interior West, yet miners could still receive a haulage allowance to compensate for the region's poor roads. But the government was trying to fix that, too; the AEC spent millions on road improvements. Taken as a whole, the uranium program merited a contemporary description as "the first government-promoted, government-supported, and government-controlled mineral rush in American history."[33]

The popular press generally downplayed the subsidies, however. "Uranium hunting is . . . a job cut out for the small-time shoestring operator, for the amateur prospector who's got the guts to buck the long odds with his last few bucks," wrote one. "Uranium is the one last treasure in the earth that's left for the little guy." Magazine articles overflowed with references to "modern Forty-niners" on the "last frontier." If you were to believe the literature, the U-boom was the result of rugged men with guts and vision and lust for adventure. The jeep and Geiger counter had replaced the mule and pick, but little else had changed—or so the story went. "In a sense," wrote one historian, "viewing the activities that occurred on the Colorado Plateau at midcentury in terms of the Old West provided the nation with a familiar, if mythic, counterpoint to the frightening realities of a world on the brink of nuclear devastation." And the Old West imagery probably seemed apropos to those U-boomers without prior experience in the canyon country. Prospecting for uranium often meant long trips into remote, uninhabited desert. Despite this, or because of it, some ten thousand prospectors (overwhelmingly white males) came to the Colorado Plateau with a dream: "Pick up a rock. If it ticks, you're rich."[34]

By far the most famous and enchanting success story belongs to Charlie Steen, an unemployed geologist who lived with his family in a cramped trailer in the railroad town of Cisco, Utah. Subsisting on potato chips and bananas, bereft of even a Geiger counter, Steen staked his dream on his scientific intuition and his run-down jeep. He hit pay dirt on 6 July 1952, in Lisbon Valley, south of Moab. Charlie filed a claim and opened the Mi Vida mine, which contained some of the richest ore ever found in the Colorado Plateau. An overnight millionaire, Charlie built a mansion, bought a plane, and continued to prospect in southern Utah. His story, which received wide national attention, inspired countless others and marked the beginning of the bona fide boom.

Naturally, for every Steen were a thousand busted dreams. The trick wasn't so much finding uranium as turning a claim into a business venture. That took more capital than most prospectors enjoyed. Despite the federal incentives meant for individuals, corporations came to dominate the uranium market. Company-owned mines were more efficient and more lucrative than private "dog hole" mines—but no less dangerous. Most lacked even basic ventilation systems. As might be expected, a high percentage of mine workers later came down with lung cancer; the problem has been particularly acute on the Navajo Reservation. Though the AEC knew the health hazards of uranium and wielded complete control over the industry, it did nothing to promote safety. The nation needed bombs: the power to destroy exacted some destruction in return.[35]

The fever for uranium peaked around 1955. Perhaps the busiest town was Moab, Utah, the new home of Charlie Steen and the Miss Atomic Energy pageant. Here beside the Colorado River, Grand County officials struggled to accommodate the influx of fortune seekers. Fruit orchards went to the axe for trailer parks. Sewage lines spilled over; phone lines were tied up. Yet the excitement was even greater than the growing pains. Moab was full of money, gossip, and dreams. In 1955, the town boasted seventy-nine mining companies (of which forty-seven would fold the next year). Using the "Uranium Capital of the World" as their base, prospectors took jeeps, bulldozers, and planes into the backcountry in search of their pot of radioactive gold.[36]

On the Colorado Plateau as a whole, approximately eight hundred mines delivered a total 1.5 million tons of ore to the AEC in 1955. The government subsidies were working: soon the Defense Department would have enough yellowcake for the next generation of nuclear weapons. In November 1958, the AEC made the announcement that its future purchases would be limited to those under contract. Prospecting was suddenly pointless.

The U-boom had busted, but not before leaving its mark. Mobile homes and radioactive tailing piles were now fixtures of the landscape. Mining jobs as a component of total employment in the five-county region of southeastern Utah rose from 5 to 26 percent between 1940 and 1960. During this same period, employment in agriculture (mostly ranching) plummeted from 56 to 15 percent. Overall, the economy benefitted, though not equally across the region. Uranium commerce concentrated in two counties, Grand and San Juan. In the early 1950s, the assessed valuation of property in San Juan County had been $3.8 million, making it one of the poorest areas in the nation. By 1960, mineral exploration and speculation had inflated the property value to $132 million. Remarkably, prospectors had laid claim to 40 percent of the 7,725-square-mile county—and that was counting only the *valid* claims. The county recorder in Monticello had to hire fourteen assistants just to keep pace with the paperwork. This sleepy Mormon town was suddenly up and running. The population doubled to 2,500 in three years. Over a million dollars was spent on new structures, including six trailer courts. Infrastructure like sewage and water systems grew and improved considerably. "But as with other booms of the past," says a local historian, "one of the largest and most permanent contributions of this era was the development of roads." As one contemporary put it: "Where there had once been barren wastelands, virtually impenetrable by man, there were now well-marked Jeep trails, gravel roads, and even paved highways."[37]

Though any mining boom—particularly one in the twentieth century—creates its share of roads, this boom was exceptional because the federal government subsidized the bulldozing. By the logic of the cold war, the roadless areas of the Colorado Plateau stood in the way of national security. "One of the major drawbacks [of the AEC uranium program] was the inadequacy of roads in this remote canyon area," reads an official history. "The AEC felt obligated to help rectify this situation." The agency claimed authority under the Defense Highway Act of 1941, and the Federal-Aid Highway Act of 1950, which stated, "There is a need at the present time to provide for emergency highway funding to essential defense installations in the event of a national emergency." In 1951, the AEC made a list of "emergency" road improvements and initiated its Access Road Program, which ran through 1958. At a final cost of nearly $17 million, the AEC subsidized the construction or improvement of 1,253 miles of roads in the uranium-producing states of the American West. Southern Utah received the lion's share, about six hundred miles. For all of this road work, the

Defense Department picked up 95 percent of the tab. The state paid the difference, and the counties assumed maintenance duties. It was an unbelievably low price for a network of new roads.[38]

With a dream and a backhoe, prospectors and mining companies cleared a lot of roadway, too, but no mileage figure is available. The upshot, however, is clear: in roughly one decade, road development in the canyon country moved forward a half century. Again, San Juan County provides a good case study. After the epic, opening work of the Hole in the Rock pioneers, road building had moved at a pedestrian pace. The harsh country resisted. Most of San Juan remained roadless until a gold rush in the 1890s and an oil boom in the early twentieth century. Outsiders poured in, prowled about, and left a concentration of trails and roads in the southern end of the county. A more general form of outside assistance arrived in 1916, when Congress passed the first Federal Highway Act. This bill offered matching funds for "post roads"—access to places where mail delivery was difficult and expensive. Federal participation in local road work increased again in 1921, when Congress agreed to subsidize certain projects at the percentage of federal land within each state—about 75 percent in Utah. This law underscored the interior West's spaciousness, its small tax base, and dependent economic status. As of 1921, slow-to-grow San Juan County reported just 116 miles of state road and 728 miles of county road, none paved, none graveled. And though the government helped improve a few arteries during the 1920s and 1930s, the big improvements had to wait until after World War II. At that point, the county experienced a fit of road building, with the U-boom at the center of things. Between 1951 and 1955 alone, the government paid for the improvement of 243 miles of roads in San Juan County.[39]

Significantly, several of these AEC projects would become segments of paved highways:

Utah 46	La Sal to Colorado state line
Utah 211	Monticello area to southern Canyonlands National Park
Utah 261	Natural Bridges area to Mexican Hat
Utah 95	Blanding to Hite
U.S. 191	Blanding to Bluff
U.S. 163	Bluff to Monument Valley[40]

These are the scenic byways on which tourism in San Juan County now depends. Unintentionally, the AEC helped promote a different kind of rush. While the progression from mining to tourism is hardly uncommon in the American West (consider the Colorado ski industry, with dozens of resorts built from the remnants of old boomtowns), few of the U-boomers anticipated the era after the inevitable bust. The most prescient commentary came from the editor of Moab's *Times-Independent* in 1956: "The uranium prospectors found a lot of beauty in the country. The uranium industry built a lot of access roads into some of those spots. The roads are still no more than 'jeep roads,' but they are starts in the right direction. . . . Someday, the tourists will 'discover' the West. And when they do, the Four Corners area should come in for more than its share of tourists and the tourist dollar."[41]

He was right on all counts. The hundreds of thousands of tourists who now visit Canyonlands National Park, or Dead Horse Point State Park, or Goblin Valley State Park, or Natural Bridges National Monument, follow the paved tracks of prospectors. And though the majority of uranium roads remain unpaved, they too have been put to good use. Today, mountain bikers and four-wheel-drive enthusiasts flock to southern Utah. Where else can you find so many roads in the wilderness? It's one of the peculiar legacies of the cold war. Were it not for the local presence of radioactive minerals, or the national desire for weapons of mass destruction, Robert Marshall's map of southern Utah might have stayed substantially the same. Before the uranium craze, big chunks of the canyon country—the San Rafael Reef, the Henry Mountains, the Circle Cliffs, to name a few—were all but inaccessible to vehicles. This is not to say they were free of roads and trails; Indians and Mormons had left their marks of passage. Most uranium roads, in fact, followed Mormon stock routes. But it seems fair to reiterate Marshall: these old trails "made little change in the character of the country."

Yet at what point did significant change occur? Though the greatest loss of Utah's roadless lands happened in the 1950s, the vast majority of contemporary observers interpreted it not as loss but as improvement. In 1957, *Arizona Highways* (whose longtime motto was "Civilization Follows the Improved Highway") published an extensive article on the places opened up by the uranium boom. The author took a deep breath at Grandview Point—high above the canyon of the Colorado River and the city of rocks known as the Needles, the heart of what is now Canyonlands National Park, a scene as grand as the Grand Canyon—and offered thanks: "As we stood on that awesome rim . . . we reminded ourselves that there is no scenery like this anywhere on the world, but on the Colorado Plateau. And we bowed again to the cattlemen and the prospector who have so conveniently opened the secret passages into all this once inaccessible country and pointed the way to the Land of the Sleeping Rainbow."[42]

To better understand the excitement of the time, it's useful to look at another regional publication, *Desert Magazine,* which offered a unique blend of exploration narratives, lost treasure fables, and practical advice on prospecting and rockhounding. It was truly a magazine for desert rats—those folks who owned a jeep, a metal detector, and a file of topographic maps. Founded in 1937 in El Centro, California, *Desert* proved remarkably resistant to change, mostly because the original editor, Randall Henderson, stayed on through 1960. After his departure, *Desert* gradually changed its image to reflect the changing American West. In other words, it degenerated into a conventional touring magazine, not unlike *Arizona Highways.* In its earlier incarnation, however, the magazine was, in its own folksy way, one of the best sources of information on the public lands of the interior West. Articles came from the pens of amateur explorers, not paid professional travelers. Thus it meant something when, in the early 1960s, *Desert* published a series of special issues on southern Utah—"America's Last Wilderness Frontier."

The series was timely because a number of transportation developments had converged in the 1950s. The creation of uranium roads, the improvement of regional highways, the wide availability of jeeps and other off-road vehicles, and the full-fledged emergence of the tour-guide business in southern Utah combined to make this wilderness suddenly accessible—if not vulnerable. Americans know what happens to "last frontiers." They close. The big dam under construction at Glen Canyon highlighted the impending change. In the meantime, however, what a glorious opportunity:

> We all dream of far-away places where the only sights are those of a land untouched by the hand of man, where the only sounds are the murmurings of nature, where the only reality is a pure and artless man-to-earth relationship. To survive in today's complex urban society, man must do more than dream—he must go into such places where the spirit can be recharged. Happily, the wilderness wonderland of southern Utah is less than two-days driving distance for 80 percent of the people who will read this magazine.[43]

Travel articles about southern Utah from the 1950s and 1960s are breathtaking. Several times a year in *Desert* or *Arizona Highways* or *National Geographic*, writers reported the "discovery" and naming of hidden valleys or natural windows such as Druid Arch, Angel Arch, Grosvenor Arch, La Gorce Arch, and Castle Arch.[44] Some of these discovery claims were completely bogus; others were true in the narrow sense that no one before had publicized the existence of the landform. But the excitement was very real. Outsiders simply couldn't believe that someplace so magnificent could be so little known. In 1965, travel editors from thirty-five publications took a trip to Moab courtesy of the state of Utah. Anne Chamberlin of the *Saturday Evening Post* said she was "rather encouraged to know there are places still so remote. If people knew what it was like they would come in great numbers. But then, that might be the beginning of the end of the wilderness."[45]

Tourism boosters in southern Utah—particularly Grand and San Juan counties—sensed they had a commodity. They tried to appeal to the adventure-loving traveler. In the 1960s, the Moab Chamber of Commerce dubbed its city the "headquarters for the new rugged tourist mecca," while San Juan County touted itself as the "untouched tourist mecca of Utah." According to one of San Juan's brochures, "This unspoiled grandeur is now available by paved or hard-surfaced highways." However, it suggested "for maximum safety, that road accommodations be checked with the Chamber of Commerce or Information Offices."[46] That caveat spoke volumes. Very simply, it meant the difference between modest tourism and mass tourism. Not until people could venture out uninformed and unafraid at any season of the year would tourist revenue amount to much. As late as 1951, the state road map offered this recommendation for the *entire* southeastern corner of Utah: "Travel in this area not recommended without guides."

Zeke Johnson and a few others had offered guided pack trips since the turn of the century, and Norman Nevills had begun his famous river running business in the late 1930s. However, the first entrepreneurs to take advantage of southern Utah's midcentury road boom were Kent Frost (a former boatman of Nevills) and his wife, Fern. Using jeeps, this couple from Monticello began taking friends and acquaintances into the outback in 1953. One of their early patrons was Randall Henderson of *Desert Magazine*. His articles helped create a clientele for the Frosts, who by 1960 had the resources to advertise. "Utah has our nation's last extensive wilderness," read one of their brochures. "It is the unspoiled wilderness that the traveler expects to see west of the Mississippi and seldom does."[47] The

Frosts' favorite region surrounded the confluence of the Green and Colorado rivers, a region that became Canyonlands National Park in 1964.

The canyonlands had first been described in print by Captain J. N. Macomb of the U.S. Corps of Topographical Engineers. Macomb received the assignment to locate the confluence of the two great rivers, and he failed. "I cannot conceive of a more worthless and impracticable region than the one we now found ourselves in," he reported, trying to excuse himself. It was 1859—no American had seen such country before. It was worthless but wonderful. In stunned admiration, Macomb described the Needles, "a long line of spires of white stone, standing on red bases, thousands in number, but so slender as to recall the most delicate carving in ivory or the fairy architecture of some Gothic cathedral; yet many, perhaps most, were over five hundred feet in height, and thickly set in a narrow belt or series some miles in length. Their appearance was so strange and beautiful as to call out exclamations of delight from all our party." Macomb's men wandered around the spires and canyons, knowing they were close to the confluence, knowing they were lost. The captain yielded to the land; it was "impassable to everything but the winged bird."[48]

Needless to say, Macomb didn't anticipate the jeep. Following the trails of ranchers and uranium miners, who ingeniously found routes between the Needles, adventurous drivers pushed into the country in the years after World War II. The establishment of Canyonlands National Park didn't immediately change things, because the Park Service adopted a permissive attitude toward off-highway vehicular use. For many early visitors, driving on the rocks was the highlight of the trip. Breathless, one left "feeling as though we had just won the West, single-motoredly." Said another, "You're not pampering yourself when you travel on wheels to view Canyonlands' visual treasures. You'll be feeling just a little more rugged after only a day of slamming and lurching along in a jeep." Another: "It's one of the last frontiers for Jeeps and adventurous drivers. . . . It's a place where a man can prove to himself that he is a 'driver' and where he won't be annoyed by traffic cops, speed limits or signal lights."[49]

Hearing comments like these, entrepreneurs caught on quickly. By 1969, Kent and Fern Frost faced competition from two other jeeping guides in Canyonlands. Southern Utah suddenly had eleven such outfits, along with eight scenic air flight operators. These businesses were pioneers in the modern service economy. Though mining (mostly petroleum and potash) made a small comeback in southeastern Utah in the 1960s, the industry offered little long-term security. Tourism, on the other hand, seemed to have a bright future. To realize the economic potential of Canyonlands as a tourist attraction, however, the last frontier for jeeps would have to give way to a new frontier for station wagons.

This transformation had been anticipated by Canyonlands National Park's lead sponsor, Senator Frank Moss of Utah. He spoke of the "two great space races" confronting the nation. "On the one hand, there lies a great challenge of outer space," he said. "On the other, there is the problem of play and living space for the American people. We dare [not] neglect either." During the congressional hearings preparatory to the creation of Canyonlands, speaker after speaker, including a representative from the AFL-CIO, concurred with the senator. American families needed more room to relax. Ross Musselman of Moab said it best: "With the exploding population, and America on wheels, and the stress under which people are living, we're going to need more and more places for them to get away from all that." This statement echoed the conclusions of the presidentially appointed Outdoor Recreation Resources Review Commission, which released its twenty-seven-volume report in the same year, 1962. Of course, to get away to Canyonlands, or anywhere else, Americans demanded paved roads—part of "all that" they hoped to leave behind. "Millions of dollars will be spent in access roads to open up the park," assured Frank Moss. "It has been estimated that an outlay of $15 million for such roads will open up this treasure to man. It is now locked up to all but a hardy few."[50]

Moss was a liberal Democrat who considered himself a conservationist. On most issues, including Canyonlands, he had the support of national conservationist groups. The senator grew rhapsodic talking about this "unsullied and unspoiled" section of his home state where "man stands small beside the spectacular monuments fashioned by the Creator." Yet he had a man-made dream for this natural beauty. In the future as Frank Moss saw it, all of Utah's national monuments would be upgraded to parks, and all of the parks would be connected by modern highways. The canyon country would then welcome the world. It was the "manifest destiny" of southern Utah to be a "tourist mecca," he wrote.[51]

Moss's political opponents, led by fellow senator Wallace Bennett and Governor George Clyde, didn't want to put all the region's eggs in one basket labeled tourism. They wanted a Canyonlands park that allowed "true multiple-use," including mineral exploration. They were, to quote one historian, "seemingly unwilling to accept the notion that the energy boom in the Four Corners had, for all intents and purposes, played itself out." And they lost. As ultimately drafted by Congress, Canyonlands was the economic domain of tourism. Capping four years of legislative negotiations, the bill received President Johnson's signature in September 1964. In Grand and San Juan counties, reaction was mixed. As one contemporary writer suggested: "The designation of the national park is finding local dwellers . . . living in a paradox. Many of them will be increasingly involved in catering to—and profiting from—the thousands of tourists the park will bring. But deep down, they'd really rather have their homeland left alone."[52]

THE GOLDEN CIRCLE

After the Green and the Colorado rivers blend their colors in Canyonlands, they abandon their smooth meanderings for a steep, straight section of whitewater called Cataract Canyon. Mile for mile, Cataract contains more rapids than the Grand Canyon. But if river runners can navigate Satan's Gut and the Big Drops, they are received downstream by the preternatural calm of Lake Powell. Starting in 1963, the impounded water of Glen Canyon began pushing its way upstream, drowning the bottom-end cataracts. Since water storage marked the end of the Bureau of Reclamation's job, the dam building agency relinquished management of the reservoir area to the National Park Service. Combined with adjacent Canyonlands National Park, the Park Service now controlled a vast stretch of dead and living river, the heart of Robert Marshall's Colorado River roadless section. But Glen Canyon National Recreation Area was a new kind of creature. In its own way, the dam and reservoir engendered as many roads and developments as the contemporaneous uranium boom.

In his charming book *Uranium Fever*, prospector Raymond Taylor recalled his business-minded amazement that the government would build a dam in the slickrock desert:

Some of this incredibly spectacular country was so broken it had been seen only from the air. A great deal of it required pack trips with guides and horses, putting it out of the reach of most tourists. But the lake would make the fantastic canyons fingering into it accessible to any tourist who wanted to hire a boat with an outboard motor for a few hours. It was within what boosters were calling the "Golden Circle," a cluster of scenic attractions. . . . With Lake Powell the hub of the Golden Circle, here was a land development project that just couldn't miss.

As soon as he learned the planned route of the access highway to the dam, Taylor began scheming. Forgetting uranium for the moment, he scouted for available roadside property. "People who'd grinned at sight of the crazy-fool prospector out on the moose pasture west of Kanab—where everybody knew there was no uranium—didn't know I was after something better. Uranium is self-depleting. Every ton of ore produced means one less ton remaining. But the longer you hold good land, the more it's worth." Kanab became the Bureau of Reclamation's temporary project headquarters in August 1956. That same month, graders put the finishing touches on a brand-new seventy-mile jeep road from Kanab to the rim of Glen Canyon. This road—and another leading from U.S. 89 in Arizona to the opposite rim—preceded the official groundbreaking ceremony in October. However unglamourous, road building was the first priority. In the first three years of the Glen Canyon project alone, the Bureau of Reclamation spent $13 million on roads. That figure was unprecedented because Glen Canyon was the first big dam built by the Bureau without the services of a railroad. Instead, a round-the-clock fleet of cargo trucks delivered mountains of supplies from Flagstaff and Kanab.[53]

On the opposite Utah and Arizona sides, work initially occurred in isolation. "It seems to give one the feeling of driving into a lost world," a visitor wrote in early 1957. He camped on the southern side, at the site of the future government town of Page, Arizona. "Except for a bulldozer and a few pieces of structural steel, the area was totally barren. . . . I don't remember ever feeling quite so alone."[54] Though he saw lights immediately across the canyon, it would have taken him an all-day drive of 190 miles to cross the intervening 1,200 feet.

For one of its earliest subcontracts, the Bureau of Reclamation commissioned a bridge—the highest steel-arch bridge in the world, 680 feet above the Colorado River. As a stopgap, construction crews built a stomach-turning suspension footbridge that swayed in the wind. Made of chicken wire, the walkway offered an unobstructed view straight down. Not a few men refused to cross the canyon until the steel bridge opened on 20 February 1959. By this time, the government had paved the access roads on either side, thus completing a new highway where but months ago no cars

Ends of the earth, 1956. (Photograph by Fred S. Finch.)

had ever been. "The new four-million-dollar-highway bridge at Glen Canyon ends the isolation and near-inaccessibility of the vast exciting 'inverted mountain' country," said the *Salt Lake Tribune* in an editorial following the dedication.[55]

Everyone expected the tourists to come. "The West is in for its greatest boom," wrote a reporter in 1961. "This time it's not the lure of gold, free land, oil or uranium. It's a concerted quest for the most valuable of our natural resources: recreation." The article cited "travel experts" who predicted three million visitors at Glen Canyon by 1963. The National Park Service was a bit less immodest, looking forward to one million visitors by 1966. To make it a reality, the agency requested an appropriation of $16 million for lakeside recreational developments. "A prodigious project?" asked the superintendent of Glen Canyon National Recreation Area. "Yes, but one that will forever reflect its value in economic returns to the Nation and returns of physical as well as mental health to its people."[56]

Road work was part of the project, of course, but the biggest single "road development" in Utah history was already in place at Glen Canyon Dam. The reservoir was a superhighway made of water. In motorized vehicles, tourists could now cruise the former river, then exit onto any of the ninety-odd feeder roads known as side canyons. For a nation that loved to burn gasoline, here was heaven.

With Lake Powell in business, Utah turned a covetous eye on boating returns. Up to this point, the $243 million Glen Canyon project had been something of a letdown for the state. "We haven't begun to feel the economic impact," said governor Calvin Rampton.[57] The dam was in Arizona. The construction town was in Arizona. The first, largest, and most important recreational development, Wahweap Marina, was in Arizona. Utah claimed about 95 percent of the reservoir, yet it lacked a single paved road leading to the water. The state felt stung.

Utah's best location for a marina was Bullfrog Basin, one of the few large bays on Lake Powell. In 1966, the state received a federal matching grant to pave an access road to Bullfrog. The $2.7 million appropriation came through the Economic Development Administration (EDA) on the basis that the local county, Garfield, was economically depressed. The county had few industries and lots of open space; the government controlled 92 percent of the land area. Unlike some of its neighboring counties, Garfield had benefitted little from the uranium boom of the 1950s. Lake Powell was a godsend—but that wasn't self-evident to everyone. Governor Rampton had to lobby in person for the EDA grant because the federal administrator of the funds "couldn't see how the road would aid economic development in the area."[58] No wonder: the thirty-seven-mile road didn't originate from any town, nor did it lead to any. Yet, as the governor no doubt emphasized, the National Park Service had already spent $1.5 million at Bullfrog clearing the land for a boat ramp, marina, motel, restaurant, visitor center, and campground.

Rampton and his peers hoped that Lake Powell would be the long-awaited catalyst for mass tourism in southeastern Utah. The state legislature had already shown its commitment to the cause by passing liberal road appropriation bills in the 1950s, and by creating the Utah Tourist and Publicity Council (1953) and the Utah State Park and Recreation Commission (1957). In its first report, the commission noted disapprovingly that Utah ranked fortieth among the forty-eight states in tourist revenue, far behind California, or even neighboring Colorado. According to the commission, Utah had nothing to lose and everything to gain by pushing its scenery onto the market. By the mid-1960s, tourism had replaced energy development as the number one industry in the Four Corners states, and no one knew its limits. The Park and Recreation Commission quoted Henry Kearns of the U.S. Department of Commerce: "Tourism is a miraculous cake that you can eat and still have. When a country exports its products, it is drawing on its reserves of natural resources. But no matter how much tourism draws on natural resources, they never wear out."[59]

Similar thinking permeated the National Park Service, as illustrated in a 1950 report on the area's recreational resources:

> The Colorado River Basin lies directly across all lines of travel between the rapidly increasing population of California and the densely populated eastern half of the United States. To a large extent in the past, it was considered just a vast space one had to cross on the way to California. Now, with the Pacific Coast more fully developed, people seeking undeveloped, uncrowded areas are beginning to discover the Colorado River Basin. . . . There is a limit, which has been reached in most sections, on the number of domestic animals that can be grazed. But the possibilities for the development of the recreational use of the basin are almost unlimited.[60]

A short time later, at the national level, the Park Service began a "mission" to modernize the park system for its golden anniversary in 1966. In essence, Mission 66 was a road-building program; not surprisingly, the American Automobile Association backed the project from the start. In Utah, tourism boosters took Mission 66 the next step: they wanted not only to improve park roads but also to connect all of the splendor spots of the Colorado Plateau with a network of highways. This dream came to be known as the "Golden Circle" (sometimes called the Magic Circle, Great Circle, or Grand Circle). Though the concept dates at least to the 1930s, it gained great impetus in the 1960s after the creation of Canyonlands National Park (1964) and the completion of Glen Canyon Dam (1963). The governors of the Four Corners states threw their support behind the plan, as did Stewart Udall, Kennedy's interior secretary. With the support of the federal government, the Utah State Road Commission published a prospectus called *Access Roads for the Golden Circle, America's Newest Playground* in 1966.

This document came to a brash conclusion: "$60,000,000 are needed for 600 miles of road improvement to provide the service required to make full utilization of the area during the next ten years." Sixty million dollars amounted to roughly one-quarter of the total cost of Glen Canyon Dam.

The Road Commission wanted nothing less than a full-scale tourist boom and justified its request on both economic and civic grounds. "The nation ... [has] a responsibility to build roads to places that are different than the places they left behind," the report suggested; harried Americans needed to "escape" to pristine country without worrying about bad roads.[61]

The "backbone" of the Golden Circle was Utah State Route 95, the road and river ferry that connected Natural Bridges National Monument to Capitol Reef National Monument. Since opening in 1947, the route had been improved in increments. In the 1950s, the state used AEC money to realign the stretch between Blanding and the Happy Jack uranium mine near Natural Bridges National Monument. In the 1960s, the U.S. Bureau of Public Roads paid for three steel bridges to replace the soon-to-be-submerged river ferry. Then, in a series of grants, the feds paid for paving the entire 133-mile route. Utah 95 was finished in 1976 at a total cost of $23 million.[62]

Despite this success, the proponents of the Golden Circle fell short of their full-access dream. Only 272 of the 600 miles have thus far been completed. What remains remarkable, however, is the original list of "cooperating agencies" for the access roads program. The National Park Service, the Bureau of Land Management, the Bureau of Indian Affairs, the Utah Parks and Recreation Commission, the Utah Department of Fish and Game, and the Utah State Historical Society all lent their support to a plan to cut the roadless lands of southern Utah into bite-sized pieces. The most audacious proposal was for a federally funded road linking U.S. 89 near Page, Arizona, to Bullfrog, and from Bullfrog to newly built I-70 north of Moab. The Lake Powell Parkway, as it came to be known, went entirely against the grain of some of the roughest terrain on the planet. The proposed route crossed the dissected benchlands of the Kaiparowits Plateau, the slickrock drainage of the Escalante River, the towers of the Waterpocket Fold, the aptly named Maze, and the Green River within Canyonlands National Park. In the course of its 280-plus miles, this road would intersect one town.

What was the rationale behind this Road to Nowhere? Simple: it promised to boost Utah's tourist revenue at Lake Powell at a minimum cost to the state. Utah felt it deserved no less. The highway to Bullfrog Marina had made the reservoir more accessible to the majority of Utahns, but it did little to lure Californians, the most coveted tourist population. They faced the same problem as the Hole in the Rock pioneers: there was no easy way to get from southwestern Utah to southeastern Utah. With the parkway, however, the all-day trip from Page to Bullfrog would become a one-hour scenic drive. Road proponents placed the southern section of the parkway, the Trans-Escalante Highway, at the top of their priority list. Utah's congressional delegation embraced the plan and managed to insert a section authorizing the highway into the 1972 act that reset the boundaries of Glen Canyon National Recreation Area.[63]

But a strange thing happened along the way. The Trans-Escalante Highway ran into opposition. Up until this point, roughly 1970, very few people had questioned the benefits of more and more roads in the canyon country. No organization fought the unprecedented bulldozing that occurred in the 1950s and 1960s. Though environmental groups grieved at the loss of Glen Canyon, they didn't take an active interest in southern Utah until the decade after the dam was completed. Environmentalists drew their first line in the sand on the Kaiparowits Plateau, where Southern California Edison wanted to build a coal mine and power plant.[64] Originally proposed in 1965, the Kaiparowits project became a national issue about the same time the Trans-Escalante Highway gained momentum. In fact, the highway route passed near the proposed coal development, and locals supported both as complementary projects. Environmentalists, led by the Sierra Club and the Salt Lake City–based Wasatch Mountain Club, also linked the road and the power plant: a twin assault on the redrock wilderness. With Glen Canyon Dam, they argued, the canyon country had paid its dues to progress. Now the land needed protection. In defiance of the proposed highway, the Wasatch Mountain Club drafted a wilderness proposal for the canyons of the Escalante River—often called Glen Canyon in microcosm. The Sierra Club published a propaganda book, *Slickrock: Endangered Canyons of the Southwest* (1971), with words by Edward Abbey and photographs by Philip Hyde.

The Golden Circle had spiraled into a debate over wilderness, democracy, and progress, and the debate was sometimes ugly. The Escalante Chamber of Commerce took out advertising space in the two major Utah dailies, the *Salt Lake Tribune* and the *Deseret News,* to say, in part: "These Protectionists are totally unrealistic, unjust, and ruthless. They would kill the economy of a country to gratify their passion for exclusive use of territory that has scenic values." No one disputed the rare beauty of the canyons, but not everyone agreed what the beauty was for. Danny Reid of Escalante offered his own opinion: "What this area needs is access so that people can see God's best piece of work on earth, not to lock it up so that just the young and very healthy are all that will know of its existence. This area is so immense, that no person can see it all in a lifetime of walking. This road would no more desecrate the area than I-80 ruins the whole state of Utah."[65]

Though people in Escalante didn't want to hear it, environmentalists weren't entirely unsympathetic to their concerns. Even these "people haters" wanted tourism to flourish in Garfield County; even they believed some version of the Golden Circle was essential. "What is needed," said Jack McClellan of the Sierra Club, "is a road with scenic variety, a road to tie together the scenic wonders of our state, not one that rips through them like a dull knife."[66] He and other environmentalists touted the Canyon Country Parkway, a plan to pave existing roads only. From U.S. 89 near Kanab, the proposed route went north on the unimproved Cottonwood Canyon road to Cannonville, then east on Utah 12 to Escalante and Boulder, then north on the graded country road over the Aquarius Plateau to Torrey, then east on Utah 24 through Capitol Reef National Park to its junction with Utah 95 at Hanksville. An alternative route went directly from Boulder to Bullfrog via the Burr Trail, a dirt road. Compared to the blast-as-you-go Trans-Escalante Highway, this plan would cost far less, and, according to its proponents, benefit the local economy more, as the route passed through several small towns.

As things turned out, the controversial and phenomenally expensive Trans-Escalante Highway failed to receive federal funding. Meanwhile, responding to bad publicity and worse economic forecasts, Southern California Edison dropped the Kaiparowits project in 1976. Residents of Garfield and Kane counties were crushed, for they had placed their primary economic hopes on industrial development. They didn't think they could base their economy on catering to tourists, and they didn't particularly want to try. Jobs in the tourism industry were typically low paying and seasonal. They lacked benefits, not to mention a certain credibility among rural Utahns who wanted to make a living from the land. The producer ethic resisted the service mentality. But until another Kaiparowits came around, the counties adopted the concept of the Canyon Country Parkway by default. In the mid-1980s, Garfield County set out to do just what conservationists had endorsed: pave the Boulder–Torrey road and the Boulder–Bullfrog road. While the first went through without a hitch, the second became the most controversial road project in Utah history.

RIGHT-OF-WAY

The Burr Trail was seemingly made to be a scenic byway. After leaving Boulder, it winds around giant beehives of Navajo sandstone before dropping into narrow, red-walled Long Canyon, which eventually opens up into a huge basin surrounded by the Circle Cliffs. After crossing the basin, the road comes to the abrupt, awesome edge of the Waterpocket Fold, an uplifted monocline within Capitol Reef National Park. In a series of spectacular switchbacks, the road drops from the fold to the blue-shale desert near the base of the Henry Mountains and turns southward toward Lake Powell.

The route takes its name from John Atlantic Burr, a pioneer stockman. Starting in the 1880s, ranchers used the Burr Trail to move their livestock from summer pasture on the Aquarius Plateau to winter pasture in the Circle Cliffs basin, what they called the "Lower Country." In 1882, a local woman commented on the trail: "It is mostly uphill and sandy knee and then sheets of solid rock for the poor animals to pull over and slide down. I never saw the poor horses pull and paw as they done today." In the early twentieth century, a few random prospectors, geologists, archaeologists, and tourists traveled the Burr Trail by mule or horseback. A third option—wagons—opened up in the mid-1930s, following trail improvements. Cars (what few of them existed in Garfield County) couldn't handle it until 1947, when the Boulder Cattleman's Association and the BLM sponsored the first bulldozer work. At last, the Burr Trail was a "road." Additional improvements, including the switchbacks down the Waterpocket Fold, date to the uranium boom. "Even before the road was completed," wrote one local, "prospectors in jeeps spread over the country staking claims." Finally, in response to Lake Powell, the county upgraded the road once more and continuously maintained it thereafter.[67]

As the only direct link between western and eastern Garfield County, the Burr Trail became vitally important in the late 1970s, when a mining firm built a new town near Bullfrog. Ticaboo, as it was called, owed its existence to a resurgent uranium market. Its mine and mill accounted for nearly half the tax base of Garfield County in the early 1980s—less an indication of uranium's value than of the county's poverty. Garfield typically had unemployment figures double or triple the state average.

By improving the Burr Trail, the county hoped to revive its economy. A paved road would, it believed, ease cross-county transportation, facilitate mining and mineral exploration, and enhance tourist revenue. The existing road received ten to fifteen traffic counts per day; the county hoped to boost the average to 250. "The paved road will open up this country to tourism," said Del LeFevre, commissioner of Garfield County. The title of the road engineering study said it all: *Boulder–Bullfrog Scenic Road: A Vital Link in the Grand Circle Adventure*. Utah senator Jake Garn championed the project and tried unsuccessfully to secure matching federal funds. The county found a more receptive audience in the state legislature, which approved a preliminary funding bill in 1986, over the objections of environmentalists. Justifying the expenditure, the bill's lead sponsor asserted that federal land regulations "have just about wiped out all potential for economic development [in southern Utah]. We're left with tourism to fill the economic void." Eager to get moving, Garfield County opened the first road bid in February 1987, but only days later the entire project landed in federal court. The lawsuit named four plaintiffs: the Sierra Club, the National Parks and Conservation Association, the Wilderness Society, and the Southern Utah Wilderness Alliance (SUWA).[68]

Barely five years old, SUWA represented a new generation of environmentalists in Utah. Formed in response to the BLM's wilderness inventory process, the group had one priority: preserving the maximum possible acres of roadless land as congressionally designated wilderness. SUWA rejected the philosophy that to preserve wilderness you had to compromise and allow development somewhere else. Though it preferred tourism over other industries, the group believed that the highest use of the land—to be left alone—wasn't an economic use. SUWA had seen enough "improvement" in the canyon country. It fought for a wild Escalante River and an unimproved Burr Trail, not one or the other.

In opposing the road project, SUWA underscored its potential impact on adjacent Wilderness Study Areas and Capitol Reef National Park. But there was a surprising auxiliary concern mentioned in SUWA's literature: the dirt road itself. "There is something beyond the immediate sensory pleasure that makes driving the Burr Trail such a special experience. There is an awareness felt once on the trail that civilization just disappeared in the cloud of dust flying behind you. A clarity of thought emerges, proclaiming that you are truly at one with the earth."[69] This marked a new development in attitudes about roads in southern Utah. In the 1950s and 1960s, wilderness lovers could look past (or even look forward to) new roads because so much primitive country remained. By the 1980s, however, wilderness in the canyon country was perceived as threatened, dwindling. New or improved roads were unacceptable because roads destroyed wilderness. However, certain existing dirt tracks—exceptionally remote or scenic ones—became, by their association with the vanishing wild, objects of nostalgia, even reverence.

Of course, environmentalists were not the first Utahns to associate roads with hallowed ground. Mormons in southern Utah had their own deep feelings about the purpose of roads in wild country. To understand, it helps to return to the Hole in the Rock pioneers and the incredible trail they blazed. In 1940, the Mormon residents of San Juan County organized a commemorative trek to the slickrock dugway at the rim of Glen Canyon. In advertising the event, the local newspaper emphasized the proper attitude: "While the trip will be most fascinating from the standpoint of scenery and associations, it is not going to be a lark or vacation—but a serious pilgrimage. It will be an earnest and reverent group going to a shrine." This language, though unusually explicit, expresses a cultural viewpoint common in rural Utah. (Garfield County, for example, is over 90 percent Mormon.) As Wallace Stegner once wrote, "Symbols of the trail rise as naturally out of the Mormon mind as the phrase about making the desert bloom as the rose—and that springs to Mormon lips with the innocent ease of birdsong." In Mormon historical consciousness, the trek across the plains to Utah ranks second only to the restoration of Christ's gospel by Joseph Smith. Besides the prophets, the great heroes of Mormon history are the pioneers, the trailblazers, the road builders. In rural Utah, this reverence for road building has, until recently, been reinforced by personal hardships due to poor transportation. Supplies, medicine, mail, family—all of these were only as close as the roads were passable. Roads were among the most basic and essential forms of progress, and the all-weather highway constituted the ultimate dream, a fulfillment of the good work begun by the pioneers.[70]

To summarize, urban environmentalists looked at the Burr Trail and mainly saw the work of nature surrounding it, while rural Mormons mainly saw the work of people supporting it, improving it. "Since the time Brigham Young sent our ancestors to settle Southern Utah," said Cal Black, former commissioner of San Juan County, "we have been told and have worked and waited for the time when our area, in which most of us here were born, and have remained by choice, would be opened up so that all people could come and enjoy the scenic beauty that we have always known and loved. This has also meant, in our dreams of the future, that we would be more easily able to make a livelihood for our families, to provide them with the educational and other opportunities our City cousins have always taken for granted." Case in point: in the 1980s, Margie Lee Spencer of Escalante drove the Burr Trail twice a week for nine months of the year to reach her job in Ticaboo. She taught school. When questioned as a court witness, Spencer said she met all sorts of drivers on the road: health officers, tourists, ranchers, boaters, prospectors, sheriffs, insurance salesmen, backpackers. They came in compacts, trucks, vans, campers. Not all were prepared; Spencer pulled more than one station wagon out of the mud with her Ford Bronco. "I've passed cars with Alaska license plates," she said. "I stopped and talked with people from I swear almost every state in the union." When asked if she believed the proposed road improvements would "take away from the wilderness characteristics" of the area, Spencer replied, "I don't see how it could. It would just make it so there weren't deep ruts in the road and so that people didn't slide off the road. And it would just make it so people could actually see more of it."[71]

Isn't that what environmentalists wanted, too? After all, three of the four plaintiff groups had earlier testified in support of the Canyon Country Parkway. When confronted with that history, however, environmentalists dismissed it as irrelevant because fifteen years had passed since the hearings, and in the meantime the National Environmental Policy Act and the Federal Land Management and Policy Act had become law and now applied to the area. Before any roads were paved, the wilderness groups wanted to see a comprehensive regional plan for tourism. Garfield County rejected the idea. Understandably, it believed environmentalists were employing a double standard where they had no business in the first place. At one point in the Burr Trail controversy, citizens of Escalante became so frustrated by outside interference they hung the directors of SUWA in effigy.

The conflict came to a temporary resolution in 1987, when a U.S. district judge ruled that the county had a right-of-way to at least the first twenty-eight miles of the Burr Trail, from Boulder to Capitol Reef National Park. An appellate court later affirmed that decision, and road work began in 1988. Soon after, four of the county's bulldozers were sabotaged by one disgruntled environmentalist, accomplishing nothing. Work proceeded to the western boundary of the park, beyond which the right-of-way was still in question. When the Burr Trail reopened, it was partly surfaced, partly dirt. No one was happy.

BOULDER BLUES

I remember the Burr Trail. I first read about it when the lawsuit by environmentalists failed. Immediately I planned a driving trip. I had to arrive before the bulldozers, and I made it just in time. Actually, my dad did all the driving, since I was underage. I merely had to stare. It was a perfect October day, warm, vivid, a day for breaking hearts. Once back home, I wrote an essay, the first time I'd ever felt compelled to record something in words. I'd been on a voyage to a new world for the first and final time. Never had I seen so much beauty: the foreknowledge of loss gave me unprecedented, passionate awareness.

It was four years before I could return. When I went, I drove at a crawl on the asphalt, looking for rocks and feelings I remembered. I couldn't find them. I missed the dust, the clarity. I drove away depressed.

Next time I saw the improved Burr Trail was with friends who'd never been. To them it was beautiful, and looking through their eyes I had to admit it was—still, it wasn't the same. On a brand-new concrete bridge I spied some sympathetic graffiti: "KEEP IT LIKE IT WUZ!" Of course, you can only keep things like they are, not like they were. That's the poignancy of the spray-painted message: it speaks to the paralysis of nostalgia and the bitterness of hindsight. It didn't occur to me until later that people in Boulder might be nostalgic, too—not for the rough road itself, but for some of the rural qualities safeguarded by roughness.

Boulder has a remarkable history with and without roads. The town sits in a small valley surrounded on one side by the eleven-thousand-foot Aquarius Plateau and on the other by the canyons of the Escalante River. Mormon ranchers discovered the rich pastureland above Boulder in 1879, but homesteading didn't begin for ten years more. Technically, these people were not homesteaders but legal squatters, since the government hadn't surveyed the land (and wouldn't until the 1930s). Boulder grew haphazardly; the founding date may be considered 1898, the year the Mormon church became aware of this far-flung congregation. Even by Utah standards, the town was remote. Boulder claims the distinction of being the last place in the continental United States to receive its mail by mule (until almost 1940). The route of the "mail puncher" consisted of twenty-eight miles of cairns stacked across slickrock hills and canyons. There's a story of two women friends who once walked the mail route from Boulder to Escalante. Sally May King remarked that the man who made the trail should be rewarded or shot. Her companion responded emphatically, "'Kill him, damn him,' that's what I say."[72]

Boulder residents learned to live without—or be creative. One man is said to have disassembled a pickup, packed it over the mail trail, then reassembled it in Boulder. Another time, "when a serious slump hit and then hung on to the cattle market, the resourceful ranchers got the idea of milking their cows and shipping the cream as a small money crop. Uncle Sam had conveniently enlarged the facilities of his parcel post service at that time; so five or six slim legged, surefooted mules, each laden with five five-gallon cans of cream, picked their way three times a week along the narrow trail."[73]

Boulder residents endured their isolation until the 1930s, when Uncle Sam came through in a big way with the Civilian Conservation Corps (CCC). First, the CCC men built an alpine road from Escalante to Boulder that circumvented the canyons except for a single spot, where workers floated an incredible wooden bridge between knife-edged ridges. Hell's Backbone, they called it. But since hell froze over each winter, the CCC went to work on an alternate, all-weather route across the slickrock lowlands. Not to be outdone, the corps also began a road leading north from Boulder to Torrey in Wayne County. By 1940, all three automobile roads—each one a marvel—were completed, and Boulder threw a barbecue party. The town had gone from zero to three roads in less than a decade.

Boulder's primary access became the lowland route from Escalante, which received pavement piecemeal over the years. Ultimately, in 1971, a continuous strip of blacktop led to Boulder—and stopped. It was still a dead-end town. This condition persisted until 1985, when state road crews finished paving the Boulder–Torrey road, thus completing Utah State Highway 12. Ironically, it was this road, not the controversial Burr Trail, that would have the greatest impact on Boulder and eastern Garfield County. Highway 12 crosses the broad eastern shoulder of the Aquarius Plateau, which offers some of the finest views of the canyon country. "The explorer who sits upon the brink of its parapet . . . forgets that he is a geologist and feels himself a poet," wrote geologist Clarence Dutton in 1880. "It is the extreme of desolation, the blankest solitude, a superlative desert."[74] Predictably, after the paved route opened, *Sunset* magazine dubbed it "The Most Scenic Highway in America." More to the point, tourists could now drive directly from Capitol Reef National Park to Bryce Canyon National Park. The canyon country was no longer divided by bad roads. Everyone doing the driving tour of southern Utah now took the highway through Boulder, and everyone liked what they saw. In the words of the old state guidebook, the town offered "amazing contrast to the desert wastes and rocky vastnesses surrounding the community." A podunk town never looked so enchanting.

"The secret valley—or its counterpart, the undiscovered island—has had a perennial appeal for the western imagination," notes Utah author Edward Geary.

> With so many imaginative overlays, it is hardly surprising that these places at the world's end, if they exist at all, often prove somewhat disappointing. . . . [Boulder], however, proved to be one of the rare expectations not disappointed in fulfillment. When I crested the last sandstone ridge and caught my first sight of the intensely green pastures and hayfields nestled among honey-colored slickrock hills, the primitive "rip-cut" fences running up and down the slopes, the copious streams flowing through the meadows, I was struck by an almost overpowering feeling that I would remain here forever. I would write to my wife and children, inviting them to join me if they chose, but I would never leave this valley at the world's end.[75]

This is not an uncommon response. All are struck by the beauty of Boulder; more than a few ask for a realtor. In the early 1990s, several new homes and a resort appeared. The town was still tiny—fewer than two hundred people—but it suddenly lost the social cohesion of a small Mormon cattle town. Relying on ranching had meant living on the edge, yet certain Boulder residents hankered for the days before outside money rolled in on the fresh-laid tar. In 1996, the Associated Press distributed this feature:

> BOULDER—Any other small town losing its economic moorings would probably consider a new road bringing in tourists and their money a godsend.
>
> But not this community that cherishes its isolation amid some of the most spectacular scenery in the country. To its chagrin, Boulder has been discovered, and worse, fractured by the fallout.
>
> "We wanted it for us, not tourists," says rancher Del LeFevre, trying to explain why he pushed for paving state Route 12 and upgrading the popular Burr Trail road as a Garfield County commissioner in the 1980s.[76]

But wait: hadn't Garfield County intended the improvements for both groups of people? Previous comments from local officials indicated that the county wanted to revive traditional rural industries while generating additional revenue from tourists passing through. Naïvely, however, road backers didn't anticipate the sheer number of outsiders who would come, or those who would be enticed to stay.

Throughout the canyon country, tourism became a hot topic in the 1990s. Wayne Wonderland's gateway community, Torrey, was finally receiving some appreciable tourist revenue, yet the new service jobs were not the kind that supported families. Even worse, land speculators had discovered the place. Tourism paved the way, it seemed, for a modern form of colonialism: outsiders shaping the future of small towns without the townspeople's consent. Native residents began to worry that Torrey could go the way of Moab, which had, overnight, become a cause célèbre in southern Utah, something like Jackson in Wyoming, or Aspen in Colorado. Around 1990, the long-anticipated tourism boom finally hit Grand County, bringing new wealth and concomitant anxiety. No one knew how to rein it in.

Compared to Moab, or even Torrey, Boulder was changing slowly. But because of its small size and history of isolation, the town didn't adapt well to any change. Boulder had become a dysfunctional town, disabled by feuds between old-timers and newcomers, Mormons and non-Mormons. And the immediate future looked no brighter: inevitably, more people would buy land in this now-approachable hidden valley. Its spell was too great. In reaching out to the world, Boulder had relinquished much of its control: the outside could now reach in. This wasn't the first time, though, that a southern Utah outpost had experienced the ironies of road building. An even starker example comes from beneath Lake Powell, that stunning, watery graveyard.

DANDY CROSSING

Hite, Utah, took its name from Cass Hite, a prospector. He came to the Colorado River in 1883 with the help of some Navajo friends, who told him of gold in Glen Canyon: shiny flecks in the damp red sand. It's hard to get rich by sluicing, but gold is gold, and Hite's discovery lured family members and prospectors to southern Utah. The men congregated at "Hite City," located on a river bar a half mile wide and two miles long in upper Glen.

Tributary canyons debouched on opposite sides: Trachyte Creek on the north and White Canyon on the south. By canyon country standards, the approach from either direction was easy—thus Hite's other name: "Dandy Crossing." Prospector and river runner David Rust remembered this rhyme about it:

> O farmers drop your grubbing hoes
> Your shovels and your picks
> Don't linger any longer
> And work the water ditch
> But leave your wife and family
> All out in the cold
> And shove for Dandy Crossing
> To hunt the shining gold[77]

Several hundred miners used Hite as their jumping-off place at the peak of this minirush in the late 1880s. Many of them ventured downriver in handmade boats. Soon the entire canyon was staked. Little came of the claims, however; the country proved too rough, and the gold too fine. By 1890, the excitement had played out. Nonetheless, a few die-hard prospectors, those content to break even, hung on. The post office at Hite managed to stay open until 1914, the same year Cass Hite died in his humble cabin on the Colorado River.[78]

Getting the mail—or anything else—to Dandy Crossing was a chore. From the nearest railroad stop, Green River, Utah, the trip took about a week. Even pack animals struggled over the last fifty miles from Hanksville (a ranching hamlet and the only wayside settlement). By the standards of the automobile age, this lower road didn't count as a road until 1932, when a local man put his shoulder to the wheel to improve it.

Arthur Chaffin more than earned the epitaph on his headstone: "Developer, Prospector, Builder." Over his ninety-five years, Arthur (Arth for short) witnessed and assisted some great changes in southeastern Utah. Originally from Cedar City, he came to Glen Canyon in 1894 to help his father and brothers with placer mining. He wasn't yet ten. Later, as an adult, Chaffin operated a trading post on the river. After a mining stint in Nevada, he moved back to Utah and lived in Wayne County, where he served as a commissioner from 1922 to 1926. While in office, he became a disciple of good roads. It was the beginning of a life crusade. In 1932, when Arth tired of town life and decided to return to Glen Canyon, he decided to do something about the road to Hite. He went to Price, Utah, pleaded with the local representative of the state highway department, and left with a Caterpillar tractor and a grader on a ten-day loan. Rather than following the established route through the canyon of Trachyte Creek, Chaffin took the Cat down North Wash, a wider, gentler canyon. From the wash's mouth, the roadbed hugged the right-bank cliffs of Glen Canyon down to Hite, four miles away.

At first, few people noticed the road improvements. In the 1930s, Hite was a ghost of its former self. Some years Chaffin had neighbors—stray prospectors or families—but in others he had none. Fortunately, Arth was too busy to be lonely. With his own two hands he built a house, a toolshed, a machine shop, and a corral, not to mention the irrigation works for his twenty-acre pasture and garden. Sheltered by sandstone walls, Hite (elevation 3,300 feet) boasted a nine-month growing season, and Chaffin took full advantage by growing peaches, figs, plums, apples, walnuts, watermelon, cantaloupe, pomegranates, dates, pears, and grapes. He even had a state permit to make two hundred gallons of wine. Barbara Ekker of Hanksville remembered that townsfolk "would bundle up the whole family and take all their canning stuff and stay down there [at Chaffin's], and bottle, and pick fruit[,] but it was an all day deal like now it's an hour drive."[79]

It took all day because of North Wash. When bulldozing the route, Chaffin had no choice but to cross the streambed when it meandered. Consequently, whenever a flash flood ripped down the wash, parts of the road went with it. Everyone who drove the old road recalls the rough crossings of North Wash, but everyone recalls a different number: 26, 38, 53, 60, 68 . . . Enough to lose patience, anyway. Arth erected a warning sign at the head of the canyon, but he wished he could do better. True to his developer's spirit, he eventually did. The details are sketchy, but by most accounts Chaffin made a trip to Salt Lake City in 1944 or 1945 to petition for funds to improve the road. At the capitol he received an enthusiastic hearing from Ora Bundy, head of the new Department of Publicity and Industrial Development. For years, the state had wanted an automobile road connecting Capitol Reef National Monument to Natural Bridges National Monument, and Wayne County to San Juan County. So Bundy offered a deal: If Chaffin would assume responsibility for the establishment and maintenance of a ferry at Hite, the state would dig up some money for the road.

How do you build a ferry? The answer came naturally to Chaffin. He had proven his handiness before by building all manner of boats, including a scow run by automated paddle wheels. Whenever he traveled to town (the distant communities of Rabbit Valley—Loa, Bicknell, and the rest), he would collect scrap iron and haul it back to his riverside junk pile. Likewise, on his trips through Glen Canyon he rummaged through abandoned mining sites. No wonder people called him "Pack Rat Chaffin," though "mechanical genius" would have worked, too. His ferry was a thing of rustic beauty. It consisted of a wooden platform supported by army-surplus pontoons, guided by twin steel cables, and operated by a winch powered by an anchored Model A Ford. With his practical skills, Arth also served as an advisor for the road project, which began in 1945, after Ora Bundy transferred sixty thousand dollars from his department to the state highway department. The construction workers came from Wayne and San Juan counties, both of which had accepted the road as a county route, meaning they would maintain it in the future. Only Garfield County refused. The road's middle section fell within its boundaries, but in this case, boundaries meant nothing. Excluding Hite, every town in Garfield lay in the west, beyond the Henry Mountains, the Waterpocket Fold, and the canyons of the Escalante River. To reach the new road, Garfield County graders faced a two-hundred-mile journey via two neighboring counties. They might as well go to Nevada.

Even without Garfield County's involvement, the road and ferry were big news in southeastern Utah. About four hundred people, including the governor, showed up at Arthur Chaffin's ranch on 17 September 1946 for the dedication. Not since the gold rush had Hite seen so much excitement. Sadly, only weeks later, Chaffin's ferry sank in a nighttime flood. Not to be discouraged, he went right to work on repairs, and the ferry resumed service in 1948—this time without a ceremony.

At first, few people rang the bell by the river to ask for a lift. But change was on the way. In 1949, the Vanadium Corporation of America opened a mill near the mouth of White Canyon. Ore came from the Happy Jack Mine, fifteen miles to the southeast. Originally developed in the 1890s as a copper mine, Happy Jack had never been profitable because the copper was contaminated with uranium. The mine sold for five hundred dollars in 1946 and was up for sale again when the AEC announced its uranium buying program in 1948. The owners, two men from Moab, immediately withdrew the sale, entered the uranium business, and netted some $25 million. Happy Jack became one of the richest mines in all of southern Utah. At its peak, in the early 1950s, it sent some thirty tons of ore per day to the White

Canyon mill. To facilitate the out-shipment of uranium, the AEC financed a new all-season road from Blanding to the Colorado River. There, across the river from Hite, a whole new town arose. A heap of tents, trailers, and semipermanent homes sheltered over a hundred people, including "every kind of expert and greenhorn prospector, and a full contingent of weirdos."[80]

Hite, too, was growing—at its own pace. In 1947, Aaron Porter bought a portion of Arthur Chaffin's property to live on with his family. In 1948, Chaffin married Della Taylor Hickman (the widowed wife of Joe Hickman, booster of Wayne Wonderland); also, Dan Miller and Jack Pehrson relocated to the river. With ten school-aged children, Hite could finally justify hiring a teacher, Rosa Gerhart. An abandoned CCC barracks from Blanding served as her one-room school. Pushing Hite even further into the present, Chaffin and Miller cleared an airplane landing strip, which uranium miners instantly put to use. Every day, it seemed, another pie-eyed prospector showed up by plane or jeep. Tourists, too, free from World War II travel restrictions, were beginning to explore the country. Trying to cash in, Arth built several guest cottages on his property. Someday, he hoped, Hite would become a haven for tourists. He envisioned daily river cruises, motel accommodations, and, most important, a paved highway with scenic overlooks. Repeatedly he petitioned the state to upgrade the Hanksville–Blanding road.

In the short term, however, Chaffin and his wife were ready for a long vacation. In 1952, they entrusted the ferry to Ilda and Elmer Johnson, who lasted as long as they could—three years. "There was not enough money in it," they said when they quit. The primitive school was another big factor. Out of necessity, Arth returned to the ferry, but he found that his heart wasn't in it anymore. Soon he wanted out, as a contemporary newspaper reported:

> Chaffin, one of the real pioneers of southeastern Utah, explains his decision to sell by saying the rush of uranium business into the heretofore isolated area just created too much excitement and confusion for an old cowpoke, miner, world-famous riverman, Indian trader, and rancher.
>
> Mrs. Chaffin, better known as Della to her friends, concurs. Ferry boat crossings on the always changing Colorado river at all hours of the day and night, plus a steady stream of prospectors, geologists, miners, and strangers unfamiliar with and unsympa-

thetic to the 'Cañon Country' leave no time for the top host and hostess of the Robber[s] Roost to visit with friends and tourists.[81]

But if the uranium boom was the catalyst, the clincher was the dam. According to a friend of Chaffin's, "When the construction of the Glen Canyon Dam was authorized [in 1956], he gave up. He knew Hite would be flooded out and the tourist facilities and marinas on the reservoir would eventually be developed as a monopoly big business with the full backing of the government and the small operator would have no chance at competing or be allowed to compete."[82]

In 1956, Chaffin unloaded the ferry on Reed Maxfield. Though Maxfield drowned in the river the next year, his widow (and their seven children) carried on. When the ferry sank in 1957, the state built a new one and hired Mrs. Maxfield as a government employee. She stayed until November 1959, when Woody Edgell took the position as well as the mayorship. Effectively functioning as the town, Mayor Edgell operated Hite's only tavern and tent motel. Like Chaffin before, he had big dreams about tourism. He too would be disappointed. The lake behind the dam promised to be a recreational hot spot, but Dandy Crossing was not in the forecast; the government intended to condemn the private property along the river. In the early 1960s, the Bureau of Reclamation informed the remaining residents that all their belongings had to be removed or burned before the reservoir arrived. By this point, the uranium mill, like the uranium boom, had died, a preview of things to come. The last of the river people left in 1963, with dead water lapping at the door. "We people who have lived at White Canyon and Hite and on the river are heartbroken that so much is lost beneath the lake," Pearl Baker said later. "Nothing that Lake Powell can ever give to the visiting public can even begin to compare with the damage that it did in the wonderful . . . fabulous places it covered."[83]

All that was left was the ferry. In 1965, its terminal year, each passenger received a commemorative certificate signed by the governor of Utah. Some people traveled all the way to Hite just to score this souvenir—a reminder of a passing era. As for Arthur Chaffin, he had made his own commemorative trip. In preparation for Lake Powell, he built one more masterpiece: a barge made of eight empty fifty-gallon drums strapped to the bottom of pontoons. Above that floating base, he mounted a floorboard (taken from the schoolhouse), a full-sized stove, and a double bed within a giant canvas tent. A heavy outboard motor propelled this peculiar creation—

Arth Chaffin handles the Hite ferry on its last official day, 5 June 1964, as Woody Edgell looks forlornly on. (Photograph by W. L. Rusho.)

Lake Powell's first houseboat. On it, Arth and Della floated over the rising reservoir to make final photographs of petroglyphs and final checks of mining claims.

When it came to his underwater ranch, Arth refused to accept the government's compensation of a few dollars per acre. He wanted to trade for twenty-eight acres at the base of the Henry Mountains, where he hoped to start a tourist camp. The feds wouldn't hear of it. Chaffin sued, arguing that the government had ignored the worth of his property as a placer operation and a potential riverside recreational development. In early 1966, a jury awarded him eight thousand dollars, "four times what the Gov. offered us—but their offer was so low this didn't amount to much. Not enough to pay the expense & worry of fighting them. We did learn that the B.L.M. & Reclamation are so 'Rotten' that no citizen should be proud of them."[84]

So Arth cut his losses and left the river for good.

He left behind a legacy, however. By building and operating a river crossing, Chaffin helped ensure that Utah established right-of-way for the highway route, Utah 95. Thus, when the government submerged the Hite ferry, it had to make amends. In 1964–65, the feds allocated $3 million for a lake crossing in the form of three steel bridges: one across the flooded Dirty Devil River, one across the former Colorado, and one across White Canyon. All three bridges were dedicated in June 1966. About the same time, crews began paving the entire route.

As the only automobile road in Utah to cross the canyon of the Colorado River, Utah 95 deserved to be called the "backbone" of the Golden Circle. Dandy Crossing—some form of it—was essential to that long-held dream of locals—the "opening" of scenic southeastern Utah. Were these new, dandy bridges above Lake Powell a true realization of that dream? The answer is yes and no. To understand, it helps to go back to 17 September 1946 and the dedication of the original Hite ferry. Luckily, William E. Rice, a recorder from Richfield, Utah, transcribed the proceedings and published them as a souvenir booklet.

"We are reenacting scenes of our pioneer fathers," said E. P. Pectol, master of ceremonies. "All who made this trek will go into history as pioneers for the future automobile road and the future development of this great Wonderland. You will have something to tell your children and to tell your grandchildren and your great grandchildren; and as the years go by you will be proud of this wonderful journey that you have made today. You are today pioneers of a greater civilization of tomorrow."[85] Zeke Johnson, representing San Juan County, was likewise ebullient. He couldn't contain his love for the land. "It has been said that when the Lord made this earth He had a lot of trash left over and He dumped it down and made San Juan [County]," he remarked. "I want to tell you San Juan is one of the beauty spots of the world—there never will be a more beautiful place." J. M. Adams, a Wayne Country delegate, agreed but added this caveat: "[Even] if a region has the finest climate, the best soil and every other natural asset, if it cannot boast of a good road, it is still a waste land." He and every speaker looked forward to the day when the outside world discovered the beauties of southern Utah and smooth, wide roads would be built to accommodate them. This beauty should not be hidden, Pectol believed. The booster from Wayne County expressed his feelings in a song lyric:

> You have read of a land of great beauty,
> Far out here in this land of our God;

You have read how its walls have been fashioned
By a Sculptor from heaven's abode.
In this land there is rest for the weary,
In this land there is peace for the soul;
But not half of this wonderland's beauty
To mortals has ever been told.

Roads would end this neglect. As Arthur Crawford of the State Department of Publicity and Industrial Development stated, "There is little question that if we can maintain this road, these trips will become one of the most popular vacation experiences in all America." He further anticipated the stimulation of vanadium-uranium mining and the reinvigoration of towns near Capitol Reef and Natural Bridges. The way the dignitaries talked, there would be prosperity all around. Lord knows, it was a long time coming:

The Pioneers who helped to build this country
Had dreams of building roads like these some day;
Wherever they are now, we know they're happy,
To see their dreams fulfilled in such a way.

. . . .

The Ferry on the River Colorado
Means a better life for me and you.

While the dedication had a surfeit of musical numbers, it almost concluded without its keynote speaker. Governor Herbert B. Maw showed up late because, embarrassingly, his car got mired in the brand-new road. When he took the podium, Maw changed the mood with his hard-hitting message: "Neither the state nor our counties nor our cities have ever done anything to date to make it possible for tourists to see anything that we actually have." According to the governor, Utah's only accessible attractions were Temple Square in Salt Lake City, developed by the Mormon church, and Bryce Canyon and Zion national parks, developed by the Union Pacific. "But where else," Maw asked rhetorically, "can a tourist go who comes to Utah unless he gets on a horse and goes out into the wilds?" Of the two million tourists who came to Utah each year, most took no more than a half-day's break from their beeline to California, the governor reported. If these people could be persuaded to stay just one more day in Utah, the state would receive some $25 million additional revenue. But tourists, like

Maw, desired good roads: "I should like to have an opportunity to look around a little and see what I am going through, and not keep my eyes glued on the road for a rut." Two years before, the governor gave up on Capitol Reef National Monument because of washboard and washouts. "I pretty near had my teeth shaken out . . . and had to turn back," he said. "Today you come down here and you are praising this road. It isn't such a hot road [applause]."

And Wayne Wonderland wasn't the only hard-to-reach beauty spot in southern Utah, Governor Maw continued. He recounted how he had been "humiliated and shamed" by a copy of *Arizona Highways*: "They had page after page of beautiful pictures, and in there Arizona had a beautiful picture of the Natural Bridge[s] in San Juan County, and of the Goosenecks [of the San Juan River] down there, and advertising that as a part of Arizona's publicity because the only way people can get into it down there is by way of Arizona." He urged the legislature to fund road development in the scenic areas of the state so that Utah could receive its fair share of the tourist dollar. Roads were vital to a "great industrial future," Maw said. He echoed Arthur Crawford, who said the state was finally ready to "claim its share of tourists and of world travelers who seek out the lands of legend and of story—the quiet beauty spots of the world, the last frontiers of loneliness."

Most striking about this last comment—and the whole dedication ceremony—was the mixture of nineteenth-century symbolism and twentieth-century dreams. Rural Utahns wanted paved roads, they wanted tourists, yet they wanted to maintain their way of life. They saw tourism, ranching, and uranium mining as compatible economic activities, all of which stood to benefit from improved roads. To the men and women gathered by the Colorado River, there was no apparent contradiction between promoting the country to tourists and keeping it like it was. Southern Utah was so big, so empty, it couldn't fill up. The last frontier of loneliness could never run out.

At the dedication, the Sage Brush Quartet from Blanding sang the familiar western song "Don't Fence Me In." The performers and the audience couldn't imagine the day when federal courts and environmental assessments would decide whether a road could be paved. They couldn't imagine the millions of automobile tourists that would eventually come to their homeland and threaten to transform, not merely supplement, the traditional rural economy. They couldn't foresee that Zion National Park, whose success they hoped to emulate, would grow so crowded by the century's end that land managers would institute a shuttle bus system. Finally, Arth Chaffin could never have expected that a reservoir would, in less than twenty years, submerge his home, and with it the substance of his dream.

CODA

Edward Abbey took the Hite ferry in 1953 and published an essay about it in 1971 for his anti-road-development book *Slickrock*. "The words seem too romantic now," Abbey said—though clearly he missed the romance:

> So, one day we loaded the tow chain and the spare spare, the water cans and gas cans, the bedrolls and bacon and beans and boots into the back of the truck and bolted off. For the unknown. Well, unknown to us. . . . At Blanding we left the pavement and turned west on a dirt road into the sweet wilderness. Wilderness? It seemed like wilderness to us. Till we reached the town of Green River 180 miles beyond, we would not see another telephone pole. Behind us now was the last drugstore, the final power line, the ultimate policeman, the end of all asphalt, the very tip of the monster's tentacle.[86]

Beyond Natural Bridges National Monument, the road became "unimproved." "Good," he wrote. "The more unimproved the better, that's what we thought. Assuming, of course, in those innocent days, that anything good would be allowed to remain that way." After following a red ledge above White Canyon, the road dropped into the sudden green of Glen Canyon. At the river, Abbey shook the hand of the ferryman, Arthur Chaffin. Then, "off we went, across the golden Colorado toward that undiscovered West on the other side."

The power of Abbey's essay lies in its self-conscious invocation of the lost. The reader knows from the beginning—from the very title, "How It Was"—that this sweet world is gone. Abbey concludes with characteristic bluntness:

> Today the old North Wash trail road is partly submerged, the rest obliterated. The state has ripped and blasted and laid an asphalt highway through and around the area to link the fancy new tin

bridges with the outside world. The river is gone, the ferry is gone, Dandy Crossing is gone. Most of the formerly primitive road from Blanding west has now been improved beyond recognition. All of this, the engineers and politicians and bankers will tell you, makes the region now easily accessible to everybody, no matter how fat, feeble or flaccid. That is a lie.

It is a lie. For those who go there now, smooth, comfortable, quick and easy, gliding through as slick as grease, will never be able to see what we saw. They will never feel what we felt. They will never learn what we know.

Abbey, who didn't know the long history behind his road to discovery, had more in common with Chaffin than he could have guessed. In separate but convergent ways, both men followed a dirt road in search of an improved world, and found it, briefly, only to reach, in the end, a river of loss with no ferry in sight.

PART 2

EXPLORATION AND THRILL

THE MOVING PEOPLE

In the early decades of the twentieth century, John and Louisa Wetherill operated a trading post and lodge in Kayenta, Arizona, on the northern edge of the Navajo Reservation. Their partner, Clyde Colville, managed the books, while Louisa spent her time as host and Indian liaison. John, meanwhile, was usually gone doing guide work. From the Wetherill place—a tidy stone structure enclosed by a landscape of rock—he led his customers to deep canyons, cliff ruins, and, above all, incomparable Rainbow Bridge. The world's largest and most beautiful natural bridge was officially discovered in 1909 by a party that included John Wetherill. Soon after the announcement, seekers began arriving on his doorstep; they too wanted to travel the moonscape passage to Bridge Canyon and its secreted namesake. To Louisa, coauthor of the family hagiography, these tourists were the latest in a procession of "Moving People." On the heels of the overland pioneer came the prospector; "after him the trader and settler; then the scientific explorer, excavating, surveying, and mapping; and now the heirs to those who had wrought life from a hard land—the men who came to accept it as their playground."[1]

The Wetherills lived long enough to see automobiles crawl across the red rock and sand, and airplanes cross the indigo sky. In 1927, the old-timers boarded a plane for their first ride. Chartered by International Newsreel, the light craft rose above desolate, photogenic canyons and mesas, over Monument Valley, on past Rainbow Bridge and Glen Canyon of the Colorado River. From the height of clouds, rare in this arid country, John and Louisa saw their homeland with new eyes. Had their vision gone far enough, past the horizon of time, they would have looked over water where none used to be. They would have seen motorboats interrupting the impossible blue of an improbable reservoir, the conveyances of a new kind of Moving People. Only five decades after the discovery of the rock rainbow, Lake Powell arrived on the scene.

The idea of Moving People is disagreeably systematic and racially selective—Navajos, with whom the Wetherills daily interacted, are nowhere to be found—yet it suggests a significant fact: tourism is contingent on specific places, peoples, and times. It has a history.

In the previous section, I examined some of the developments that would, by the late twentieth century, permit industrial tourism in the canyonlands. Now I turn to the people called tourists—defined here broadly as pleasure travelers—starting with those relatively few who came to the country *before* it was "discovered" and "developed." The focus will constrict to Glen Canyon and the land to its immediate south, including a sliver of Arizona. The San Juan Country, as it's sometimes called, is the roughest, least travel-friendly part of the canyonlands, yet it boasts a remarkable history of travel. Chronologically, I'll consider three groups of visitors: (1) those who came to Rainbow Bridge from 1909 to roughly 1950 via overland trails; (2) those who floated down Glen Canyon (and hiked to Rainbow Bridge from the river) from roughly 1940 to 1963; and (3) those who boated on Lake Powell (and walked to the bridge) from 1963 to roughly 1968.

Though differences exist within and between these groups, they share two common denominators: an explicit identification as explorers and a related, implicit identification as whites. All of the available evidence suggests that the tremendous majority of tourists were Euro-American. For my purposes, "Euro-American," like "white," is a conceptual term as well as an ethnic catchall. Whiteness is a concept akin to gender, class, and race. Regardless of their specific European and/or American ancestries, tourists used their economic status to assume the masculine role of white explorers in dark, exotic territory. In southern Utah and northern Arizona, tourists found what seemed like a new world—or at least a throwback to a simpler, and somehow superior, America. Early Rainbow Bridge visitors tended to identify this semimythical place as the "frontier"; river runners and boaters tended to call it "wilderness." Both words evoked excitement, as they had for earlier Americans, but with newer connotations of peace and renewal. Overwhelmingly, people *liked* Glen Canyon and, later on, Lake Powell. They liked it the way they found it, in no small part because places and place-experiences like these were hard to come by anymore. To the extent that they were discontinuous with everyday life, they can be termed sacred—literally out of this world.[2]

Clearly, the canyon country of Louisa Wetherill's generation (and even the next) was not really a "playground" in any trivial sense. For here in

Utah, in the twentieth century, you the tourist could still find perfect kivas and pristine vistas. You could stumble on places where—just maybe—no one had been before. And with a little effort, you could actually discover arches and bridges, and ruins, and give names to unnamed canyons.

The great western surveys of the nineteenth century had largely bypassed the Glen Canyon region. The Powell Survey floated right down the middle, of course, but did surprisingly little work beyond the river (one important exception being the excursions of geologist Grove Karl Gilbert into the island peaks of the Henry Mountains). Much later, in the 1920s, dam surveyors worked the river, but the region as a whole was bereft of good maps until the 1950s, when the uranium boom propelled the U.S. Geological Survey into action. Before then, the best (and sometimes only) information on topography, climate, and history were found in the geologic reports of Herbert Gregory, who began his fieldwork in 1909, the same year Rainbow Bridge was discovered. "That a geologist who made his primary contribution during the second and third decades of the present century should have been still exploring virgin land seems an audacious idea," writes historian Gary Topping. "It is true, nevertheless." True in the sense that the land was "virgin" to scientific exploration—and likewise to tourist exploration. As the following narrative shows, the two weren't always separable.[3]

At one level, the long record of twentieth-century exploration in the San Juan Country demonstrates the real ruggedness of the canyonlands. But it also suggests the significance of the frontier in white American culture. According to Frederick Jackson Turner, one of those rare historians to achieve the status of legend, the frontier experience made Americans out of Europeans. He first presented this thesis in 1893, arguing that the transformation of "free land" (that is, Indian land) engendered American ingenuity, prosperity, and democracy. It was an optimistic, even heroic interpretation of the past; no wonder people liked it. Yet it had a stinger: the frontier—and with it, a great era in American history—had closed in 1890. So said Turner. He took his cue from the U.S. census director, who declared in that year that it was no longer possible to identify a continuous line separating settled country from the unsettled "frontier," defined by the presence of less than two people per square mile.

Among most professional historians, Turner's sweeping, impressionistic thesis fell from dominance by the 1940s. More recently, a cadre of scholars has attempted to bury the "F-word" for good. At issue, in part, is the racism of the frontier thesis. An old-fashioned Turnerian take on the American West marginalizes Native Americans—and by the same token, Hispanics, Asians, and all the other "others." That is, Real History (as opposed to "prehistory") doesn't begin until Euro-Americans introduce it. Real History moves from east to west: it's the narrative of the Moving People. To the frustration of many academics, this linear, Eurocentric interpretation lives on in popular culture. Turner's 1893 explanation of the nation's past has shaped (and since been shaped by) Hollywood, Nashville, NASA, foreign policy, and—most important here—tourism and environmentalism.[4]

Beginning in the early twentieth century, significant numbers of white Americans lent their support to the emerging conservation movement. They sought to preserve remnants of the frontier as national parks and primitive areas. From books and magazines, they devoured stories of wilderness exploration. Better yet, in rugged pockets of the American West—places like the canyonlands that still met the people-per-square-mile criterion—they acted out frontier narratives long after the frontier had supposedly passed away.[5]

That it would pass away, probably soon, was always the assumption—and part of the thrill; being among the last was momentous, not unlike being first. This contradiction crops up repeatedly in travel accounts from the early years of Rainbow Bridge. In a typically American turn, visitors regretted the transformation of this far country even as they took advantage of its increasing accessibility. Likewise, while most pleasure travelers expressed antimodern sentiments—or, at the least, delight at temporarily escaping modernity—their very presence signified the encroachment of the modern world, a world that would, inevitably, bring changes to the land. But rather than dwell on this future, visitors seemed to "ease uncertainty by holding on to the landscape of an ephemeral present."[6] As a tactic, this wasn't always successful; some people had to concede firsthand the closing of Utah's "frontier." All agreed on one thing: the age of exploration couldn't last.

In short, many visitors anticipated specific forms of loss at Glen Canyon. By the late 1950s, of course, the all-encompassing form had a name: Glen Canyon Dam. The unavoidable reality of a rising tower of concrete served to reinforce an unspoken admonition: *Go now, explore while you can. Maybe you'll end up with a broken heart, but your memories will be golden.*

THE SUMMER OF 1909

The "discovery" of Rainbow Bridge was the last great find—on the wonder scale of Yellowstone and Yosemite—in American geographic history. Practically every subsequent travel article and brochure begins by mentioning the event. It has become something of a myth, a story of beginnings. Forget about the geologic record; from the perspective of tourism, real time at Rainbow Bridge begins with the words, "First visited by white men August 14, 1909." That line appeared on the first page of the first permanent visitor register, placed beneath the bridge in 1923. The author was Neil Judd, a member of the original party. In careful black ink he summarized his adventure for posterity. For many years, every bridge visitor read—and, by adding his or her name to the register, implicitly affirmed—the discovery story.

The 1909 party was actually two parties combined, one under the leadership of William Douglass, a General Land Office surveyor, another under Byron Cummings, a University of Utah professor. What brought the discoverers together was not camaraderie, but a dispute over archaeology—a dispute best explained through the family of Cummings's guide, John Wetherill.

The five Wetherill brothers settled on the Mancos River in southwestern Colorado in 1882. Soon after, they began exploring the river's headwaters in Mesa Verde. Thrilled by their archaeological discoveries, they neglected their ranching business in favor of full-time exploration. The brothers—particularly the eldest, Richard—felt they had found their life's calling. Richard went on to conduct excavations in Utah's Grand Gulch, Arizona's Tsegi Canyon, and New Mexico's Chaco Canyon. Though basically self-taught, he knew as much about archaeology as a lot of "professionals," since the field was just emerging as a science. However, because he was outside the academy, and seemingly outside the law, institutional archaeologists came to despise Wetherill. They developed a new term for him—pothunter—and lobbied for federal intervention. Luckily for the Wetherill haters, the prevailing politics of the era, Progressivism, placed great faith in professional science. Starting around 1900, the General Land Office (the forerunner of the Bureau of Land Management) did its best to discourage Wetherill and the legion of faceless pothunters—most of whom, it should be said, deserved the title more.

The most significant discouragement was the 1906 Antiquities Act, which made it a felony to excavate on federal land without a permit. In addition, it gave the president the power to reserve land of scientific or historic interest as a national monument. Though the legislative intent of this act was to protect localized archaeological sites in the Southwest, various presidents, starting with conservation-minded Teddy Roosevelt, have broadly exercised its power (a recent, controversial example being southwestern Utah's 1.7-million-acre Grand Staircase–Escalante National Monument, created by Bill Clinton on the eve of his reelection in 1996).[7]

Roosevelt designated Utah's first monument, Natural Bridges, in 1908. The three great bridges of White Canyon had been locally known since the 1880s, but gained national attention only in the first decade of the new century, when the *National Geographic* and other magazines gave them publicity. Until then, the largest well-known span was the Natural Bridge of Virginia, originally surveyed by George Washington, later owned by Thomas Jefferson. Though something of a minor attraction today, the Natural Bridge of Virginia was a world-famous attraction in the nineteenth century, sometimes named the "seventh natural wonder of the world." Early accounts of Utah's natural bridges typically noted how they surpassed their eastern counterpart. As the *New York Times* wrote of the largest of the three, "It would require five bridges of the size of the Natural Bridge of Virginia placed side by side to match this one in the width of its span." Before being upstaged by Rainbow Bridge National Monument and later Arches National Monument, Natural Bridges represented southeastern Utah's greatest drawing card for tourists. Arches and bridges excite the imagination as few other natural features. "By a curious coincidence while traveling in Japan," wrote a Salt Lake man in the early twentieth century, "I ran across a wealthy Belgian, a world traveler, who, when showing me his collection of photographs and curios, invited me to behold the greatest prize of all: a series of colored photos in a special electric lighted cabinet, of his trip to Utah's world famous Natural Bridges."[8]

In 1908, soon after the president signed the proclamation, the General Land Office dispatched a surveyor, William Douglass, to Natural Bridges. For assistance, Douglass hired a local Paiute man, Jim Mike, from whom he learned of a "larger and prettier" bridge shaped "like a rainbow" eighty or ninety miles west of Bluff, Utah, the surveyor's base of operations. About the same time, Douglass got a different lead from John Wetherill (who at that time was operating a trading post at Oljato, Utah). The trader spoke of Anasazi cities in the Tsegi Canyon system in northeastern Arizona. Though winter set in before Douglass could investigate, he persuaded his superiors in Washington to designate a monument in the region as a preliminary action against pothunting. So, sight unseen, the government created Navajo National Monument in early 1909. Come summer, Douglass intended to survey the new monument and hunt for Jim Mike's bridge.

As fate would have it, another man had almost identical summer plans. His name was Byron Cummings. An easterner by birth, a classicist by training, he had been associated with the University of Utah since 1893. There, over time, he turned to administration for work and archaeology for fun. During the 1909 academic break, he hoped to make explorations and excavations in Tsegi Canyon. He also hoped to locate the fabled natural bridge shaped like a rainbow. Cummings had heard about it from Wetherill, his guide, who in turn had gotten the information from a Navajo customer, Blind Salt Clansman.

Here some background is in order. Certain Navajos had known about Rainbow Bridge since the late nineteenth century, when the tribe began pushing into southeastern Utah. The initial push was born of crisis: in 1863, a federal military force under Kit Carson incarcerated perhaps two-thirds of the Navajo people. Those who escaped the "Long Walk" to Fort Sumner, New Mexico, fled west and north, beyond the periphery of their traditional land (the Dinetah). One of these renegades was Hashkeneinii. Traveling lightly, and often by night, he set a relentless pace for his family group, thereby earning his name—usually translated as "Giving Out Anger." The group survived on seeds and the occasional rabbit; Hashkeneinii wanted to save his twenty scrawny sheep for breeding stock. "Finally we reached the south end of Navaho Mountain," the headman's son recalled through an interpreter, "and came to a nice little stream with grass. Mother sat on the ground and she said she would go no further. Father tried to make her go on but she would not, so we made camp there, and lived in that place for six years."[9]

That grassy nook—a few miles, as the crow flies, from Rainbow Bridge—was so deep in tough terrain that Hashkeneinii avoided all contact with the two great enemies of his tribe, the Americans and the Southern Utes. But a third, non-hostile group, the San Juan "band" of Southern Paiutes, already called this region home. They knew all about Rainbow Bridge. The Paiute population, numbering perhaps a couple of hundred, centered in two localities: Willow Spring (near present-day Tuba City, Arizona) and Navajo Mountain. That the mountain now goes by that name says a lot about the recent history of the San Juan Paiutes—predominantly a history of loss. Though it's little known today, the whole strip of Utah south of Glen Canyon and the San Juan River was briefly a Southern Paiute reservation. Today, the "Piute Strip" (as it used to be written) falls within the boundaries of the Navajo Nation, a result of the Navajos' aggressive territorial expansion during the post–Fort Sumner period. In the last three decades of the nineteenth century, the Navajo population doubled to at least twenty thousand. Their sheep flocks grew even more impressively. Meanwhile, the number of San Juan Paiutes and their animals stayed roughly the same, and they struggled to compete with Southern Utes, Mormons, and especially Navajos. Though Paiutes would never disappear from the Rainbow Bridge region, most would acculturate into Navajo life through intermarriage and interaction. Perhaps the best-known San Juan Paiute had a Navajo name: Nasja Begay (Ná'áshjaa' Biye'), Owl's Son.[10]

And so the narrative resumes:

In August 1909, Nasja Begay was hired by Cummings for his knowledge of the rainbowlike bridge. For Cummings, this had already been a summer to remember. With the help of some Navajos, his party had located two magnificent cliff dwellings, Inscription House and Betatakin, in the Tsegi country. The professor and his three students (one of whom, his nephew Neil Judd, would go on to became a noted archaeologist) set about excavating. They worked under a permit issued to Edgar L. Hewett, head of the School of American Archaeology in Santa Fe, though Hewett himself had little to do with the digs. Like Richard Wetherill, Cummings was a self-taught archaeologist; the difference was his academic connection. Unfortunately for him, however, the man behind the new monument, William Douglass, didn't bow to the academy. Hoping to revoke Cummings's permit, the government man trailed the professor through the first part of the summer, taking notes to bolster his case. Aware of the impending conflict, John Wetherill arranged for the two men to meet and suggested the idea of a joint discovery expedition. Oddly, they agreed. The two glory seekers, Cummings and Douglass, made a symbolic pair. As Hal Rothman observes, the civilian expert and the government professional represented the past and future of this public land region: from unfettered exploration to rule-bound management.[11]

They set off on 11 August. Douglass's guide, Jim Mike, was there from the beginning, while Cummings's guide, Nasja Begay, caught up a couple of days late, and not a minute too soon. Travel over the "Glass Hills" had been slow, sometimes bewildering. Horses were bleeding from their hooves. Before Nasja Begay arrived, Jim Mike had recommended retreat, but John Wetherill kept the party going—and kept going in the right direction, fueling recent speculation that he had located the bridge the year before but had kept it to himself.[12]

In any event, the bridge was reached with rations and tempers running thin. "A spirit of rivalry developed between Professor Cummings and myself," Douglass admitted in his field notes, "as to who should first reach the bridge. . . . For [the last] 3 hours we rode an uncertain race, taking risks of horsemanship neither would ordinarily think of doing, the lead varying as one or the other secured the advantage over the tortuous trail."[13] Both men, particularly Douglass, wanted prestige; the surveyor wanted it for his agency as much as for himself. As it happened, however, Wetherill overtook Douglass at the last moment to become the first white man to pass beneath the rainbow. Yet the theatrics continued: for years afterward, Douglass and Cummings (and even more, Cummings's friends and family) sparred over who should receive credit for the discovery. On 14 August 1909, however, there was glory to go around. Starting a tradition of "firsts," Cummings became the first white man to glimpse the bridge, Douglass the first to measure it, Judd the first to photograph it.

Ever since that sweltering day in 1909, observers have tried and inevitably failed to describe Rainbow Bridge. The scene begs awe. The largest natural bridge in the world is also the most symmetrical and graceful. Unlike every other, Rainbow lacks a flat top or "roadway." Instead, the whole structure curves in a near-perfect half-circle. One side enters the ground by itself, standing free like the foot of a rainbow. Long ago, Bridge Creek flowed around this abutment—then the terminus of a canyon wall—in a tight meander. At the meander's inside corners, the stream gnawed against the wall, and eventually broke through, forming a thin tunnel, the beginnings of a bridge. Subsequent spallation in the uniformly structured Navajo sandstone greatly enlarged the opening. The creek, meanwhile, continued to cut downward so that Rainbow Bridge now spans a narrow canyon-within-a-canyon. Over 350 feet separate the streambed and the top of the bridge. By itself, the bridge measures 290 feet high. To most people, 290 feet is just a number; to visualize size, they need a comparison. Start-

The first photograph of Rainbow Bridge from the point of first sighting, by Neil M. Judd, 14 August 1909.

ing as early as 1910, observers claimed that Rainbow Bridge could sit comfortably over the dome of the Capitol in Washington, D.C. A slight exaggeration, it turns out, but a memorable comparison. Some others from the period:

Statue of Liberty	151 feet
Niagara Falls	158 feet
Arc de Triomphe, Paris	164 feet
Mormon temple, Salt Lake City	210 feet
Bunker Hill Monument, Boston	221 feet
Flatiron Building, New York City	285 feet

By any yardstick, Rainbow Bridge was a wonder. It seemed predestined to be the last great American discovery in the Lower Forty-Eight.

According to several of the self-proclaimed discoverers, the "real" credit belonged to the Paiute guides. Though probably well-meaning, the sentiment was unavoidably ethnocentric. At the time, Nasja Begay and Jim Mike (and Dogeye Begay, a Navajo packer) had no reason to want credit for the "discovery." That obsession belonged to whites. "What is it that confers the noblest delight?" Mark Twain once asked.

> What is that which swells a man's breast with pride above that which any other experience can bring to him? Discovery! To know that you are walking where none others have walked; that you are beholding what human eye has not seen before; that you are breathing a virgin atmosphere. . . . To be the *first*—that is the idea. To do something, say something, see something, before *anybody* else— these are the things that confer a pleasure compared with which other pleasures are tame and commonplace, other ecstasies cheap and trivial.[14]

Of course, only one person (or group) may attain this ecstasy of originality. After 1909, no one would feel Byron Cummings's pure sense of discovery when spying the curved form of Rainbow Bridge. Everyone else who visited the place had first seen a photograph. But so what—there was room for more adventure. Maybe it was too late to be the First White Man, but here in the San Juan Country, where Indians numbered in hundreds and Anglos in handfuls, visitors could still taste the frontier, the way the West used to be—or was meant to have been. It's most fitting, then, that among Rainbow Bridge's earliest postdiscovery discoverers were Theodore Roosevelt and Zane Grey, two major purveyors of the western myth.

DESERT DUDES

Rainbow Bridge was the second of Roosevelt's three planned adventures in the Southwest in 1913 (the culmination being the Hopi Snake Dance). Like nearly everyone who came to the bridge in those early years, T.R. relied on John Wetherill to show him the way. The route was long and rough, at one point crossing an incredible expanse of naked sandstone hummocks— petrified sea waves, as someone later described them. After several days on the trail, the presidential pack train descended into thousand-foot-deep Bridge Canyon, where a streamlet, the patient sculptor of Rainbow Bridge, occasionally surfaced and gathered in scooped-out pools. Directly beneath the bridge, the full-bodied ex-president took a backfloat.

The "triumphal arch" soaring above was "surely one of the wonders of the world," said Roosevelt. The bridge, however, received but a single paragraph in his many-paged travel account. Rainbow Bridge's subordinate part was suggested by the title: "Across the Navajo Desert." Though fascinated by the Navajos, Roosevelt felt ill at ease in their territory. The landscape was of "incredible wildness, of tremendous and desolate majesty," to be sure, but it wasn't as inviting as the shade trees planted by the Mormons in Tuba, or the rose and hollyhocks tended by Louisa Wetherill in Kayenta.[15]

Roosevelt didn't give a justification for spending weeks on a horse in the desert. To him it was probably self-evident. For more context, it helps to read the book—Roosevelt's last—in which "Across the Navajo Desert" was anthologized. Prefacing *A Book-Lover's Holidays in the Open,* T.R. extolled the manly joys of exploring "the wide, waste spaces of the earth." He conceded, however, that such activity normally comes in the vigor of youth, "before the beat of the blood has grown sluggish." What was Roosevelt, an aging heart-attack candidate, left to do? Luckily for him, satisfaction could also be found on the "outskirts of adventure." By that he meant places that were relatively remote yet accessible: not-too-distant lands where you could, nonetheless, be a genuine adventurer. At Roosevelt's moment in history— after steam locomotion but before the modern automobile—those outskirts were expansive, from Africa to South America to the American Southwest.[16]

In 1913, Roosevelt's adventureland encompassed Rainbow Bridge. The national monument lay as far from a standard-gauge railhead as one could get in the continental United States—about two hundred miles by stage to Flagstaff, Arizona, and the cars of the Atchison, Topeka & Santa Fe; or 170 miles to Thompson, Utah, and the Denver & Rio Grande. "And it is even farther than it sounds," wrote an Indian trader, "for we don't measure distance in miles so much as in depth of mud and the length of time it takes to get anywhere." But all the same, it was *only* two hundred miles. The Rainbow Bridge country was, to invert a phrase, so far, yet so close. In places like Navajoland, wrote T.R., "the beauty and charm of the wilderness are [the older man's] for the asking, for the edges of the wilderness lie close beside the beaten roads of present travel." He was describing, quite simply, the best of two worlds. With your home base in civilization, you could, like a child, jump the backyard fence to roam in the wild world—and be back again for supper.[17]

Zane Grey, who visited Rainbow Bridge three months before Roosevelt, endeavored to stay close to this frontier. "Men love the forbidding and desolate desert because of the ineradicable and unconscious wildness of savage nature in them," he wrote. "Harness the cave-man—yes! . . . but do not kill him." Grey was a primitivist, a believer in that nostalgic concept of the superiority of "uncivilized" life. Primitivism, as one scholar has written, is the "paradoxical product of civilization itself . . . born of the interplay between the civilized self and the desire to reject or transform it." Grey himself was transformed in 1907 on a trip to the Grand Canyon. "No boy suddenly dropped into the West could have had a more magnificent adventure than I had," he wrote. "That wild, lonely, purple land of sage and rock took possession of me." Grey was a thirty-five-year-old dentist—soon to be ex-dentist. A native of Zanesville, Ohio, he returned to Arizona more than twenty times in the succeeding years as his new career took off. During the teens and early twenties, only McGuffey's Readers and the Bible outsold Zane Grey's westerns.[18]

Following his first trip to the Rainbow—a trip made with Wetherill, Nasja Begay, a cook, a supply wagon, and two women friends—Grey penned a lucid travel essay, "Nonnezoshe" (an anglicization of a Navajo word for "bridge"). Elements of this piece found their way into his 1915 novel, *The Rainbow Trail*, the sequel to the hugely popular *Riders of the Purple Sage*. Like many of Grey's romances, *The Rainbow Trail* borrowed heavily from real landscapes and people. John Wetherill became John Withers, and Nasja Begay became Nas ta Bega (now a full-blooded Navajo, but otherwise described the same: "dark, stately, inscrutable"). In the book, the desert-wise Withers has a frank tongue and a skeptical eye. In real life, Grey came to Kayenta three times before overcoming Wetherill's deep skepticism that the writer had the mettle for the two-week pack trip to Rainbow Bridge. Why did Grey want to go? He was enchanted by the spell of open spaces, much like his literary characters. In fact, sometimes Grey sensed life and fiction converging. West of Kayenta, along the canyon trail to Rainbow Bridge, "there rushed over me a strange feeling that *Riders of the Purple Sage* was true," he wrote. When Grey quoted sections of "Nonnezoshe" verbatim in *The Rainbow Trail* to describe the feelings of the protagonist, John Shefford, it wasn't merely a writer's convenience. To some degree, Shefford *was* Zane Grey.[19]

The novel goes like this: As a boy, Shefford dreams of an artistic career, but his family steers him to divinity school. He becomes a preacher, only to doubt the religion he preaches. A scandal follows. Disgraced and confused,

Shefford decides he must leave the Midwest. Where to go? Where else but the West? Shefford makes an obsession of a tale he had once heard of a maiden sequestered in a hidden rock valley in Utah. Answering "the wild call to the kingdom of adventure within him," he embarks on a quest to recover her. Once in Utah, the preacher toughens up; he learns to ride a horse and shoot a gun. Through a series of trials—including being tied and left for dead on a mound of fire ants—Shefford becomes a man, molded in the "stern and fiery crucible of the desert." In the climactic action, Shefford and his rescued girl, guided by the sage Nas ta Bega, escape rabid Mormon polygamists by descending Nonnezoshe Boco—Bridge Canyon, home of the rainbow. At Rainbow Bridge, Shefford finds the realizations of his dreams: brotherhood, romantic love, and spiritual faith. The experience of the wild desert has been invigorating, redemptive; it has offered a whole new start. And though the hidden natural bridge is but a temporary destination (Shefford ends his odyssey back home in Illinois), it's a place where personal growth crystallizes.[20]

Fiction again meets truth: Charles Bernheimer, a flesh-and-bones character who found new vigor exploring the canyonlands, was a big fan of Zane Grey. In fact, during one of his fifteen expeditions between 1915 and 1936, Bernheimer named a canyon after the writer. It's a story worth telling.

A wealthy German-American Jewish businessman from Manhattan, Bernheimer was the most conspicuous in a line of eastern gentlemen explorers (not unlike Byron Cummings) who came to the Four Corners region in the early twentieth century, attracted by the relics of the Anasazi and the vastness of the land. Bernheimer was well into middle age before he decided to go westering. He attributed it to "the urge of the subconscious." His boyhood dream, ignited by Cooper's Leatherstocking Tales, refueled by Zane Grey's romances, "fixed [on] Arizona as the land of mystery to be penetrated only by the most hardy and brave." His excitement eventually focused on the land surrounding Rainbow Bridge. In 1916, geologist Herbert Gregory described this as "the most inaccessible, least known, and roughest portion of the Navajo Reservation. . . . The deep canyon trenches are practically impassable and the buttresses flanking the cathedral spires are so narrow, smooth, and rounded that passage from one to another and access to the capping mesas have so far not been attained." "Why visit such a hazardous land?" asked Bernheimer in his 1924 book,

Rainbow Bridge. "The desire to do this is as old as man. . . . The charm and lure of exploring, once one yields to this craving, become irresistible. It is a real sport, for it develops endurance, abstinence, courage, and skill."[21]

In fact, Bernheimer was the unlikeliest of desert expeditioners; two regional historians have described him as a "skinny, sunken-chested" hypochondriac "utterly unqualified by heritage, training, or physique." No matter: he had money. Each summer before age and the Depression overtook him, the New Yorker would kiss his wife goodbye, ride the train to Arizona, then take a horse (later an automobile) to John Wetherill's place in Kayenta. There he would lay down a sum for food, pack animals, camp hands, and guides. Then it was off to the land of discovery. No one had circled Navajo Mountain before; no one had mapped the surrounding canyons; no one had pinpointed every Anasazi ruin. For Bernheimer, these summertime activities provided something like rebirth. According to one contemporary newspaper, "He was a tenderfoot and getting old, but he struck the gold-hued trail of romance into the forbidden unknown. . . . It gave his life an intensified vitality and velocity which reversed the rate of what were supposed to be his 'declining years.'"[22]

This doesn't mean that Bernheimer became a frontiersman. Even in the wild he would don his vests and fashionable knickers; only reluctantly did he abandon the necktie. Quick to credit his constant pair of well-paid guides, John Wetherill and Zeke Johnson (who, as good businessmen, let Bernheimer make "discoveries" when he wanted to), Bernheimer recognized the humorous incongruity of his presence. In his field notes, he once referred to himself as a "dude-explorer." Nevertheless, he took his expeditions seriously—and generally overrated their significance, as his tedious travel accounts attest. Though inspired by the dreams of boys, Bernheimer wanted his expeditions to be judged by the science of men. Toward this end, he extended an open invitation to Earl Morris, the respected southwestern archaeologist, to join him, and on Bernheimer's tab. Morris accepted on five occasions, and those five field seasons accounted for nearly all of the scientific achievements of the Bernheimer expeditions.

As for the gentleman leader, he gave names to geographic features and placed those names on his decent self-made maps. With the help of Wetherill and Johnson, he eventually succeeded in circling Navajo Mountain and blazed a new trail to Rainbow Bridge. A better word would be *blasted*: one narrow spot in "Redbud Pass" required several sticks of dynamite. Bernheimer wrote about it in the *National Geographic*, and later his book, which, according to his publisher's advertising, "describes to you an America you never dreamed of—a territory centuries dead at the time of Columbus, untouched for thousands of years, protected from invasion by cliff and desert and canyon and burning sun—suddenly opened up and given to the nation by the initiative and persistence of this cliff-dweller of Manhattan."[23] Was that all it took to "open" the New World of Utah—for some New Yorker to write a book? Maybe so, since the territory was only partly physical, another part perceptual. The latter could change independently or in tandem with the first. But one irony didn't change: whenever and however you "opened up" a wilderness, you risked losing the very qualities you hoped to draw near. Roosevelt's outskirts of adventure were attractive but fleeting; you had to be in the right place at the right time. Some could sense that their time was passing.

In 1923, returning to Kayenta after several years, Zane Grey noted some disturbing changes in his landscape of inspiration. It seemed the Navajos had been introduced to the two great evils of the day: influenza and greed. The Wetherills' outpost, though undeniably remote, no longer felt "wild and lonely." Automobiles had begun to travel the red-dirt trails. Others had found Grey's refuge. He was no doubt aware of what Gary Topping calls "the phenomenal rise of Kayenta as a tourist destination during the Roaring Twenties," a time when primitivism was fashionable among the arts community in America: "Kayenta became a refuge for jaded artists and writers during summer flights from the increasing congestion and pressures of urban life. Kayenta never became an artists' colony like Santa Fe during the same period but . . . it fulfilled the same function." "At the Wetherill's," wrote a free-wheeling woman from Boston, "we found homeliness, a bountiful table, and marvel of marvels, the bath-tub furthest from an express office in the States. A few miles further north, all traces of civilization drop out of sight, and you are living the Day after Creation." Despite its mundane bathtubs, Kayenta appeared to her as "a gateway, like Thibet, to the Unknown. It is a frontier, perhaps the last real frontier in the States. Only Piutes and Navajos brave the stupendous Beyond."[24]

To Zane Grey, Kayenta was the gateway to Rainbow Bridge, one place still removed from "the crass materialism and the aftermath of the Great War, the rush and fever and ferocity of the modern day with its jazz and license and blindness. . . . Too unknown, too remote, too hard to reach, Nonnezoshe still survived. Humanity had not marred it." To reach the bridge in 1923, Grey challenged John Wetherill to take him via "a trail never ridden by white men." Wetherill did (or, more likely, convinced Grey he did), but untrodden trails were a finite commodity, even here.[25]

Ironically, this was a business trip for Grey. He traveled to the bridge with Hollywood producer Jesse Lasky to scout out movie locations. Like most of Grey's novels, *The Rainbow Trail* made it to the silent screen (three times, in fact). The novelist was active in the production and promotion of the film adaptations; he more than played his part in publicizing this enchanted land to millions. But when people and regulations started coming—just the first small wave—Grey went berserk. In 1930, after a spat with the state of Arizona over out-of-season hunting permits, Grey vowed never to return. The state no longer resembled the land of freedom described in his books. To use a metaphor he would have appreciated, Grey was a pioneer in loss. According to one biographer, "Zane Grey needed the excitement of new discoveries to inspire his writing," and for a time he recaptured this excitement by exploring the northern Navajo country. But eventually he "exhausted all he could from it."[26]

Not everyone had such uncompromising standards for the undiscovered West. In 1930, one John Stewart MacClary drove to Kayenta to meet John and Louisa Wetherill. By this time, the aged couple had become regional legends, beloved relics of pioneer simplicity and hospitality. True to form, the Wetherills invited dust-caked MacClary to their dinner table. After satisfying food and conversation, the traveler retired to his guests' library. The Wetherill's collection, enormous for such an outpost, included a guest register. MacClary read through it, then added his entry, a poem:

> You've read in your novels of "great open spaces",—
> Of stern lands "out where the men are men".
> Perhaps you have laughed at the novelist's zeal,—
> Maybe doubted the words of his pen.
>
> But, if you are weary of smoke and of noise,—
> If you're looking for Nature supreme,—
> Come out to our West-land,—we'll show you the best land,
> A land that is fairer than dreams.
>
> . . . .
>
> This is the land that was meant to endure.
> Its rugged spires tell you that's true.
> It is healthful, inspiring, —a kingdom apart,—
> And it's spread here for me and for you.

It's the strength of our nation,—the backbone itself.
Words fail when its beauty's observed.
It's sweet, undefiled, rough, rugged and wild,—
The one land that God has reserved.[27]

If one is to take MacClary at his word—that God Himself reserved this last morsel of the frontier for his generation of (white) Americans— God had done so by making the land rugged. Of course, to claim this divine bequest, Americans needed to smooth over some of that selfsame ruggedness. In a later magazine article, MacClary was miffed to report that Rainbow Bridge remained "well nigh inaccessible to the average tourist" for years after its inclusion in the park system. To float there down the Colorado River was risky, to take the ten-day chartered pack trip was expensive. "Splendid adventure, perhaps, for wealthy people with unlimited time and money—yet all classes were entitled to the privilege of viewing the natural wonder, since Uncle Sam had reserved it as property for all the people."[28]

America's park system, organized in 1916, had its roots in nationalistic pride and insecurity. For the new republic, ageless natural beauty represented the best answer to European cultural antiquity. Who needed a castle when you had a chasm? After its aggressive westward expansion in the nineteenth century, America could point to scenery that rivaled, even exceeded, the Alps. Reserved as parks, the great scenic lands of the West served both to celebrate the nation and to commemorate its frontier past. "Our National Parks will continue for generations to come to be the No Man's Land, the Undiscovered Country, the Mysterious Old West, the Land of Romance and Adventure," wrote prominent parks booster Enos Mills in 1917. He hoped the parks would foster admiration for land and civilization in America, and the union he saw between the two. But first the public had to get there. Roads, however unromantic, were a must. Mills approvingly noted plans to make Rainbow Bridge National Monument "easily accessible."[29]

An access road finally came in the 1920s. Another layer of inaccessibility was peeled away—by entrepreneurs, however, not by Uncle Sam. In truth, the feds had little to do with the national monument. The fledgling Park Service lacked the resources. Besides, at Rainbow Bridge—the least-visited unit in the park system—management seemed unnecessary. The monument managed itself. The titular custodian, the ubiquitous John Wetherill, got a one-hundred-dollar stipend for periodically assuring the Park Service in Washington that the bridge hadn't fallen down. The bureaucrats didn't know about the new road or the responsible party—the Rainbow Natural Bridge Transportation Company—until the business was up and running.

The owners, S. I. Richardson and Hubert Richardson, were prominent traders on the Navajo Reservation. Rainbow Bridge National Monument had presented them with the opportunity to expand into the tourist business. The only problem was transportation. Charles Bernheimer had made a decent trail; now they needed a road to the trailhead. After acquiring the necessary permit from the U.S. Indian Bureau, the Richardson brothers hired some Navajo hands to blast and fill a winding hundred-mile route—ostensibly an old "Ute War Trail"—from Red Lake, Arizona, to the base of Navajo Mountain, near the Utah state line. According to the Richardsons, the fifty-thousand-dollar improvement project was slowed down by Navajo saboteurs hired by competing white traders. In any event, the Rainbow Trail opened for traffic in 1924. At the end of the road, the newly built, newly rustic Rainbow Lodge greeted visitors. In its opening year, eighty-eight people stayed over. Of those, twenty-two went on to Rainbow Bridge. Located less than twenty miles away, it could be reached by horse or mule in two or three days, round trip. Price: one hundred dollars per person, slightly more than a round-trip train fare from Chicago to Seattle. Over the next ten years, the price dropped to forty dollars—cheaper, but still no giveaway. This was never a poor person's vacation.[30]

For their guiding business the Richardsons received all-around praise. Their road, lodge, and stable permitted the best of two worlds—an accessible wilderness. So long as the road stopped here. "For after all," wrote one visitor, "it is the isolation, the difficulties of reaching [the bridge], together with the final glorious reward for hardships endured, that in part make it so appealing." Great appeal remained, assured the proprietors: "*Visiting the great arch is still a romantic adventure!* . . . Come to where the term 'great open spaces' is no mere figure of speech; where you can truly rest, both mentally and physically. Give yourself that needed vacation from business problems. Nothing could be more beneficial, inspiring and instructive." Like Zane Grey, you traveled over "the Rainbow Trail," only you could do it in an automobile. At Rainbow Lodge, you traded your car for a horse and followed Charles Bernheimer's trail to the bridge, but unlike the "cliff-dweller of Manhattan," you didn't have to fritter your whole summer away. "Yours may be the great adventure for but a fraction of the time and money expended by the famous [Bernheimer] expedition." Rupert

Larson, the author of this promotional language, observed in Los Angeles–area newspapers that the distance between southern California and southern Utah was "only" seven hundred miles, "a truly pleasant three-day journey, unique in that it carries one into the least known portion of the United States." Larson himself drove it "without so much as a tire puncture."[31]

He was lucky. It could take an entire day to negotiate the last hundred miles to the lodge. In rain or snow, the road was impassable. And never mind calling; the lodge had no telephone. Assuming you got there, though, it felt wonderfully like the edge of the world. Ironically, what lured the tourists—being Out There—precluded a high profit margin for the Richardsons. Road and shipping expenses ran sky high. The brothers continued to make their money trading with Navajos, not by outfitting well-to-do tourists. Management of the lodge turned over in 1926 and again in 1928, when some very capable relatives of the Richardsons, Bill and Katherine Wilson, settled in. The Wilsons lasted a quarter century and became synonymous with Rainbow Bridge. In their guest log appeared the names of many luminaries, including John D. Rockefeller, Jr.[32]

The millionaire, like many others, arrived via Indian Detours, a business arm of the Atchison, Topeka & Santa Fe Railway. Starting in May 1926, train passengers to or from California could lay over in New Mexico and receive one of several tours of the Land of Enchantment. It worked like this: a "de-tourist" rode in the back of a Packard Eight while a driver with a ten-gallon hat watched the road and a "courier"—a young, attractive woman weighted with turquoise and silver—interpreted the sights.

Indian Detours owed its existence to recent developments in American culture. Foremost was the "new vogue of the Southwestern desert that had developed since the 1890s and reached spectacular dimensions" by the 1930s. After scorning the desert for generations, Americans finally developed (with the help of writers like Mary Austin and John Van Dyke) a landscape aesthetic that embraced it. The same *fin de siècle* era saw a resurgent interest in the outdoors, especially the wide-open spaces of the West. As unprecedented urbanization, industrialization, and immigration challenged what it meant to be an American, native-born whites intensified their westward gaze. The once-expendable frontier—what was left of it—was deemed worthy of preservation as a living history museum, the place where Americans had become Americans. By extension, the native peoples of the West, once despised or neglected, became valuable relics of a mythic national past. Not coincidentally, the emerging fields of American archaeology and anthropology found their main inspiration in the desert Southwest. Great ruins such as Mesa Verde and modern pueblos such as Taos provided Euro-Americans with an enlarged sense of their national culture. That is, they enlarged their own antiquity by appropriating from other peoples.[33]

Tourists flocked to the "Southwest," a multi-ethnic travel region largely created by the railway and the Fred Harvey Company. Here Indians hadn't "vanished" as they had in most of the nation. Implicit in the selling of the southwestern tribes, however, was the notion of the vanishing authenticity of their traditions. Doomed cultures, like doomed places, make compelling attractions. Wide-eyed tourists crowded onto the Hopi Mesas to witness the Snake Dance; they photographed camera-leery Navajo shepherds, "Bedouins of our last frontier."[34]

The interaction between tourists and Native Americans was a bit different at Rainbow Bridge. Here nature rather than people was the main attraction. Since no one lived in the immediate vicinity, tourists only encountered Indians as guides, packers, or cooks. From the tourist's point of view, this service relationship affirmed the mythic roles of white explorers and native scouts. According to the dominant cultural logic and its racist assumptions, Indians couldn't discover things, but they could do good by showing Europeans what to discover. Call it the Sacajawea complex. At Rainbow Bridge, the Indian-as-accessory was celebrated in the form of a bronze plaque with the following inscription: "To commemorate the Piute Nashja Begay, who first guided the white man to Nonnezoshe, August 1909."

The plaque owed its existence to Raymond Armsby, a "prominent clubman" and "capitalist" from San Francisco. Photographs show a middle-aged man in a stylish sweater, coat jacket, and knickerbockers. Pipe smoke floats above his gray mustache. Armsby was a typical Rainbow Bridge tourist from the era before World War II—white, wealthy, well-educated, worldly. He first came to the bridge— "the most romantic spot in the United States," he believed—in 1922. He decided right then and there that "the Indian who led the white man here should be commemorated." He wrote to the National Park Service with an offer to pay for the construction and placement of a bronze plaque. The agency's director, Arno Cammerer, approved the preliminary plan (a deviation from usual practice), and it went to the agency's landscape architect for final design and approval.[35] There was some confusion as to which Indian guide from the 1909 expedition—Nasja Begay or Jim Mike—should be honored. (Apparently no one considered honoring both.) When consulted on the issue in 1924, John Wetherill came out in strong support of his friend, Nasja Begay. "Jim [Mike] bowed up saying that the Whiteman's horses could not get over the rocks," Wetherill wrote disparagingly. "It was very evident that Jim did not know the trail and took this method to hide his ignorance. I at once sent for Nasja Begay and he led us in without any trouble. I do not feel that Jim is entitled to any credit whatever."[36]

Wetherill's input seems to have been decisive. Armsby hired Jo Mora, a Monterey sculptor noted for his depictions of Native Americans, to make a relief of Nasja Begay. The finished piece, forty-two inches high, showed a horse rider with tied-up hair, necklace, and waist wrap. Packed in a sturdy wooden frame, the bronze traveled by train and automobile as far as Kayenta. Here, at the end of the road, the job went to Phoebe, one of Wetherill's mules (the same animal that had carried portly Theodore Roosevelt years before). The delivery took five days. Trying to describe the trail—a generous word—a reporter from San Francisco employed some urban references:

> Imagine a mule 17½ hands high, weighing 1,100 pounds, with two 16-foot drags fastened to a pack-saddle and carrying at her heels a precious bronze tablet weighing about 400 pounds, going down the California Street hill, into the Merchant's Exchange Building, up nine flights of stairs, through a narrow window to the roof of the Insurance building, and then down the fire escape of that building to the street again and you will have a dim idea of Phoebe's journey to the Bridge.[37]

About fifteen people followed Phoebe for the unveiling ceremony on 22 September 1927. Raymond Armsby presented the plaque to Frank Pinkley of the National Park Service; John Wetherill did the actual unveiling; and Louisa Wetherill read a Navajo prayer. Meanwhile, Pat Gannon of International Newsreel captured the day on film. The resulting newsreel, seen at Saturday matinees everywhere, showed, among other things, that not everyone participated in the ceremony. While everyone else huddled beneath the bronze on the canyon wall, a twosome squatted a distance away, looking none too interested. They were Navajo packers, the only Native Americans on hand. Ironically, no Paiutes, no relations of Nasja Begay, were present. In fact, none of the surviving publicity and news coverage says anything about the life and times of Nasja Begay except that he guided the First White Man. By implication, of course, the Indian had died. Expensive commemorative plaques don't generally go to the living.[38]

Tourists read the historical marker at Rainbow Bridge, 1967. (Photograph by Mel Davis.)

Nasja Begay's story—what little can be pieced together—is more modern and tragic than the plaque would suggest. In 1918–19, an influenza epidemic spread across the planet. As a modern history of the Southern Paiutes notes, "High death rates were found primarily in isolated areas where nutrition, medical care, and housing all tended to be of poor quality." All of these characteristics applied to the Navajo Mountain community of San Juan Paiutes. Nasja Begay, a prominent member of the community, left for Blanding, Utah, with his four sick children to get medical help. None made it.[39]

Depending on your situation, then, "frontierlike" conditions could mean travail or luxury. What Rainbow Bridge tourists called "roughing it" was softened by technology. Thanks to the automobile, they could, in an emergency, reach a hospital in a day or two. That distance amounted to a comfortable degree of danger, a thrill. The bridge was Out There but not too far out. As an Indian Detours brochure said: "Rainbow Bridge has become known the world over, but the trail to it still holds the rare thrill of discovery. Few have actually seen it and there is but one white man's house within 60 miles of Rainbow Lodge."[40] Merely by stepping out (or gazing out) of the touring car, you crossed into what the company called "terra incognita." You were among the first to see the land since it had been opened; you followed safely in the footsteps of the explorers.

But in fact, in the 1930s, "de-tourists" playing explorer sometimes encountered the real thing: members of the Rainbow Bridge–Monument Valley Expedition (RBMVE). This ambitious survey, the brainchild of Ansel Franklin Hall, covered a three-thousand-square-mile region "still *terra incognita* to the white man." Hall was an educator with the National Park Service, with an office at the University of California. One associate characterized him as an "irresistible blurb," and also, more kindly, an "unlikely combination of shrewd promotor and romantic idealist." Who else would try to launch an expedition during the Great Depression?[41]

"WANTED: TEN EXPLORERS BETWEEN 26 & 45 WILLING TO PAY UP TO 4.30 PER DAY," read an advertisement in the Berkeley alumni magazine. "Does it seem strange," Hall asked on the same page, "to ask a man to pay for the privilege of working hard, living entirely out of touch with civilization?" Apparently not. Seventy-five well-to-do men (including field staff) participated the first year, 1933. Over the expedition's six-year life, more than 250 people signed up for what has been called the "largest self-supporting, multidisciplinary expedition ever conducted in North America."[42]

The RBMVE had two main objectives: to provide a school of outdoor education, and to gather scientific data for federal land managers. Ansel Hall hoped that the reports from the expedition would serve as the basis for a management plan for the northern Navajo country—preferably as a national park. He had the blessing of the Park Service and the backing of a distinguished board of directors, including Herbert Gregory and John Collier, commissioner of the Bureau of Indian Affairs. The aging John Wetherill, Hall's constant source of practical advice and geographical information, was eventually named associate director.

Hall solicited equipment in addition to money and personnel. In one sweet deal, he obtained a fleet of new V-8 Fords by agreeing to let the company take newsreel footage of the machines in action. Soon after, consumers saw on the big screen that Ford built vehicles tough enough to penetrate America's "Gobi Desert." According to one trade magazine, "Ford trucks and station wagons carried the explorers into the remote corners of the land. It may be said that a few Piute Indians living near the muddy San Juan are the last of the American aborigines to be introduced to the motor car. Astonished, they have gazed from their brush lodges to 'see the Fords go by.'"[43]

To be a Ford explorer—to be among Hall's pit crew—cost about three hundred dollars per person, including a fifteen-dollar fee for the two absolutely required items: accident insurance and an air mattress. Yet Hall gave his recruits this warning: "This is *not* a deluxe expedition." You worked hard, sweated hard, got red-orange sand in your hair. But it was worth it. Undergraduates, the bulk of the participants (the minimum age having been lowered), received college credit for their work. Moreover, it was a once-in-a-lifetime opportunity to go back in time. Reporting on the expedition, the *New York Times* proclaimed, "The Wild West is still not entirely tamed." Echoed Hall: "The frontier is *not entirely gone!*"[44]

Were these men (no women allowed) really frontier explorers? Well, they certainly acted the part. Expeditioners used Indian guides and packers; they divided into reconnaissance groups; they excavated ruins, drew maps, made photographs, and wrote reports. They discovered Jurassic fossils and many pre-Columbian relics (though one overeager member incorrectly announced the "discovery" of a large Anasazi ruin later identified as Poncho House, already photographed by the Hayden Survey in 1875 and excavated in 1923). Some unqualified students deserved ridicule— "a bunch of rich college kids looking for a way to spend their summer vacation," recalled the granddaughter of John Wetherill—but others went on to become noted archaeologists. Several of Hall's field staff were excellent scientists, and at least one important publication resulted directly from the RBMVE.[45]

These accomplishments notwithstanding, the impetus behind Hall's program— "the thrill that goes to men who are privileged to push into new country"—was hardly restricted to expeditions with advisory boards. Indeed, sometimes it was hard to separate the "authentic" explorers from the rest. Here Ansel Hall's career is suggestive. After the RBMVE shut down in 1938, the educator went on to operate the concession at Mesa Verde National Park and later the Explorer's Camp for Boys. Much like the Boy Scouts, this camp was meant to turn soft young men into hardy specimens of adventurous Americans, the country's future leaders. From their base in southwestern Colorado, enrollees divided into "Indian tribes" led by "chiefs" in order to go on "expeditions" to ruins and wonders rumored to be "somewhere out there."[46]

"The appeal of the undiscovered is strong in America," Frederick Jackson Turner once observed.[47] Yes, but how long could it last in the canyon country? How long before everything was discovered and explored, before "the last frontier of the Old West" finally closed? A contemporary familiar with the region, Clyde Kluckhohn, saw closure on the horizon.

In 1922, during his freshman year at Princeton, Kluckhohn became chronically ill. Concerned, his parents sent him to northwestern New Mexico to recuperate with relatives. Though he quickly regained his health, he became addicted to the cure: he couldn't get enough of the desert and its peoples. His subsequent fieldwork among the Navajos bolstered a distinguished career in anthropology at Harvard.

One of Kluckhohn's contemporaries, anthropologist Edward T. Hall, lived on the Navajo and Hopi reservations from 1933 to 1937. A half century later, he nostalgically remembered the time and place:

> It was still the *frontier*. . . . Try to imagine a place with no roads, no radios (they were available but people didn't use them), no bridges, only the most primitive automobiles: Where the Indians got around on foot, on horseback, and in wagons. Where it was possible to drive for an entire day and not see another human being. When the attitudes toward Indians held by most whites were framed by convictions that the Indians were inferior and the only solution was to make them over in the white man's image. Yet when one penetrated beneath the surface of that world, there was a truth, a veracity, which is difficult if not impossible to find today. The Indians, particularly the Navajos, were still themselves and relatively untouched by the white man's culture; only a handful of the fifty thousand spoke English.[48]

Into this foreign land an eighteen-year-old Clyde Kluckhohn embarked on a summerlong pack trip in June 1923. Of the many highlights, Rainbow Bridge was indisputably the best. Kluckhohn and his traveling companion were among the first five hundred to record their names in the register there. Afterwards, the pair made their way by horseback to the South Rim of Grand Canyon. The view downward into the geologic past generated undiluted awe, but it was with "mingled feelings" that Kluckhohn turned about to face the region's future—the hotel, shop, railway depot, and other appurtenances of mass tourism. "Brave but bewildered," he wrote, "we wandered among the fashionably dressed people hurrying about in an effort to see the most sublime sight in America in twelve hours."[49] Some of them inquired whether the scruffy wayfarers were western actors hired by Fred Harvey.

With familiar ambiguity, Kluckhohn viewed such tourist developments—an extension of America's industrial growth—as inevitable but regrettable. In his second and more interesting travel book, *Beyond the Rainbow* (published in 1933, the same year as the beginning of the RBMVE), he reported the depressing truth: the magic of the country was going, going . . . The auto-friendly Rainbow Trail had opened since his 1923 trip (during which, by an appropriate coincidence, Kluckhohn passed Zane Grey on the novelist's final trip to Rainbow Bridge; the two parties were among the last to ride the long horse trail from Kayenta). Back then, sighed Kluckhohn, the place seemed so impenetrable. Now, in 1927, it was only a matter of time: tourists—as opposed to respectable *travelers*—would reach the stone rainbow.

Kluckhohn, now an Oxford fellow on summer vacation, was forced to seek new horizons. Beyond the Rainbow, across Glen Canyon of the Colorado River, he found his goal: Wild Horse Mesa—Zane Grey's romantic name for the Kaiparowits Plateau—a vast, forested flatland bordered on three sides by imposing cliffs. Here, Clyde Kluckhohn dreamed he would find the real item, The Last Frontier, the place Rainbow Bridge was no more. The "American" spirit in him—the "lust for danger and adventure in exploration and discovery"—called out for the mesa.[50]

Kluckhohn and some friends reached their destination but not before a deflating talk with Ben Wetherill, guide and Indian trader, and son of John Wetherill. Wild Horse Mesa was not as wild as Kluckhohn had led himself to believe. Ben had been there in 1915 with geologist Herbert Gregory. Kluckhohn learned, to his further disappointment, that Mormon stockmen from Escalante had ranged their animals on the plateau for years. Navajos sometimes crossed the river to hunt deer there. "Our frontier gone!" moaned Kluckhohn. Had he and his party, the Filthy Five, known these facts earlier, they would have gone elsewhere, someplace indisputably unknown. But now it was too late; they had to complete the journey. In the end, they were pleasantly surprised. "Now that we were here," Kluckhohn wrote, "the Mesa was so perfect, so absolute a thing in itself that whether others had been here or not mattered no longer." Why not? "Psychologically, Wild Horse Mesa was still the one virgin outpost of the vanishing frontier. Psychologically we claimed the Mesa as our domain by right of discovery."[51]

Likewise, psychology, not physiography, made the difference between Herbert Gregory's Kaiparowits Plateau and Zane Grey's Wild Horse Mesa. The names described one place, two states of mind. Kluckhohn's perception of the mesa as wilderness was shaped by powerful cultural attitudes about the American West. In the words of historian Richard White, "The mythic West imagined by Americans has shaped the West of history just as the West of history has helped create the West Americans have imagined." *Beyond the Rainbow* is a fine micro-example. The opening chapter, "The Last Frontier," describes how Kluckhohn couldn't bear to see a western film lest the urge to roam possess him. Finally, after reading a *National Geographic* article by archaeologist Neil Judd (one of the discoverers of Rainbow Bridge) about a "practically unknown and unexplored" section of Utah, Kluckhohn and some friends decided to "pull a Grey" and go. In other words, Kluckhohn modeled his adventure after the fictional works of an author who based his writings on his own planned adventures. Furthermore, inspired by movies (including, no doubt, Zane Grey adaptations) and intrigued by a magazine that "created" mysterious lands and exotic peoples as much as it ostensibly examined them, Kluckhohn contributed his own adventure text. He laid yet another layer of interpretation on this grand sedimentary landscape. This derivation doesn't necessarily undermine the authenticity of his adventures. Far from it: his exciting narrative describes numerous close calls in the back of beyond. My point is simply that Kluckhohn's trip and the book depicting it are enmeshed with other depictions—and deceptive perceptions—of experiences in the "wild."[52]

Kluckhohn understood some of this. He showed his insight when he referred to the Glen Canyon–Rainbow Bridge region ironically as the "next-to-last-frontier country." He couldn't guess, however, that this country could retain that title indefinitely. By reimagining the last frontier, or redefining it, newcomers could postpone its demise. They could, for example, redefine by comparison: Rainbow Bridge, though relatively accessible, offered an exhilarating contrast to Grand Canyon's full-service scenery. No coach cars or hotel suites here, reported syndicated humorist Irvin Cobb in 1940. To approach the Rainbow, he wrote, "You must cross about as rude a stretch of wilderness as is left in this country and brave some mighty brooding solitudes. And these adventures, even when negotiated with no special amount of danger, give the green horn a Daniel Booneish satisfaction."[53]

Cobb and other early tourists genuinely enjoyed getting out and getting a little dirty. Though they sometimes griped about the trials of transportation, they reveled in the fact that decades after the discovery of Rainbow Bridge they could be among the first ten thousand to sign their names there. No matter that theirs was a dude trip. They could still feel a bit like Boone—yet not too much. Dude wranglers permitted that agreeable middle ground: exploration with security. "Trust your guide, and obey him completely," advised the Work Projects Administration's *Utah Guide* in 1940. "It may mean your life."[54] On top of that, a very good meal. On a typical pack trip, guides started the Dutch oven steaks and biscuits while their guests stretched their legs for a close-up look at the bridge. Camp at Rainbow Bridge was tucked into a hollow a half mile upcanyon.

The place was called Echo Camp. Though now in disuse, the site is covered with memories. Some are tangible. Mounds of rusting tins rise like industrial anthills above the crusty red sand. A decrepit outhouse and numerous bed frames litter the scene. Most of the spring supports are still functional, some remarkably comfortable, even though the mattresses have been hauled away. Then there are the intangible memories. People used to lie here, talking, listening, watching. Embraced by slickrock, sheltered by the Milky Way, what did these people feel? What went through their heads when, in the warm morning light, they walked back for a final look at Rainbow Bridge? It's impossible to divine, difficult to generalize. But was it all manly adventure and frontier fantasy? No.

Clyde Kluckhohn repeated the oft-heard remark that no person returned from the trip an atheist. Robert Frothingham sensed a vague but "overwhelming emotional appeal" to the bridge. Will Robinson remarked on "the tremendous force of it." Hoffman Birney thought nothing could "more perfectly attest the definite existence of a Supreme Being." The visitor register contained many quotations and citations of scripture, particularly from the Psalms. In 1920, one visitor pronounced in pencil, "A wonderful work of your God, remain and worship Him in all His glory."[55]

Unfortunately, these records are incomplete; not every early visitor left a message. More to the point, not every visitor was a "visitor." Guides are notably underrepresented in the travel literature. I wonder about these men—particularly Dogeye Begay—and their reactions. He was the cook for the 1909 "discovery" party. Later he led dudes to the bridge. What did this Navajo think about all the wealthy white outsiders who came to discover for themselves this "wonder of the world," this "sublime work of God"?

For local Navajos, Rainbow Bridge was (and still is) sacred. After Blind Salt Clansman "discovered" the bridge sometime around 1870, a body of ceremonies grew up around it. On 14 August 1909, while his employers scurried to take pictures and measurements, Dogeye Begay rode up and around the freestanding leg of the bridge because he didn't know the prayer to pass beneath it. This was not the universal "Indian" response—San Juan Paiutes unacculturated into Navajo ways didn't share this sacred understanding of the bridge. Late in life, Jim Mike referred to Rainbow Bridge as "just a pile of rocks." For Navajos of the Navajo Mountain region, however, the bridge became the center of a region where deities dwelled. It's not, as many non-Indians would say, that Navajos invented traditions to explain the existence of the bridge. Rather, Rainbow Bridge helped explain and amplify old traditions, almost as if their mythology anticipated the existence of a rock rainbow. However, since Navajo ceremonial knowledge is by nature localized and individualized, different medicine men told different stories of its origin. Floyd Laughter of the Navajo Mountain community spoke this way:

In those days of long ago, when man was created, or very shortly after they had come to be, two female persons walked away from a place called Black Water. They probably just wandered from that area and eventually got lost. In their wanderings they finally reached a place where the Sun comes up and came upon the Holy People of that area. But those [Holy People] would not become used to them because they were different—People-of-the-water. And the two asked these people whether they could live among them, but the Water people refused—because it would not be a good place for them to be. "But since you are here [the Holy People said], we can help you and provide a way by which you can return to your own land." And the miraculous means was a Rainbow. They were told it would bring them down in the direction where the Sun goes down. And so they were brought back, in that miraculous manner of Rainbow, to the area of Navajo Mountain, which is the "Head of Earth." . . . At the time of this event it was also decided by the Holy People, that Rainbow would remain as Rock-arch and that it would be a place to bring offerings and prayers, also a place of refuge.[56]

Appropriately, those prayers concerned water—mostly in the form of summer rain. People offered ceremonial stones and corn pollen at Rainbow Bridge and other nearby sites, including springs and alcoves in Bridge Canyon. In fact, the hollow known to tourists as Echo Camp is known to some contemporary Navajos as a "place where Gods used to meet."[57] Evidently, the tourist camp and corral profaned the place. Of course, Navajos themselves were involved in the tourist business. A famously adaptable people, they could make room for commerce within the religious sphere—up to a point. Lamar Bedonie, who sued the federal government in the 1970s over Lake Powell's intrusion under the rock arch, earlier worked as a guide:

> I used to take White people up there after they found out about it. At that time there were no trails, and we had to make our own trails. And we made a trail, and I took only White people up there. Some were big ladies who could not ride horses. They wanted to see the Bridge. So I used to help these ladies onto and off their horses. That was my work. I also used to carry their lunches and hay for the horses. They wanted to go up there and see it, and take pictures. Every day I earned money that way.[58]

Other than guides, Rainbow Bridge only occasionally drew people at work. During the summer of 1922, the U.S. Geological Survey was busy mapping Glen Canyon and its major tributaries in preparation for a proposed dam (which, in another form, became Glen Canyon Dam). One of the crew, Harry Tasker of Green River, Utah, earned his wages balancing a heavy wooden stadia rod. It was tedious labor, usually without the benefit of shade. When the survey party made its way up Bridge Canyon, Tasker recorded his thoughts in the register:

> Some come here to see the work of God
> But I come here to hold up a Rod![59]

Tasker was in a distinct minority. But if most visitors weren't at work, their exploration wasn't entirely play, either. By exploring, tourists moved from familiar—*all-too*-familiar—industrial landscapes to "terra incognita" or the "stupendous Beyond." Rainbow Bridge became famous not simply as a wonder but as the center point of the most remote country in the country. It was, to use another phrase, a locus for the sacred. Surrounded by a sea of slickrock, the natural bridge was removed from the profane: the world of modern cities, politics, and wars. Nowadays, academics often compare tourists to pilgrims, but I suspect that early-twentieth-century bridge tourists would have preferred an analogy to the Pilgrims of 1620, who sailed west across the ocean to the New World. The pilgrimage to Bridge Canyon was distinctively American, and distinctively *western*. Sacredness fused with the western myth of regenerative masculinity as part of the metaphor—and real activity—of exploration. In published travel accounts, expressions of spirituality were almost always accompanied by or subordinate to descriptions of exploits in the untamed territory.

A slightly different example may help to reinforce this point. Willard D. Morgan and his wife came to the country with backpacks around 1930. Warnings about the perils of hiking without a guide only strengthened their resolve to make the trip alone. The attraction? They could stop for pictures whenever they desired. The Morgans were photography nuts. With shoulder-crushing packs filled with the essentials—film and water—the couple left Rainbow Lodge and entered the canyon wilderness. They made frequent halts, taking detailed notes on filters, f-stops, exposure times. Eventually, after miles of sweaty hiking, they turned a bend and sighted the end goal: "Majestic and silent, 'Nonnezoshe,' the Rainbow Arch, had become a reality. Cameras and photographing were forgotten for the moment. We were enjoying one of the grandest forms of nature in the silence and solitude which is always associated with such remote places. The traffic-jammed city which we had left only two weeks before was entirely obliterated. 'Nonnezoshe' commanded our imaginations." Next, using a drill and rope, Mr. and Mrs. Morgan ascended the canyon wall and dropped onto the slender causeway of the bridge. Having conquered the bridge, they then went crazy with their Leicas. That evening, weary and satisfied, the couple made camp beneath the rainbow. As bridge and sky merged into darkness, the photographers drifted into sleep, forgetting everything save "the daytime thrills in climbing and picture-making."[60]

The Willards' experience, like that of any visitor, was unique and partly inscrutable to the historian, but their written description reinforces a conclusion drawn from a body of narratives. In the first five decades of Rainbow Bridge as a discovered site, the majority of outsiders—the explorers and tourists and would-be explorers—earned a premium: the satisfaction of being among the first to see (and photograph) it, the thrill of being so immersed in the wild, so seemingly detached from the world.[61]

DOWN THE RIVER

Rainbow Lodge burned down in August 1951. The guest cottages survived, but the fire heralded the demise of the operation. Navajo Mountain Trading Post, located to the east, tried to pick up the dude business but with only limited success. The fire had worsened an existing condition: the decline of overland traffic to Rainbow Bridge. The automobile road had deteriorated— "so bad, in fact," wrote one visitor in 1939, "that it is impassable and those tourists who seek to make the trip to the Lodge in order to visit Rainbow Natural Bridge have been forced to turn back." In other words, this particular tourist frontier, marked by its tantalizing accessibility, was "closing" by returning to its previous, less comfortable, more frontierlike condition. In the 1940s, the situation was exacerbated. The new half-owner of the lodge, Barry Goldwater, quit maintaining the fourteen-mile trail to the bridge. It was a financial decision. "The best season we ever had, we took about 400 people down to see Rainbow Natural Bridge," the senator later explained. "That year, I only lost $1,400." And though the total number of bridge visitors was steadily (if slowly) increasing, more and more visitors chose the alternate route: down the Colorado. River runners walked from the mouth of Forbidding Canyon to its tributary, Bridge Canyon, then on to the bridge—a six-mile trip. Starting from a trickle before the war, rafter-hikers had surpassed pack-trippers by 1950. By 1960, they accounted for nearly 90 percent of the signatures in the national monument register.[62]

This transition mirrored a larger movement in western tourism—away from the elite cultural activities and toward middle-class recreational activities. Through it all, however, exploration remained a powerful draw in Glen Canyon. Consider this river trip promotion, mimeographed in 1941:

> Each year more people are taking advantage of this opportunity to penetrate the heretofore unreachable "Land of Mystery"; to thrill to the remote fastnesses of these spectacular great canyons. The unlimited number of really unexplored side canyons ever presents the challenge for investigation and exploration.—It is like going into another World.[63]

The author of this enthusiasm was Norman Nevills. In 1928, he moved to Mexican Hat, Utah, on the San Juan River. He was twenty. His father, an itinerant prospector, had arrived several years before. They labored together in the San Juan oil field until the boom that brought them busted. Against the odds, the Nevills family remained. The red rock landscape had grown on them. "Having faith in the eventual development of the roads that would open up this region," they built the Mexican Hat Lodge. To the infrequent passerby, Norm offered guided tours of nearby Monument Valley. In 1933, through one of his patrons, he landed a lucky job as field assistant to the Rainbow Bridge–Monument Valley Expedition. Over the next three summers, Nevills made some cash and connections—enough to start a brave new experiment in business. He was fascinated by rivers, especially the San Juan. After passing by Mexican Hat, the river withdrew into the rock to join the Colorado in Glen Canyon. Nevills wanted to take people there.[64]

His greatest asset was his unflagging optimism. He would need it. At the time, most people considered river running daft, if not reckless. After Nevills had been in business a few years, Utah's leading newspaper, the *Salt Lake Tribune*, ran an editorial called "Foolish and Futile Are Risks That Are Needless." "It would seem folly to persist in making the trip for nothing but thrills or dramatic obituaries," it scolded. Another contemporary appraisal was more sanguine, if overblown:

> There are still frontiers in the United States! There are still places where the civilization such as is known in the cities, towns and villages of America has barely touched. . . . Among [such] places in the great West is Mexican Hat, Utah. . . . Down where life is raw, where your past is still unquestioned, where only your performance counts in the job to be done today, lies a region that breeds men and women of the caliber that we thought belonged only in history books. . . . [Here] there has been going on, unbeknownst to the majority of the American people, a development of what promises to be not only the king of sports but a sport that presents to those who participate the ultimate in thrills, enjoyment, suspense and surprise. It is known as "river running."[65]

Whitewater rafting has yet to become the king of sports, but it boasts its share of fans and disciples. Now a worldwide phenomenon, it traces its origins to the Colorado River system (the Green, the Colorado, and the San Juan). River runners like to trace their genealogy to one-armed John Wesley Powell, who crashed and portaged his way down the river in 1869. Powell's trip was work, not recreation. He and his men broke their backs every day for the reward of rancid bacon, moldy flour, and black, black coffee. In the Grand Canyon, the relentless roar of rapids gnawed at the crewmen. Three of them opted to climb out of the chasm—a dubious prospect—rather than continue downstream. They emerged from the depths only to be killed by Paiutes (or, as some claim, Mormons).

It's difficult to identify the first example of recreational river running in the canyons. In 1896, George F. Flavell and Ramón Montéz made a full traverse of the Green and Colorado rivers with these objectives: "First, for the adventure; second, to see what so few people have seen; third, to hunt and trap; fourth, to examine the perpendicular walls of rock for gold." In 1909 (the year of Rainbow Bridge's discovery), Julius Stone, an industrialist, made the same trip with the help of riverman Nat Galloway. It was a pleasure trip, to be sure, but one with a professional objective: to create a comprehensive photographic record of the canyons. Ellsworth and Emery Kolb made a similar photographic trip two years later. Private adventures like this became increasingly popular in the second and third decades of the century. In 1932, for example, Julian Steward, professor of archaeology at the University of Utah, took a trip down Glen Canyon. His group included Charles Kelly and Hoffman Birney, two amateur historians of the West who came along for fun. The ill-prepared party had its share of adventures, mishaps, and feuds, yet Steward managed to excavate twenty-three sites in twenty-eight days on the river.[66]

Like Nat Galloway, David Dexter Rust occasionally acted as a river guide. A native of Kanab, Utah, Rust did pioneering concession work at Grand Canyon, where he was one of Zane Grey's favorite guides. Around 1915, he shifted his gaze upstream to Glen Canyon. Rust owned several two-man canvas folding boats and was willing to take anyone on the river who wanted to go. He averaged about one trip per year. In 1926, Rust guided governor George H. Dern through "the unknown part of Utah" so that Dern's administration could take a more informed position on a dam in Glen Canyon, proposed by the Bureau of Reclamation as early as 1920. As far as Dern was concerned, the only potential benefit, besides temporary jobs, was scenic: "A good deal of the present canyon would be submerged by the reservoir and a lot of the beautiful glens and beauty spots would thereby be lost, but I am inclined to think that more scenery would be gained than lost by making the lake," he wrote. "The proposed Glen Canyon reservoir might therefore prove an important asset to Utah from a scenic standpoint."[67]

David Rust's successor, Norm Nevills, did his best to prove that Glen Canyon itself was an economic asset. In the 1930s, Nevills started what may be considered the first modern outfit on the Colorado River. His contemporary, Bus Hatch of Vernal, Utah, did the same on the Green. Following World War II, as river traffic picked up dramatically, Nevills and Hatch bred imitators. The 1950s was the "Golden Age": "If someone wanted to start a river-running business, all that was needed was a couple of boats and some passengers. No rules, no regulations, no permits, just get in the boat and go." Commercial rafting soon spread to other western rivers—the Snake, the Salmon, the Rogue. Rafting received a huge publicity boost from controversial reclamation projects in the 1950s and 1960s, including Glen Canyon Dam. The sport's newfound popularity led to overcrowding in the 1960s. The inevitable result—regulations and permits—arrived in full force in the 1970s.[68]

Nevills helped start it all. In 1938, he led his first major excursion, an event-filled passage down the Green and Colorado rivers from Green River, Utah, to Lake Mead, Arizona. Because of the deadly reputation of the Grand Canyon (fewer than a hundred had successfully navigated the river) and the presence of two women in the party, the trip made news around the country. "They'll never make it," one "veteran" river explorer told the press. While the "Nevills Expedition 1938" did experience its share of clashes—with both rocks and personalities—everyone returned intact, and Nevills relished the moment of fame. The hyperbolic publicity generally obscured the fact that the women, Elzada Clover and Lois Jotter, were field botanists. Their trip was foremost a scientific expedition.[69]

Nevills tried to capitalize on the moment by planning a trip that would dwarf the 1938 expedition "in all details of interest, hazard, and accomplishment." He tried to obtain corporate sponsorship for this summerlong retracing of John Wesley Powell's journey from Green River, Wyoming, down through the Grand Canyon. Along the way, "various scientists and experts" would collect plants, plot ruins, and study geology. At the close of each busy day, they would relate their observations and adventures to a national audience via a radio carried in the boats. The listeners would "[run] rapids as they sit in their apartment or drive down Fifth Ave." Cameramen of world fame would capture the entire canyon system in natural color. "Another goal of this expedition," he wrote, "is the almost certain discovery of a great natural bridge which will be by far the largest in the world, the evidences and location of which is known only to Mr. Nevills."[70]

Most of these plans fell through; Nevills failed to secure a sponsor. In lieu of a two-way radio, his party sent messages via passenger pigeon to the

Deseret News in Salt Lake City. As for science, trip member Hugh Cutler was a professional botanist; Mildred Baker was an accomplished amateur ornithologist; and Barry Goldwater was a fine photographer—but they and the other high-paying passengers came along primarily for pleasure. Nothing about the trip suggested an organized scientific expedition. Undaunted, Nevills went ahead with his preplanned "discovery" of a little-known natural bridge in a side canyon of the Escalante River. Though large (75 by 175 feet on the inside), it was no Rainbow. Nevills' party named it after Herbert Gregory, the geologist of the canyon country. Gregory repaid the compliment the next year when he seconded Nevills' nomination to the elite Explorers Club of Manhattan. The other nomination came from Ansel Hall.[71]

Ultimately, Nevills' relentless self-promotion paid off: in the 1940s, several national magazines, including *Life,* the *Atlantic Monthly,* the *National Geographic,* and the *Saturday Evening Post,* ran features on river running. Nevills received the label "World's No. 1 Fast Water Man." That had the ring of confidence. With an excellent safety and satisfaction record, Nevills could, by the late forties, attract both women and men, young and old. The river trip was novel but no longer exceptional, exciting without the stigma of being a hazard.

Nevills' bread-and-butter run started at Mexican Hat. He and his twelve passengers followed the San Juan River on its goosenecked course until it married the Colorado in lower Glen Canyon. Here, on day four of the trip, Nevills made a number of regular stops: Music Temple (a cul-de-sac where John Wesley Powell and his men had camped and sung), Hidden Passage (a slot filled with reflecting pools), Mystery Canyon (a box canyon with beckoning but unusable Anasazi hand- and footholds), and Twilight Canyon (a slot so narrow it blocked the sun). All but the first, Nevills had named himself. Day five went entirely to Forbidding Canyon and Rainbow Bridge. The trip wrapped up on day six at Lee's Ferry, Arizona, Mile 0, where Glen Canyon ended and Grand Canyon abruptly began.

As business improved, Nevills replaced his mimeographed leaflet with a slick-paper brochure, complete with photographs and testimonials of the beauty and adventure of the San Juan–Glen Canyon trip. "The north side of the river is a wild uninhabited country," it read. "On the south is the Navajo reservation. At rare intervals we may get a passing glimpse of the Indians themselves. This is a remote and in parts unexplored region." One of Nevills' guests concurred: "The San Juan flows through a slice of the American Southwest as it was before the white man came with his guns, axes, explosives and bulldozers. Each San Juan traveler is richer for having experienced a week living as our pioneer forefathers did in a country which has not yet been 'improved' and humanized."[72]

Nevills died in a plane crash in 1949, at the height of his improbable career. In his day, the "World's No. 1 Fast Water Man" had little competition for the title. The second Glen Canyon outfit, Harry Aleson's Western River Tours, didn't form until 1948. There *was* another operator in Glen Canyon, but Art Greene ran such an unusual business that it hardly qualified as competition. Forget about weeklong float trips—Greene used motorboats to go *up* the river to Rainbow Bridge. He and his extended family operated a trading post near Lee's Ferry, Arizona. In 1943, hoping to supplement the trade, Greene began experimenting with various boats and motors. Finally, in 1948 he came up with a combination that worked: a twenty-two-foot flat-bottomed boat mounted with a 450-horsepower airplane propeller. He named it the *Tseh Na-ni-ah-go Atin'*, Navajo for "trail to the rock that goes over." Greene's air-powered trips took only three days, including one to hike to the bridge. The only drawback was the deafening roar of the airplane prop. Passengers wore earplugs. Despite this handicap, travel writer Joyce Rockwood Muench seemed to hear her pulse. She used heart-pounding language to describe Green's inaugural upriver trip—another "first" for "Twentieth Century adventurers" in "wild land still unsurveyed." There in Glen Canyon, she wrote, "no hint of the outside world is had and with the grand feeling of isolation, the stupendous scale of the chasm, the world seems well lost."[73]

Thanks to Greene, Nevills, the media, and word of mouth, the glory of Glen Canyon became known to a sizable audience in the 1940s. "By 1950 there was almost a need for traffic lights," wrote river expert Otis Marston.[74] And that was just the beginning. By 1960, no less than a dozen groups were offering Glen Canyon adventures. About three-quarters of these were owned and operated by professional river runners. Most of these folks had known or worked for Nevills, all of them knew each other, and they formed a close, if sometimes dysfunctional, family. They suffered from a common, joyful affliction: "canyonitis." They didn't go into business for the money—any of that was a bonus. They ran the river because that was their life. Nothing felt better or freer than to push off from shore, enter the current, and disappear into a canyon.

Now for a portrait: Harry Aleson, a Norwegian-American from Iowa, returned from the trenches of World War I with a disability pension and a desultory future. He finished high school, started college, got married, and wandered in and out of various jobs. Then he saw the Grand Canyon. Soon after, he boated into the lowermost section, as far as Lake Mead intrudes. He fell permanently in love. "So you want to go live at Meade [*sic*] Lake," his soon-to-be-ex wrote him in 1941. "Of course I don't have to tell you how I feel about it." Alone, Aleson moved his belongings to a tent camp in an isolated cove of the reservoir. "MY HOME, Arizona," he called the place—always using capital letters. Though he did sporadic guide work, he gained his initial reputation as a daredevil. With Georgie White—another future river runner—he twice floated the lower Grand Canyon in nothing but a life jacket. "Damnably cold," he later remarked. Gradually, Aleson turned to professional river guiding, an idea encouraged by his association (and short-lived partnership) with Norm Nevills. In the late 1940s, Aleson transferred his base camp from MY HOME to the comparatively plush Johnson Hotel in Richfield, Utah. From there, he organized trips down the San Juan, the Green, and the Colorado. As a guide, Aleson was known for his varied menu, offbeat humor, and encyclopedic knowledge of canyon history, particularly that of Glen Canyon.[75]

Aleson liked the Glen so much that he returned in the off-season to explore. Between 1952 and 1955, Aleson made several extended trips with Richard Sprang and Dudy Thomas. Not just trips—"We *lived* in the place," Sprang wrote. They never thought once about obtaining permits; where would they apply? Equipped with good food and good books, they stayed in the Glen for four to six weeks at a time. On one trip, the trio averaged one mile per day in the course of a month. They had a name—Canyon Surveys—and a goal: to study Glen Canyon and all of its glens in one-tenth-mile increments, taking notes, making maps, and shooting photographs. "Ambitious?" asked Sprang. "God! Never in our lives could we fill all those blank spaces."[76]

The most exciting blank was Mile 132, where a side canyon entered the river from the south. Aleson, Sprang, and Thomas named it Forgotten Canyon because the dam surveyors of the 1920s missed it on their maps. The canyon boxed up quickly, but the trio didn't give up. By enlarging some Anasazi footholds near the mouth of the canyon, they gained access to the upper section, where they discovered an untouched ruin. Now known as Defiance House, it is famous for the warriorlike pictograph above it. Describing this and many other inscriptions and ruins, Aleson filled ninety-eight pages of his journal in 1952. Even though he and his friends never came close to achieving their goal, they had a marvelous time exploring a marvelous place.

Canyon Surveys focused on the history and archaeology of Glen Canyon. The first extensive biological survey of the canyon occurred in 1955, when Gus Scott—a close friend of Aleson, Sprang, and Thomas—spent three weeks on the river with Robert Robertson. Scott and Robertson were science majors and former roommates at Stanford. Their Glen Canyon expedition was not a school project but "a way of imparting a theme or a purpose to their river trip beyond that of mere recreation." Their boat, the *Glen,* carried a plant press, notebooks, and a library of reference books. The fine acoustics of one glen inspired the men to shout scientific terms such as "prezygapophysis and other words which have probably never echoed from these walls." At Mile 130, the duo explored another side canyon that had escaped the notice of the USGS river survey. They named it Beaver Canyon after the heavy presence of the web-footed dam builders. Scott and Robertson made detailed observations of five species of amphibians, twelve species of reptiles, and eighteen species of birds. They also collected sixty-five botanical specimens. Following the trip, the summer-vacation students wrote an exhaustive final report. According to Gary Topping, the "Scott-Robertson expedition was possibly the best documented river trip ever made anywhere, and compares favorably with almost any other scientific survey." Unfortunately, like Canyon Surveys, the work was never published.[77]

A nonscientific but more time-intensive exploration of Glen Canyon was undertaken by Katie Lee. A folk singer by occupation, Lee fell in love with life on the river in the mid-1950s. She had a deal with Frank Wright, the co-owner of Mexican Hat Expeditions, the successor to Nevills' outfit: she would sing and play the guitar for the guests in return for her passage down the river. For Lee, these trips provided a much-needed break from the nightclub circuit. Soon she decided she never wanted to leave. "After the river had totally captivated me, I just became an addict and it was one of the things that I just couldn't survive without," she remembered. "It was just like having a soothing balm rubbed into me for two or three weeks or a month while I was there. And I would go back completely cleansed and feel like a whole new human being." To feed her addiction, Lee began to take long "exploratory trips" with Frank Wright and Tad Nichols during the off-season. Over the course of several years, the trio investigated every last alcove and glen. They gave names to more than two dozen side canyons—

several of which have been adopted by the U.S. Board on Geographic Names. One of them, Dungeon Canyon, Lee described in her journal: "It is so dim . . . so eerie . . . so quiet and humanless . . . so cool . . . that only a photograph could explain it. . . . We feel creation all around us, deep in the womb of Mother Earth. We touch her scars and now and then, with the wonder of it, there are tears in our eyes. We feel we have been let in on a great secret—and we have!" The date was 10 October 1956, four days before blasting began on Glen Canyon Dam, forty-two miles downstream. "When I think ahead," wrote Lee, "I begin to choke . . . this will all be under water."[78]

Since learning about the proposed dam the year before, Lee had written letters to Congress and spoken out to her concert audiences. Likewise, the members of the Western River Guides Association (WRGA), formed in Salt Lake City in 1954, had scrambled to make themselves heard, but the voices were too few against a power too great. In Washington, D.C., where the Colorado River Storage Project was debated, conservationists had their hands full fighting proposed dams in Dinosaur National Monument. Glen Canyon Dam wasn't a priority. No one paid much attention to Lee, the WRGA, or two small Utah groups: the Utah Committee for a Glen Canyon National Park, and Friends of Glen Canyon.

Ken Sleight, one of the founding Friends, was introduced to river running in 1951, and he loved it from the start. Two years later, after seeing Glen Canyon, he decided to pursue his love despite the financial risk. He quit his managerial job at Firestone, bought some used boats, and opened a guiding business. Simple as that. Over the first three years, as he built a clientele, Sleight and his family survived on his off-season salary as a substitute teacher. By the late 1950s, however, he was making a modest living from Glen Canyon and his Wonderland Expeditions. Most of his business came from repeats and referrals—people who liked his laid-back style and strenuous pace. At every opportunity, Sleight paddled to shore to go hiking—both to favorite spots and to side canyons new to him. "Those were the Golden Days," remembered Sleight. "It was just right for me. It was a period of adventure and exploration. There were always new canyons to explore, new things to see."[79]

Like most guides, Ken Sleight owned a small fleet of World War II surplus neoprene pontoons. The army had used them to cross rivers, but they worked just fine for floating, too. They could be augmented with oars or more typically an outboard motor. Baloney boats, as they were called, held more people in more comfort than the trim (and wonderfully maneu-

River runners in Glen Canyon, ca. 1950.

verable) plywood vessels used by Norman Nevills. Better yet, the new un-sinkable tubs were cheap. With some cash and some leisure time—both more plentiful in the postwar era—anyone could be a river rat. Expertise was optional. If you started at Hite, the most popular put-in, you could look forward to a 162-mile run without a rapid worth the name. Swift currents, powerful eddies, and stiff winds could all cause trouble, but the run in Glen Canyon required only average outdoor skills. Bert Loper, who lived in Glen Canyon from 1907 to 1915, called this section the "Kindergarten of the Colorado."

In the 1950s, a wide variety of people, both paying guests and private adventurers (including the occasional uranium miner and petroleum geologist), came to the Glen. Probably the most common visitor was the Boy Scout. In the 1940s, Boy Scout leaders in Salt Lake City had searched for a superactivity to count as the final requirement for the Explorer badge. The idea of a river trip was tested in 1947, when Bert Loper led an electrified group of boys down the Colorado. Thereafter, troops from the Wasatch Front, Phoenix, and southern California made Glen Canyon a yearly tradition—with, and later without, the sponsorship of the BSA. By 1959, 1,252

Explorers from Utah had been initiated in the Glen. Some troops went on their own, but Ken Sleight, Georgie White, Al Quist, Malcolm Ellingson, and John Cross each regularly carried scouts. Another guide, Kenneth Ross, led several groups of boys through Glen Canyon as part of Southwest Explorations, the remnant of Ansel Hall's Explorer's Camp for Boys. According to Ross, passage by boat through "America's loneliest wilderness" could "hardly be called original exploration." Nevertheless, "such a voyage reminds one of the finest adventures left in an overcivilized age. . . . Not all the slit-like canyons of the San Juan or the glens and alcoves of the Colorado have echoed to the footsteps of men. Adventure still lurks around every bend and up every hidden gully."[80]

Boy Scouts will be boys, and these trips undoubtedly featured as much horseplay and mayhem as adventure. Indeed, Glen Canyon endured its fair share of teenagers. The Phoenix YMCA and a Salt Lake–based outfit called Socotwa introduced hundreds of young people to river running. Socotwa stood for South Cottonwood Ward—the Mormon equivalent of a parish. Its groups were so large (and notoriously unprepared) that Socotwa developed a flag system to aid communication between boats. Red meant danger ahead; yellow meant hurry up; white meant go to shore; blue meant "Great sight or wonder: look for it."

The clearest sign of Glen Canyon's swelling visitation came in early 1957, soon after the Bureau of Reclamation started work on the dam, located at Mile 15. Offhandedly, the Bureau announced that Glen Canyon—all 170 miles of it—was off-limits to travel for the duration of the project. Quickly, however, the agency changed its mind. Inundated by complaints from the WRGA and individual river runners, the Bureau limited its restriction to the dam site, and bulldozed a new access road (for the "official" reason that the Bureau of Land Management needed to check mining claims in the area). The road reached the water's edge at the mouth of Kane Creek, a lonely spot forty miles upstream from Lee's Ferry. Though it made for a premature end to river trips, there was no alternative exit.

Ironically, the dam had been authorized at the moment that river running in the Glen was coming of age. Already fairly popular, the canyon became a must-see during the construction years, 1956 to 1963. As Russell Martin writes, "Glen Canyon began to take on an *importance,* a kind of tender beauty that it had never seemed to have before—even to those who knew it intimately—once its days were numbered." Traffic on the river

Kane Creek road under construction, 1957. (Photograph by F. B. Slote.)

grew faster as the deadline drew closer. For many, the giant federal reclamation project intensified the canyon experience. A "fevered mix of discovery and farewell," Bruce Berger has called it. Canyon lovers—and, no
less, curiosity seekers—came to see the dying canyon. Outfitters pocketed
the bittersweet reward. In 1962 and 1963, Harry Aleson ran one trip after
another to meet the demand. Plenty of people had accepted his "final invitation" to see "Glen Canyon and the superb beauty in the mouths of hundreds of side canyons and glens, never to be seen by man again." Call it
terminal exploration.[81]

"I am fulfilling at last a dream of childhood, and one as powerful as the
erotic dreams of adolescence—*floating down the river*," wrote Edward Abbey in *Desert Solitaire*. The date was June 1959. Remarkably, considering
the month and year, Abbey and Newcomb—his game-legged, pipe-smok-
ing friend—encountered no other river runners or motorboat tourists. The
pair spent nine days on the Colorado at a total cost, including boats, of
$350. After pushing off from Hite, Abbey was ecstatic: "Cutting the bloody
cord, that's what we feel, the delirious exhilaration of independence." He

congratulated himself and Newcomb for carrying only one navigational aide, a fairly useless Texaco road map of Utah. "We are entering Glen Canyon without having learned much about it beforehand because we wish to see it as Powell and his party had seen it, not knowing what to expect, making anew the discoveries of others." Nonchalantly, Abbey reported that his map fell overboard in the first riffle. Not true (as his journal attests), but it makes a good story.[82]

Scholar Ann Ronald justly calls "Down the River" (the longest chapter in *Desert Solitaire*) "a synopsis of the author at his best." More to the point, it constitutes the single most influential written document on Glen Canyon. The two paperback editions of *Desert Solitaire* have stayed in print continuously since the early 1970s. Millions, perhaps, have read Abbey's moving, idealized portrait of the canyon:

> Words fail. I draw a rusty harmonica from my shirt pocket and play old folksongs and little tunes from the big symphonies—a thin sweet music that floats for a while like smoke in the vastness all around us before fading into the silence, becoming forever a part of the wilderness. . . .
>
> Down the river we drift in a kind of waking dream, gliding beneath the great curving cliffs with their tapestries of water stains, the golden alcoves, the hanging gardens, the seeps, the springs where no man will ever drink, the royal arches in high relief and the amphitheatres shaped like seashells. A sculpted landscape mostly bare of vegetation—earth in the nude.

Since Abbey never got a second chance to see Glen Canyon, his trip took on, in retrospect, great, even sacred meaning. "I was one of the lucky few," he wrote, "who saw Glen Canyon before it was drowned. In fact I saw only a part of it but enough to realize that here was an Eden, a portion of the earth's original paradise."[83]

After tasting the canyon's fruit, some couldn't bear to leave. Noted photographer Eliot Porter floated down the river in 1960, "but what I saw and tentatively entered in the short time available on this first visit left me with a feeling of frustration and determination to come back, to explore other mysterious and secret places that I knew were hidden behind the multi-colored sandstone cliffs. I knew that what I had photographed was a superficial record, the slightest vision of this wonderful place."[84] He returned several times, twice in the company of Georgia O'Keeffe. In 1963,

Porter's work appeared as *The Place No One Knew: Glen Canyon on the Colorado*. Published by the Sierra Club, it represented a *mea culpa* by conservationist leaders for their indifference about Glen Canyon during the debates on the Colorado River Storage Project. Understandably, some river runners took issue with the title. An inscription in Katie Lee's copy of the book reads, "Well, *we* knew it." A more accurate title would have been *The Place No Politically Important Conservationist Knew*.

By the 1960s, Glen Canyon was anything but unknown. Traffic cops— or river rangers—would have been a real blessing. At the mouth of Forbidding Canyon, it wasn't unusual to find a pileup of a hundred or more campers, all coming or going to Rainbow Bridge. The visitor register for June 1961 gives a snapshot look at late-term travel in the canyon. Of the 985 people who signed the register, 763 were males, 222 were females. All but twenty-seven came down the river. They came in a variety of contraptions: pontoons, inner tubes, fiberglass kayaks, jet boats. Perhaps a majority came without guides. Fifteen friends from Salt Lake City arrived on June 1 and wrote: "All girl expedition—living on linblad rations—pill & fruitcake— all the way from Mexican Hat." At the other end of the gender spectrum, five Explorer posts sweated their way to the bridge. A representative sample of their entries includes "Very beautiful"; "Too tired to know"; "Hot!"; "Hungry!"; "Wow!"; "I wish I was home"; "I miss my chick"; "Girls"; "*Girls* Water Food"; "Crummy food"; "Girls, malts, etc." The scout groups were large, ranging between twenty-one and eighty-four people, but they weren't unique. Socotwa brought groups of thirty-eight, thirty-two, and sixty-six. The budget-rate outfitter Georgie White arrived on June 14 towing forty-three river rats. The previous day, four successive entries told a story:

Too many people!

Yes, but very spectacular.

Very nice but very hot.

What a crowd!

"Glen Canyon got pretty gruesome; it was awful," said veteran river runner P. T. Reilly, looking back. "Too many unqualified people were taking boats down there. . . . They were leaving open toilet areas, flies were bad, you couldn't find a spot that didn't have a pile of human waste on it to throw your sleeping bag." Richard Sprang complained that "[river] bars were burned by the horde of let's-see-everything-in-a-hurry river travelers of that era who were down there to see what Glen Canyon looked like when it was too late to save it. One particular outfit, it has been verified, actually set fire to some of the bars to provide spectacular Kodachrome photographs. . . . This is as utterly disgusting as anything I can think of and yet it's quite fitting. You might as well cremate the damn place because it was dying."[85]

In the days before minimum-impact camping, river runners simply buried their trash or dumped it in the river. This system had worked fine in the 1940s and early '50s, but eventually it led to problems. Popular camps like Forbidding Canyon looked bad and smelled bad. Populations of ants and flies increased dramatically. Meanwhile, in the popular side canyons, filigrees of fern and moss fell apart under too many footprints. Glen Canyon was being discovered with a vengeance. During the final boating season, Woody Edgell, the ferryman at Hite, estimated he carried five hundred vehicles per month. Most of these dusty cars carried river runners. "The Colorado and its tributary, the San Juan, are seeing traffic of a sort never dreamed of before," reported the *New York Times*.[86]

One of the prospectors in this "boating rush" was Stewart Udall, congressman from Arizona. In 1960, with his wife and two of their six children (both boys), Udall took a chartered motorboat trip with Frank Wright. Udall was combining business with pleasure: his family vacation was on the tab of a congressional investigation into the anticipated effect of Lake Powell on Rainbow Bridge National Monument. A short time later, as the newly appointed secretary of the interior, Udall wrote a feature article for a syndicated Sunday newsmagazine. With nods to Teddy Roosevelt ("The Strenuous Life") and President Kennedy ("The New Frontier"), Udall urged American parents to give their children a "He-Man Vacation." As an example, he described his own river trip into "one of the wildest, most untouched, most stupendously beautiful regions in America."

> We hiked and climbed and swam. We explored canyons visited by few other human beings and prowled through cliff dwellings built 700 years ago by a prehistoric Indian tribe which, having built them, vanished without a trace. We slept on sandbars with only the stars and the sky to shelter us. We cooked our food over wood fires. . . .
> For our two boys, Tommy 12, and Scott 11, it was an exciting and rugged adventure. For my wife Ermalee and myself it was a chance

to escape from the pressures of modern society, to wake up both physically and spiritually.[87]

Secretary Udall chose not to mention that this "untouched" place was scheduled to be replaced by a reservoir he voted for as a congressman. He left it to other politicians to celebrate the impending transformation. In 1962, the governors of Utah and Arizona took the official "Last Trip down the Colorado." Guided by Art Greene, this motorboat excursion went quickly. To save time, a chartered helicopter met the dignitaries at the mouth of Forbidding Canyon and whisked them to Rainbow Bridge and back. In Page, Arizona, at the end of the "strenuous" trip, the governors unveiled a plaque commemorating the event. The wording was in the past tense: "Starting at Hite, Utah, on May 26, 1962, the Governors and their official party began a farewell exploration of the Glen Canyon area on the mighty Colorado. Three days later the party concluded their trip at Glen Canyon Dam, having covered 186 miles of the river. Upon completion of the dam, Lake Powell, with a shoreline of over 1,800 miles and destined to become one of America's great recreational playgrounds, was created."[88]

The birth/death notice was slightly premature. Oar boats continued to float the Colorado through the end of 1962. With the aid of motors, a few river rats continued into spring, after the reservoir began filling. A poignant entry from the Rainbow Bridge visitor register for 5 April 1963 reads, "Went to sleep on the Colorado last night, woke up on Lake Powell this morning."

Besides the recreational pallbearers, Glen Canyon had its own group of necrologists: the Upper Colorado River Basin Archeological Salvage Project. It could be thought of as an institutional version of Harry Aleson's Canyon Surveys. Members came from the Museum of Northern Arizona and the University of Utah; funding came from the National Park Service by the power of the Historic Sites Act of 1935. "Salvage" or "emergency" archaeology in America grew up in response to the Tennessee Valley Authority. Later, in the 1940s, Congress created a special committee on salvage work to address the hundreds of government-sponsored dams being planned. Unfortunately, the committee had no part in designing the dams; it could only respond—slowly and incompletely. In the days before environmental impact statements (authorized under the National Environmental Policy Act of 1969), action came first, reckoning later. At Glen Canyon, the reckoning was huge. The potential loss of cultural relics wasn't as great or well-publicized as in the case of the contemporary Aswan High Dam in Egypt, but the Colorado River had its own treasures in cliff ruins, pit houses, and petroglyph panels. Historical and biological studies were eventually added to the massive project.

According to project director Jesse D. Jennings, "the enterprise was begun in high romantic hope in an ecstatic state of expectation of adventure—a state of mind soon transmuted to a less emotional, but no less satisfying, recognition of the scholar's task." The magnitude of the task was, as one staff member put it, frightening: nearly every side canyon—one hundred or more of them—contained ruins. Two years alone were devoted to two major tributaries, Lake and Moqui canyons. In all, over a thousand archaeological sites were discovered. Any associated thrill was erased by the fact that only about one in ten could be excavated before their underwater burial. The field logistics were difficult; the living conditions, primitive; the heat, oppressive. A shortage of graduate students led to untrained workers doing fieldwork. Digs were quick and dirty, and even at that, whole sections of the reservoir area went unstudied. It was a losing race against time.[89]

"On the personal side," Jennings wrote much later, "learning the Glen and working in and near it for six or seven summers was a rich, emotionally charged period of my life. The vastness, the isolation, the stillness, the overwhelming beauty of the land, even (especially) the heat, the still starlit nights, the blue or brassy midday sky, all combined to make me constantly aware of my good fortune."[90]

He wasn't the only one feeling lucky. During the canyon's last years, a different, much larger crew of workers anticipated creation, not destruction. With more than two thousand men laying concrete, the dam at Glen Canyon rose at a breathtaking, round-the-clock pace. The achievement was especially impressive considering the initial obstacles: no road to the site, no way to cross the canyon, no town of any size for nearly one hundred miles. On a mesa acquired from the Navajo Nation, the government assembled the town of Page (named for a former commissioner of the Bureau of Reclamation). It was the capital of nowhere. Yet "people *wanted* to come to Page, it appeared. Like the Mormon pioneers before them, they wanted to go to a place that was virtually empty, entirely unformed, a town unfettered by convention." For these construction families, transforming the wilderness rather than exploring it connected them to a vital, ephemeral part of America. "It was pioneering and it was tremendous," remembered one worker. Added another, "It was the last frontier to be developed in America—before Alaska."[91]

THE MOST EXCITING LAKE ON EARTH

The Glen Canyon project came to a symbolic end on 13 March 1963 when the second of two diversion tunnels, the river's intravenous life support, was closed. Frustrated from its course, the Colorado River pushed against the adjacent earth-fill coffer dam. In one final act of creative energy, the river broke free on 18 April and rushed downstream—only to meet a permanent concrete face. The Colorado stopped.

Done with its job, the Bureau of Reclamation turned over management of its 1.2-million-acre land withdrawal to the Park Service. Along with prodigious amounts of driftwood, Glen Canyon National Recreation Area began to gather tourists. To the public, Lake Powell offered many enticements and one must-see: Rainbow Bridge. Between 1909 and 1963, fewer than twenty-three thousand people on record had visited the national monument. No one doubted that that figure could be matched in a single season on the lake. Natt N. Dodge, who came to the bridge by horseback in 1960, was sad yet ambivalent about this change. True, many more would get to see the great span, "but these thousands will miss the thrills of that wilderness adventure in the slickrock solitude."[92]

It's one of the great ironies of Lake Powell, however, that many people found just such a thrill. A few weeks after the reservoir started rising, a correspondent with the *Salt Lake Tribune* made an inspection tour. He reported, without a trace of regret, the demise of "one of the last great wilderness frontiers." Yet in the same article, he used words that could have described the former Glen Canyon—a place of "breathing room" and "solitude" offering "adventurous skippers and crews plenty of chances to let their exploring imaginations run wild." Many embraced this exciting incongruity—a wilderness where you could pilot a boat, a reservoir where you could feel like Columbus. Travel articles concerning nascent Lake Powell are laden with metaphors of exploration and pioneering. "Historians have called the Indian Wars the last great American adventure," wrote one Salt Laker, "but I can testify there's some left, and I've just had a taste of it." His party of six spent a long weekend at Lake Powell. Half of them had never camped before.[93]

David Brower of the Sierra Club once called 1962 the "Year of the Last Look." The town of Page, making its conversion to a tourist site, labeled 1963 the "Year of Exploration." The created landscape of Lake Powell had literally never been seen before. "We were one of the pioneers in these river trips," advertised Art Greene. "We know this land—we've lived with it for years. Yet, even to us this will be a year of exploration, of seeing new things."[94]

A characteristic traveler's report went like this: "As the water reaches into mysterious canyons, creeping into areas never before seen by whitemen, it will disclose to exploring boaters exciting country seen for the first time." Before the dam, Glen Canyon's tributaries often contained impassable drop-offs or chokestones, tantalizing barriers to the unknown. As the listless lake invaded the glens, overwhelming the ferns and cottonwoods, beaver and deer, the water surpassed these obstacles, permitting exploration beyond. Eyes aglow, boaters propelled up canyons where perhaps even the nimble Anasazi had never been. Longtime Page resident Stan Jones, a.k.a. "Mr. Lake Powell," remembers this time:

> Well, the first couple of years that I was here, I made a number of trips out on the lake that lasted as long as three weeks at a time. . . Each time I cruised the new lake I would note in my log those hanging canyons that would someday be accessible by boat; I was determined to be the first to enter, if I could.
>
> At one point during my explorations over a period of more than three years, I carried a ten-foot ladder, an aluminum ladder, aboard the boat, so that I could actually pound used automobile valves that I had sharpened on one end to pound into the rock and tie the boat. And then I would put the ladder on the deck up to the canyon floor so that I would be the first one in there. It worked because no one was dumb enough to carry a ladder on a fourteen-foot boat [laughter]. Or any kind of boat. And so I was able to climb into some of those and get back down. This was the most rewarding experience I've ever had in my life, to go into those canyons. Nobody had ever been there; no four-footed animal had ever been.[95]

No wonder Lake Powell was sometimes called "the most exciting lake on earth." Not only could you discover your own side canyon, you could zoom up the main channel alone. Most observers of the new reservoir mentioned both the geographic isolation and the personal solitude—days spent without seeing another soul. Here you could really escape the world. Several went so far as to describe the man-made waterway as "unspoiled," "untrammeled," or "unexploited."

This hyperbole made some sense. With its narrow channels and towering walls, Lake Powell resembled a river much more than a lake. And during the first months—even the first several years for some parts of the sprawling reservoir—the place did seem wild. Surprisingly, slightly fewer people (about three thousand) visited Rainbow Bridge in 1963 than 1962. It took time for Glen Canyon to become known to its new audience. Furthermore, those who came at the beginning had to live without a marina. For seven months after the dam gates closed, boaters had to drive the twenty-three miles of jarring dirt road to Kane Creek to put in. During the same time, at the very same spot, straggling river parties took out. Nearby, the Bureau of Reclamation had posted a sign. It was meant for incoming boaters, but the opening lines no doubt spoke to those taking a backwards glance at the canyon that was.

WARNING
LAKE POWELL IS BEING FILLED
DEAD END ROAD—RISING WATER AHEAD

After the reservoir flooded a portion of the Kane Creek road, boaters used a temporary launch near Page until the water finally rose high enough to service the permanent boat ramp at Art Greene's Wahweap Marina. Years before, with tremendous foresight, the riverman had leased a parcel of state property—then a trackless mesa miles from water. When the dam got underway, Greene and his family corporation built a road, then went to work on a motel and marina. Did the Arizona business pioneer have misgivings about Lake Powell? No permanent ones. "Now a whole new breed of people can come out and be adventurers in safety," Greene told the *National Geographic*, sounding like Norman Nevills two decades before. Art Greene was the only Glen Canyon guide to make a successful transition to the reservoir, though Frank Wright and Gaylord and Joan Staveley gave it a try. The majority never did, disgusted or heartbroken by the dam.[96]

"Some of my fellow guides and concessions are saying, 'although much is lost . . . much more will be opened up,'" wrote Ken Sleight in his mimeographed *Wonderland Newsletter*. "As I see it . . . all that will be 'opened up' was already there before. It was certainly open to all of you who made the effort to do a little exploring." Confronted with the new environment, Sleight made a business decision: "You will not find us on the bank of the lake operating a 'million dollar' concession but you will find us in the far reaches of a number of the tributary canyons." His favorite was the Escalante River, often called a Glen Canyon in microcosm. Sleight led backpacking trips into the canyons of the lower Escalante until they too were consumed by water. "God, what a mistake it was to build the dam," he later said. "But I also hope that no one ever again will have to experience the ordeal I had in seeing Glen Canyon destroyed, inch by lousy inch."[97]

For those who never knew the Glen, however, it was hard to feel bad about Lake Powell. In 1964, the new editor of *Desert Magazine*, Choral Pepper, took a cruise with Frank Wright, who had spent the last several years as head boatman for the Glen Canyon Salvage Project. Pepper reported excitedly that "every 24 hours, at the time of our visit, the water level rose another two feet. Canyons that had been boxed since the coming of white man were for the first time about to be revealed." When asked how he felt about the reservoir, "Frank answered that its rising waters brought him closer to tears than he'd been for a long, long time. . . . The idea of an ancient [Anasazi] ruin inundated is almost more than he can bear." Pepper tried to acknowledge the loss, but her heart wasn't in it: "This passing of an era has been lamented by other writers. I'm afraid I belong to the future . . . to the promise of Mystery Canyon which will soon be accessible for the first time; . . . to the discovery that soft red sandstone substitutes for a sandy beach—bugless, burrless and snakeless; and to the exciting advance of strong, silent, untrammeled land. This is for me. I like the new Lake Powell."[98] A good share of this "new breed of people" came from Phoenix, just one day's drive to the south, thanks to a new federal highway. In 1963, the desert state of Arizona ranked "near the top of the list in per capita boat ownership in the United States," with 20,800 registered vehicles. Phoenix alone boasted twelve boating organizations! Considering the pool of possible visitors, Lake Powell saw only modest traffic its opening summer—a reported 2,300 boats. But the mere fact that several thousand boaters would travel hundreds of miles to a reservoir with bare amenities is remarkable. There were several large developed reservoirs in the mountains near Phoenix—why go all the way to Lake Powell?[99]

Primitiveness was part of the lure. "Planning a trip to Lake Powell should not be considered with the casual offhandedness of 'just another fishing trip,'" cautioned one travel writer. "Consider yourself a latter-day Lewis or Clark and plan accordingly." At first, nothing save water and slickrock existed between Wahweap and Hite, a distance of almost 150 miles. Boaters had to carry their own gas, and plenty of it. Waterskiing wasn't allowed. There were no patrols at first, no buoys marking the maze of side channels. More than a few visitors got stranded or lost. (Not until 1967 did the U.S. Coast Guard begin patrolling the water. Lake Powell fell under its jurisdiction because the vast reservoir qualified as an "inland ocean.") The Park Service could only admonish, "Be carefree but not careless. This is a place for recreation, but it is just emerging from its wild state." The agency had plans for developments up and down the lake, but for the moment these were just plans.[100]

Come 1964, boaters had a choice of three access points: Wahweap, Hall's Crossing, and Hite, the latter two in Utah. Only Wahweap had the luxury of a paved road. The Utah locations were closer to Salt Lake City, Denver, and Albuquerque, but it required an adventurous spirit to haul a boat over the ruts and sand. Only 2,290 made the trip to Hall's Crossing in 1964. The very next year, however, some 15,000 came. Across the reservoir, visitation was up 23 percent. In 1967, a Salt Lake boat dealer reported that his annual gross sales had risen from $600,000 to $1,000,000 after Lake Powell and Flaming Gorge Reservoir (on the Green River) started filling. As the director of the Utah State Park and Recreation Committee commented, "Every time a new body of water has been created, we've increased the number of boating registrations. People for years have thought of Utah as a desert state. We are taking steps to change that image."[101]

Observing these trends in 1966, one Lake Powell visitor remarked that "the next two or three years in all probability will be the last in which this part of the West will still be at all wild." But unlike the lovers of the late Glen Canyon, most boaters didn't seem to dread this impending outcome. Then again, they too wanted to seize the moment. "From an exploring standpoint," explained the *Salt Lake Tribune* back in 1963, "boating the lake right now is the best time." It wasn't every day you found what the Upper Colorado River Commission (a pro–dam lobby) called a "veritable boater's paradise" within "a spectacular wilderness area."[102]

Here, in startling new form, was Theodore Roosevelt's old outskirts of adventure.

CLOSING TIME

Imagine a dirt road ending with a sign: "Beyond this point, the backcountry begins." (Such a placard once existed in a national park in Utah.) Leave the car and you're there: the thrilling threshold. Beyond is a place both wild and accessible. Unfortunately, though, the sign keeps moving; the road keeps getting improved. As someone once wrote about southern Utah, "If you are the rugged type who likes to get close to the land, or the type who likes to brag 'I was there then,' the time to [go] is right now."[103] If you wait a year, you'll find that the road has been graded a bit, cut a bit closer to the heart—and the end—of the wilderness. At the same time, however, this new-and-improved road attracts newcomers with their own definitions of undiscovered and undeveloped—owners of cars with lower clearance, if you will. For them, the land has been opened for exploration—or for activities not even associated with wilderness. For others, of course, part or all of the country has been lost. Regrets are voiced: "Things were better then," or "This place has been spoiled." Some adjust, some can't; some search for a new special place.

This metaphor of displacement—the road with a moving terminus—is culturally specific. It applies best to Euro-American visitors, and imperfectly at that. It would be messier but more realistic to imagine a separate road and a separate vehicle for each traveler. More realistic because in addition to the land's transformation, visitors' ideas about the land, about change itself, change too. The overlay of all of this roadwork—the interactions among culture, self, and environment—looks blurry. But the general shape of things is unmistakable: the perimeter of the wild is shrinking. The road is one-way, and it leads to a cul-de-sac.

Not coincidentally, this idea of wilderness resembles the "vanishing frontier" popularized by Frederick Jackson Turner. While Turner and others have variously defined the frontier as a process, a contact zone, or a place, popular usage favors the last: as place-words, *frontier* and *wilderness* are usually interchangeable. From a historical perspective, however, it's more useful to think of them as similar but sequential idea-words. After the seemingly infinite frontier was discovered to be finite, its vestiges were designated (in name and later in law) as wilderness. From abundance to scarcity: "Rarely has a reversal of a cultural icon been more complete," writes historian William Cronon.[104]

I would add a caveat: though wilderness in the canyonlands may be nothing but a cultural creation, the canyonlands are not. They're a real place with real history. When, in the early twentieth century, visitors described Glen Canyon as primitive, they weren't simply feeding their fantasies. At the time, this place *was* far removed from the nation—though hardly the peopleless, storyless place that tourists often imagined. More to the point, this rock land was, in a word, elemental. No one has ever denied that. If tourists made a mistake, it was in conflating that force of nature with their introduced concepts of "frontier" and "wilderness." Yet it's hard to blame them. If this wasn't wilderness, what was? It looked and felt like wilderness was *supposed* to.[105]

Likewise, it makes sense that people used the language of the wild to describe Lake Powell in its early years. Nothing adorned the shoreline—rock met water, water reflected rock. The reservoir looked, at least while it rose, shockingly pure. All the marks of canyon history had been erased. In 1963, one travel writer steered his boat into a glen, then turned the engine off. When the wake of the boat had expired, his companion raised a hand—"listen!" Reply: "I didn't hear anything!" Response: "That's the beautiful part, you can't hear anything but maybe a raven's croak or the twittering of cliff swallows. No horns, no trains, no jets—nothing."[106] The silence signified the absence—the annihilation—of Glen Canyon's terrestrial life. Ironically, vacationers could obtain release from the mechanical world by taking a boat onto a reservoir, the result of a dam, the ultimate manifestation of mechanized nature.

Glen Canyon Dam converted kinetic energy into electrical energy, but lake explorers required a third kind. After September 1965, boaters made sure to go up Forbidding Canyon—if not to see Rainbow Bridge, then to refuel at the nearby Rainbow Marina, a floating facility anchored to the submerged canyon floor. It received its gasoline from a barge christened for a regional vice president of Chevron; the pilot on the maiden voyage was a sales representative for Standard Oil. Finally, boaters could "explore the full length of Lake Powell without the necessity of carrying extra fuel," reported the *Deseret News*. The fill-up station, located about a full tank's distance from Wahweap, enjoyed brisk business. In three years it graduated from an 1,800- to a 3,000- to a 10,000-gallon tanker. Gas queues formed each summer afternoon.[107]

Beyond Forbidding Canyon, however, large areas of Lake Powell lay glistening and expectant. "The boat traffic thins to nothing," disclosed one writer in 1968, a year when 28,000 people came to Rainbow Bridge National Monument and 650,000 people to Glen Canyon National Recreation Area. He was surprised but delighted that no detailed map of the reservoir yet existed. That was part of the magic. "Go there now, before it is all 'discovered,' and make your own map. You'll never have a chance again quite like it."[108]

These words sounded like preparations for nostalgia. Bruce Berger tells of a friend who discovered the canyon only after the dam was completed. During his first day on Lake Powell in 1963, he saw nobody else. He returned yearly for "a series of fresh adventures in a new country." But each subsequent year, more people appeared and more canyon disappeared. Finally, faced with a barrage of fun seekers, he threw in the towel: "That was the end of our Lake Powell, which was a place for exploration, and its conversion into pure recreation."[109] Like all of the "wilderness areas" that preceded it, this one proved to be ephemeral.

For over half a century, wilderness exploration had been the leading tourist activity in the Glen Canyon region. Explorers came equipped with various degrees of seriousness and various motivations. To mingle with traditional Indians, to test one's toughness, to get away from it all, to make discoveries, to blaze new trails, to see new beauty, to feel sweet solitude, to sense the power of God. Or some combination. To be an explorer, whatever the guise and era, was a blessing. Early Rainbow Bridge visitors and early Lake Powell visitors knew they had it good. They had found another world. Almost always, they came away inspired. It's remarkable how many first-time river runners came away from the Glen with a different life trajectory.

To be an explorer was a privilege. Generally it was an economic and cultural privilege because it assumed the means and desire to travel for pleasure. Invariably it was a racial privilege because it assumed a Euro-American perspective. This was especially plain in the early days of Rainbow Bridge. For example, visitors typically memorized their register number, their position removed from the First White Man. Number 278, number 5,561, number 7,000—these were figures of distinction. Such people could sign their name "with the smugness of those who are aware they are members of a small coterie."[110] With similar smugness, visitors occasionally recorded their exploits. It was surrogate discovery. You couldn't *see* the place first, but you could *do* something there for the first time. Some examples:

First Utah woman to visit the Rainbow Bridge (1924)
First movies taken at the bridge (1927)

First Missourian to go on top of bridge with broken foot (1929)
First women to have spent night atop Rainbow Bridge (1945)
First man to play "Over the Rainbow" under the Rainbow on an Ocarina (1948)
First to photograph bridge with 35 mm Kodacolor (1958)
First gasoline-powered vehicles to carry travelers to the bridge area—TOTE GOTE! (1960)

The last entry was part of a sales campaign for "America's No. 1 Off Highway Cycle." On a "grueling" trip across "nearly inaccessible terrain," twelve "rugged individualists" took their mopeds for a test ride. "This was the first time," read the subsequent advertisement, "that man had attempted to reach this remote area in the southern Utah desert with motorized vehicles."[111]

After Tote Gote, it's hard to find any more "firsts" in the register. Likewise, in the late 1950s, when the number of registrants reached roughly sixteen thousand, people stopped recording their number to the side of their name. After all, what's so special about being sixteen thousandth? What's so great about a crowd? In the near future, when Lake Powell extended into Rainbow Bridge National Monument, boaters—hundreds of thousands each year—would park in sight of the span. What would these new visitors find at Glen Canyon? What would they take from it? How would they value the rainbow made of stone?

In *Traders to the Navajo*, Louisa Wetherill voiced strong nostalgia for earlier, less complicated days and pride for having been part of them. And despite the changes, despite the new roads, Wetherill expressed the conviction and consolation that much of the desert would forever stay untrammeled. Zane Grey was less hopeful. Upon leaving the Wetherills for the last time, in 1929, he registered his low spirits in their guest book: "Time is cruel. The years are tragic. The pioneers could not stay the approach of deadly civilization." He lamented the changes in the land and the "doom" of traditional Navajo ways. Yet he too found some solace in the farthest reaches of this arid, rough country. "The so-called civilization of man and his marks shall perish from the earth, while the shifting sands, the red looming walls, the purple sage, and the towering monuments, the vast brooding range show no perceptible change."[112]

By 1960, with Glen Canyon Dam under way, such faith in the invulnerability of the canyonlands—as a "frontier" or a "wilderness" or simply undeveloped country—seemed naïve. Of those who came before the dam, perhaps none was more free from illusions than Wallace Stegner, who in 1947 floated the Glen with Norm Nevills. "We are not pioneers, explorers, or even adventurers, but simply backroads tourists," declared the writer. Even so, Stegner felt excitement—mingled with profound gratitude—at seeing the remote canyon. At one point, after scaling a wall for an unobstructed look at lonely magnificence, he admitted, "We feel like explorers here." Why not linger by the Colorado, grow a beard, write a book? Stegner toyed with the idea for half a minute before abandoning the "notion of sanctuary." It wouldn't work, at least not for long. At the mouth of Forbidding Canyon, the passage to Rainbow Bridge, the essay closed with a sigh: "This is the way things were when the world was young; we had better enjoy them while we can."[113]

A rejoinder, one Stegner didn't answer then, gains force with time, at Glen Canyon and across the American West. What if you came too late?

PART 3

BEAUTY MADE ACCESSIBLE

DÉJÀ VU

First trip memories:

As the nominal leader of a Mormon youth group, I had the responsibility of organizing a summer "superactivity." The boys in my age group indicated they wanted most to visit Lake Powell. I jumped on the idea because I had an ulterior motive: I hated the reservoir, but my hate, born of books, was incomplete. Never had I been on the water—the dead river—for the very simple reason that my family didn't boat. My church advisor, on the other hand, owned all the right toys. We, the fourteen- and fifteen-year-olds, merely had to pool our cash for gas and food.

Our group made camp near Hite Marina at the upper end of the reservoir. The first day, at dusk, we fished for bass at the base of a maroon-colored butte. Déjà vu: I finally realized I'd seen this butte before—in a book. In 1871, the second Powell expedition cached a boat near here and briefly rested after the punishment of Cataract Canyon. In the photograph they took, of course, the butte stands taller by hundreds of feet.

We did the usual Lake Powell things—fishing, waterskiing, cliff-jumping—but a few of the boys insisted on going to Bullfrog, the next marina down. "We should have gone there instead of Hite," they said under their breaths. Hite was the smallest of the marinas and the one most geared toward fishing. Bullfrog had more action, more reputation. One boy had promised his girlfriend a Bullfrog T-shirt (something of a status symbol in my high school, same as a ski-lift pass hanging from your parka). Happily, our chaperon was accommodating: he burned a day's worth of gas driving us there. On the way, I looked carefully for other landmarks I might recognize from my readings on the river. The lake was lovely, I had to admit. Meanwhile, the others just pulled down their caps. "Wake us up when we get to Bullfrog," they said.

My second lake experience came a few years later. Early one mild morning I queued with other tourists at the dock of Wahweap Marina near the

Utah-Arizona border. After boarding the *Rainbow Trail*, I gazed passively from the sundeck as the noisy craft left a trail of wide wakes. For most of the trip—fifty miles made in less than two hours—we followed the old channel of the Colorado River. The tour guide made the standard intercom jokes. In time, he steered up a tributary canyon; a buoy at its mouth read "Rainbow Bridge." A few more twisting miles and there we were. Effortless. I disembarked onto the short, wide, dusty path. Looking ahead, I could see a large group clustered in the shade of the bridge, lounging, snacking, chatting. The boat captain followed me. "Listen to this," he said with a grin. Leaning back, he hollered twice in close succession: "*Hello, shut up!*" In tandem, the words reverberated six or seven times.

Ashamed, I bowed my head. I kept it down as I walked to and under and beyond the natural bridge. Only when I was out of sight and sound did I look up. By this point, I reckoned, I had crossed from Rainbow Bridge National Monument into the Navajo Nation. I kept walking. Eventually, at a bend in the canyon, the bridge came back into view: a small floating hoop in a chasm. With a chill, I recognized this perspective as the one in the first photograph of Rainbow Bridge, taken 14 August 1909.

Since I had arranged with the concessionaire to return on the afternoon boat, I got to stare at the bridge for hours (instead of the usual twenty or thirty minutes). That entire splendid time, I was alone; no one ventured past the bridge. After so much silence, the return trip by boat was jarring, morose. I couldn't stop thinking about the lost world below. I tried to recall every photograph I'd seen of this section of the Glen and imagined others to fill in the gaps.

My nostalgia was finally interrupted by a boy on a Jet Ski. His high-pitched machine made more noise, it seemed, than the eighty-eight-passenger cruiser. After we passed a houseboat—what must have been his family—he followed in pursuit. He was a wake jumper. After accelerating to a point parallel to the boat, he cut back to catch the wave. Then he revved up and did it again. And again. Mile after mile, wake after wake, he lifted his machine higher into the air. The setting sun lit his face like sandstone. Intense yet joyful, his look was compelling. A look that said, "This world is beautiful. It's mine to enjoy." Looking at him, someone who could have been my neighbor, my churchmate, I sighed: Lake Powell must be so much fun without the danger of déjà vu.

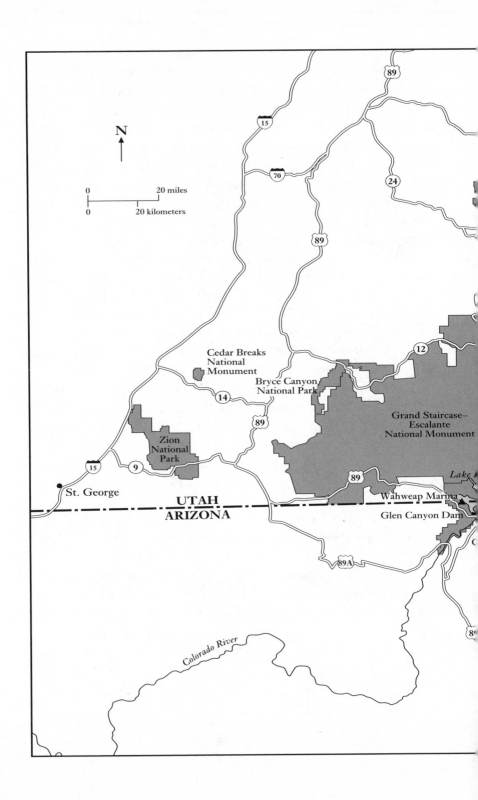

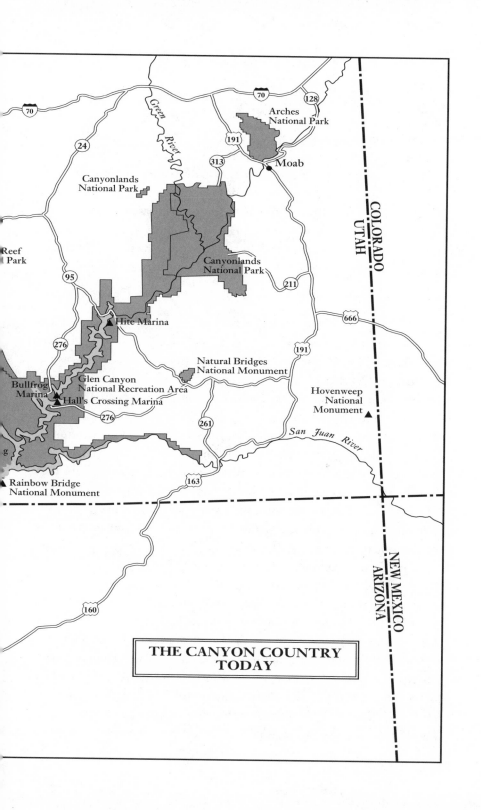

THE CANYON COUNTRY
TODAY

WAS IT WORTH IT?

Soon after the reservoir began to fill, *Arizona Highways* devoted an entire issue to Glen Canyon Dam and "America's Newest Playground." Alongside the stunning photography of Josef Muench, the contributors' text praised the dam and reservoir incessantly. The closest thing to an equivocation came from Joyce Rockwood Muench, the photographer's wife and a canyon alumna. "We had come this time, frankly mourning the death of Glen Canyon and with no intention of being easily pleased by whatever the upstart Lake Powell might have to offer," she wrote. "Yet, after one breathtaking view, we had surrendered. It was love at first sight." Muench then quoted from FitzGerald's *Rubáiyát* to underscore her conversion:

> Ah, my Beloved, fill the cup that clears
> Today of past regrets and future fears[1]

Over the years, *Arizona Highways* has published several special issues on Lake Powell, each one predictably enthusiastic. As the official organ of the Arizona Department of Transportation, the magazine exists primarily to create tourist revenue for the state. It doesn't pay to regret Lake Powell. Only once, in a 1965 article examining the new, waterborne accessibility of Rainbow Bridge National Monument, has *Arizona Highways* confronted the essential ambiguity of the reservoir. The author, Thelma Hall Towle, a resident of Winslow, Arizona, had visited the bridge four times in the days before the dam—three times by horse, once on foot from the river. The fifth time around, she took a one-day jet-boat tour. "My heart did flip-flops between pained remembrance of the River as it had been, and marvel at the new shore line," she wrote. "I have never been so torn, so hopelessly beyond words or thought to explain my feelings."[2]

All the old landmarks were gone. Some new ones had been exposed— a previously inaccessible cave, a previously invisible arch—but these too would be lost, for the reservoir had two hundred feet yet to rise. Towle hankered for the narrows and the pools at the junction of Forbidding and Bridge canyons. Someone had used the sandstone wall as a temporary signpost, painting "Rainbow Bridge," with an arrow pointing left. From here to the landing area, the water was a "mess of driftwood and twigs, on water slicked with oil. . . . This entire area thus had a scummy, mosquito-breeding look which made me heartsick."

*The mouth of Bridge Canyon on the way to Rainbow Bridge, Lake Powell, 1965.
(Photograph by Mel Davis.)*

Not surprisingly, Towle felt relieved to leave the reservoir and the noisy boat behind. From the water's edge it was a short hike to the bridge along a well-beaten trail. Towle and her husband brought their thirteen-year-old hound, "and that fact alone will stand in my mind as a denominator of the change that has taken place," she wrote. Yet the dog wasn't the only beneficiary of the new easy access. After talking with her tour-boat companions, Towle concluded that "it is a completely new segment of the population which is now seeing this no–longer–remote world." She ended her article with a personal vignette:

> We learned that of our eleven members, only my husband and I
> had been here before. One woman had yearned for years to see the
> Bridge, but her husband and family insisted she was not physically
> up to the trip, and she quite agreed. Even with the hike reduced to
> one and one-half miles, all were dubious, but she put in a do-or-
> die vote. It had been hard for her. She trailed far behind the rest of

us, but she got there. When lunch was first spread she was too exhausted to eat, but rest revived her, and the glow of her happiness in the sight of the great arch which she had expected never to see reflected on all of us. If nine people who would not have seen Rainbow Bridge under the old circumstances can now see it, and if one out of those nine is as elated as she, then I and others who so deeply regret the changes can certainly feel the sacrifice of primitiveness has been in a good cause.

Towle received a "flood of letters" in response to her publication. Replying privately to Frank Masland, another river rat, she wrote, "As to my last sentence—you'll be consoled to learn that every letter I received made the same objection to it as yourself." She continued:

There was an interesting bit of psychology there, which I couldn't put into such an article, but which I think you might appreciate. I, you, the rest of us who so loved the Glen were probably quite a lot alike in some of our reasons for it. A love of the wild places, of the loneliness, a certain gloating perhaps to be such individualists— but looming large was a love of adventure, joy in excelling over the ruggedness of the country and weather, a thrill at every small bit of danger. In contrast, here was a heavy housewife in her middle years who had none of these reasons for wanting to be there . . . in fact *all* those reasons became hardships in her case! It was *only* the beauty of the Bridge which had brought her there, and that was something she had dreamed of for many, many years. She was utterly transported with a deep and silent joy. This is something that could not help but make a deep impression on any lover of the Bridge. I don't expect that many of the new order will react so deeply, but if there was one such instance, there will be a *few* others, and I can feel that there is at least this tiny modicum of good in the great evil.[3]

Towle was right: she couldn't have published her true feelings in *Arizona Highways*. Even as it was, the magazine downplayed her ambivalence. On the lead page, the editors emblazoned, "New beauties revealed by the modern lake approach are worth the sacrifice of former rugged primitiveness." This summary statement might as well serve as the official motto of Lake Powell apologists. Ever since 1963, people have been arguing about the morality of the reservoir, and typically the debate gets down to this: Was it worth losing some of the beauty of this country when many more people can enjoy the great beauty that remains? In answering no, the dam haters argue for Glen Canyon's superior beauty and the superior quality of its recreation. The apologists, meanwhile, tend to emphasize recreational quantity—can millions of happy boaters be wrong?

What is strange about this ongoing debate is its relationship to Glen Canyon Dam. People routinely discuss the merits of the dam when they really mean the merits of the reservoir. They are not necessarily the same. The endless talk about the aesthetic and recreational effects of the dam tends to obscure the fundamental question. Why was it built?

THE RECLAMATION DREAM

Major John Wesley Powell, for whom Lake Powell is named, did more than explore the Unknown; his river exploits became a stepping-stone to a distinguished career in science and government. In 1878, he released his *Report on the Lands of the Arid Region of the United States, with a More Detailed Account of the Lands of Utah*. In it, Powell alerted his congressional audience to a big problem: two-fifths of the United States could not support agriculture without irrigation. Somewhere around the hundredth meridian, the land gave up green in favor of gray, brown, and red. And even "when all the waters running in the streams found running in this region are conducted on the lands," said Powell, "there will be but a very small portion of the country redeemed, varying in different territories perhaps from 1 to 3 percent."[4]

For Powell, even 3 percent redemption was worth the effort, but he wanted to do it efficiently. He bemoaned the fever and fraud that characterized nineteenth-century land development in America. In his *Arid Region* report, Powell outlined a series of reforms. First he would scrap the Land Ordinance of 1785, which had established a survey to map the nation into sections of one square mile. Powell would replace that grid—which made no sense against the disordered topography of the West—with a survey that followed watershed lines. Simultaneously, he would institute an economic survey that would classify the unclaimed lands of the Arid Region according to highest potential use—as rangeland, timberland, or farmland. The acreage deemed most suitable for irrigated agriculture would then be available to homesteaders, but instead of 160 acres (the standard allotment under the Homestead Act), they would receive 80 acres with water rights. Each plot would be tied to a collective irrigation district; the small farmers would work together to build dams, canals, and ditches. However, if their capital proved insufficient, Powell called on the federal government to assist in water development.[5]

Powell's proposed reforms went nowhere, but his minor thesis—that Washington would have to play a role in irrigation—was eventually embraced by the people he despised: the boosters who saw no limits, who scoffed at 3 percent. Starting in 1891, William Smythe, the self-ordained prophet of irrigation, organized annual "Irrigation Congresses" to promote national reclamation. For him and other believers, nothing less than the greening of the desert would fulfill the meaning of the verb *to reclaim*. Man proved his divinity by transforming the arid "waste," thus completing the good work of God. Likewise, America proved its promise by subduing the continent—every last piece of it. Tellingly, Smythe entitled his 1899 manifesto *The Conquest of Arid America*. He began with a poem, "Emancipation":

> *The nation reaches its hand into the Desert,*
> The wasting floods stand back, the streams obey their
> master, and the stricken forests spring to life again
> upon the forsaken mountains!

> *The nation reaches its hand into the Desert,*
> The barred doors of the sleeping empire are flung wide
> open to the eager and the willing, that they may
> enter in and claim their heritage![6]

Like many Americans of his era, Smythe believed that the conquest of nature furthered human democracy. He predicted that with the "miracle of irrigation," the West would become an egalitarian domain of small, prosperous farmers, a fulfillment of the Jeffersonian dream. By the turn of the century, however, the dream had stalled. Except in areas settled by the hypercooperative Mormons in Utah (from whom Powell took inspiration), western irrigation of the 1800s was a failure, at least by the standards of imperialism. The Desert Land Act of 1877—a variation of the Homestead Act—had promised settlers one square mile of land if they could irrigate it, but the drafters of this bill had no idea of the difficulties involved. Very few settlers turned a profit, while speculators made a killing with fraudulent claims. In time, private companies, and later states, tried to bankroll irrigation projects but with limited success. To turn the desert into the Garden required a vast inheritance—the kind of money only Washington controlled. And though the western states didn't really want a new form of federal intervention, they wanted even less to disavow the religion of irrigation. In 1902, Senator Francis G. Newlands of Nevada won passage of the Reclamation Act, which President Roosevelt approved immediately.

According to the law, the government would set aside revenue from the sale of public lands to establish a revolving Reclamation Fund earmarked for the construction of irrigation projects. Within the project areas, farmers could buy no more than 160 acres of land. The loans for their purchases, payable in ten annual interest-free installments, would replenish the revolving fund, thus permitting more and more projects. At least, that's how it worked on paper. In practice, the provisions of the Reclamation Act became mere goals: William Smythe's flood of "eager and willing" yeomen never came, and those who did went bankrupt with disturbing frequency. With its fund barely replenishing, much less revolving, the Reclamation Service decided to offer its water to large landowners, setting aside the 160-acre limit. Meanwhile, in 1910 Congress gave the Reclamation Fund a generous loan, and extended the irrigationists' repayment deadline first to twenty years and later to forty (still without interest). And what fruits did these subsidies yield? As of 1923, the Reclamation Service (soon to be renamed the Bureau of Reclamation) had put 1.2 million new acres under irrigation, an area roughly equivalent to 0.2 percent of the state of Utah.[7]

After such an inauspicious start, federal reclamation might have passed away had it not been for monumental Hoover Dam, which captured the imagination of Depression-era Americans. Significantly, however, the original support for the dam didn't come from workers or even small farmers. It came from the city of Los Angeles and the corporate farms of southern California. Irrigationists in the Imperial Valley (previously known as the Valley of the Dead or the Salton Sink) had been using the Colorado River since 1901 via a canal they shared with Mexico. Unfortunately, the canal had no headgate, and in 1905 the river broke through. For almost two years, before the Southern Pacific Railroad plugged the outlet, the main part of the stream emptied into the center of the valley, forming the fifty-mile-long Salton Sea. (Actually, this was normal behavior for the river; it had drained into the sink before and would do it again.) Undeterred, farmers tried to finance a new, "all-American" canal with a headgate, but they couldn't come up with the millions. In 1917 they went to the government for help, and the Reclamation Service responded. The agency's new director, Arthur Powell Davis (nephew of Major Powell), had an engineer's dream: a comprehensive plan to restrain the intractable Colorado River. He convinced the farmers of the Imperial Valley that a canal by itself was impractical; it demanded an upstream storage dam, one that would prevent floods, trap silt, and provide a dependable year-round flow of water. Davis acquired his second ally in 1920, when Los Angeles expressed its interest in the proposed dam. Having already grown 600 percent in the first two decades of the century and having already sucked the Owens Valley dry with an aqueduct, the city was looking for new sources of power and water.[8]

Meanwhile, upstream, the states of the Intermountain West watched with growing alarm. They feared that fast-developing California would claim the entire flow of the Colorado River even though the river originated in their snowcapped mountains. This anxiety had legal merit, based on the fundamental rule of western water rights, prior appropriation: "First in time, first in right." Translated, that means that the first entity to put water to "beneficial use" owns the right to that water, no matter where that water comes from or where it goes. Thus, by the logic of water law, it made sense to develop water you didn't really need in case you did need it later. Long recognized between individuals, prior appropriation became applicable between states following a Supreme Court ruling in June 1922. Suddenly, alarm turned to panic; the upriver states insisted that the Bureau of Reclamation postpone its comprehensive plan for the lower Colorado until the river had been apportioned. The government sent a negotiator, Secretary of Commerce Herbert Hoover, who sat through eleven tedious months of debate.

How much water should each state get? River gauging stations seemed to indicate an average annual flow of 16.4 million acre-feet (enough water to cover 16.4 million acres, or three states the size of Utah, with one foot of water). The delegates tried dividing that figure into seven pieces, but no one could agree on percentages. In the end, they opted instead to divide the river into two basins. Lee's Ferry, Arizona, the point between Glen and Grand canyons, became the demarcation point. The Upper Basin thus consisted of Utah, Colorado, Wyoming, and New Mexico, while the Lower Basin consisted of Arizona, Nevada, and California. By the terms of the agreement, the Upper Basin got to keep 7.5 million acre-feet of water as long as it first supplied the Lower Basin with the same amount (based on a ten-year average). That still left an apparent surplus of 1.4 million acre-feet, a contingency for Mexican claims. (The water rights of sovereign Indian tribes, meanwhile, were simply ignored.)[9]

All of the states but one signed the Colorado River Compact in 1922. Arizona objected because the agreement did nothing to protect its water from California; it merely protected the Upper Basin. In 1928, Congress got around Arizona by ratifying the Compact as a six-state agreement, which cleared the way for Boulder (Hoover) Dam. Construction began in 1931. By the time President Roosevelt gave the dedicatory speech on 30 September 1935, the 726-foot structure, by far the largest dam in the world, had become a symbol of the New Deal and a source of national pride—"the Great Pyramid of the American Desert, the Ninth Symphony of our day." It also represented the Bureau of Reclamation's transformation into a powerful agency of elite engineers, planners, and bureaucrats. The agency had all but abandoned its original goal of providing assistance to small farmers. The overarching goal of conquering the desert remained, but from now on the Bureau would rely on its allies in business and politics—and its ever-growing congressional appropriation. Between 1940 and 1950, the agency's budget ballooned from $79 million to $373 million.[10]

Immediately after Hoover Dam, the Bureau built Parker Dam and the Colorado River Aqueduct (for Los Angeles), and Imperial Dam and the All-American Canal (for the Imperial Valley). Flushed by the success of its comprehensive Lower Basin project, the Bureau turned its attention to the other great rivers of the West, including the Columbia, the Missouri, and the upstream Colorado.

By the mid-1940s, the Upper Basin was eager to develop its water. The regional economy had exploded during World War II, primarily thanks to the federal government. In Utah alone, military installations and wartime industries added a staggering fifty thousand jobs and a hundred thousand residents. State leaders hoped to feed and sustain the boom during the post-war period, but they worried about adequate supplies of water, power, and agricultural produce. They didn't yet need the water, but they *wanted* to need it. They wanted one of the Bureau of Reclamation's packages of dams, power plants, and aqueducts. Above all, they wanted the Intermountain West to be rich, powerful, metropolitan: a player in national politics.[11]

In preparation for development, Utah, Wyoming, Colorado, and New Mexico divvied up their water appropriation in 1948. They did it by percentages because it was unclear how much of their 7.5 million acre-feet they would actually get. In 1944 the U.S. Senate had ratified a treaty granting Mexico 1.5 million acre-feet of the Colorado River per year. This more than exceeded the "surplus" of the compact, but as subsequent stream gauging showed, there probably never was a surplus. The flow numbers used in 1922 by the state delegates had been recorded during a few exceptionally wet years. The true average discharge seemed to be closer to 16 million acre-feet per year (eventually downsized to the current best estimate, 13.5 million). But rather than fix the compact, the states thought it easiest and best to fix the "deficient" river. Happily, they had the enthusiastic support of the Bureau of Reclamation. In 1947, the Bureau released a massive compendium of data under the blunt title, *The Colorado River: "A Natural Menace Becomes a National Resource."* Today, the Bureau wrote in its foreword, Hoover Dam "only partly harnesses the wild Colorado River."

> Tomorrow the Colorado River will be utilized to the very last drop. Its water will convert thousands of additional acres of sagebrush desert to flourishing farms and beautiful homes for servicemen, industrial workers, and native farmers who seek to build permanently in the West. Its terrifying energy will be harnessed completely to do an even bigger job in building bulwarks for peace. Here is a job so great in its possibilities that only a nation of free people have the vision to know that it can be done and that it must be done.[12]

In the pages that followed, the Bureau identified 134 potential projects. There wasn't enough river for all of them, unfortunately. Over the next couple of years, the Bureau singled out the cream of the crop and packaged them as the Colorado River Storage Project (CRSP). The plan called for a handful of large storage projects (notably Echo Park Dam on the Green River and Glen Canyon Dam on the Colorado), and eleven "participating projects," which would actually deliver the water to high-country farms, ranches, and municipalities, including Salt Lake City.

The role of the storage dams was crucial. By regulating the flow of the river—holding during floods, releasing during droughts—Echo Park and Glen Canyon would permit the Upper Basin to fully develop its water allocation without fear of missing its required delivery to the Lower Basin. In other words, the Upper Basin had to build big dams so that it could build small dams. This was true politically, and fiscally, too. The hydroelectric revenue from the CRSP's storage dams was programmed to offset the cost of its participating projects, most of which were blatantly uneconomical. The Bureau had developed this form of cost-sharing, called "river-basin accounting," in 1942 and proceeded to run with it. As the historian of the agency wrote, "All benefits and income from producing units were lumped together to establish overall feasibility."[13] The rationale was familiar: dams for the sake of more dams.

But the water would be used—that was the important thing. In the minds of reclamationists, it was better to use and be wasteful than to not use at all. When confronted with its own projection that the mere evaporation from Glen Canyon reservoir would exceed the total volume of water put to beneficial consumptive use by all of the CRSP's participating projects, the Bureau of Reclamation simply answered, "At the present time there is something over 4 million acre-feet of water going down the river into the [Sea of Cortez] which is not being used at all."[14] Here was the true waste; total use was the truest conservation. Without the CRSP, the Bureau claimed, the Upper Basin could develop "only" 58 percent of its apportioned water. This scenario was dishonorable, if not inconceivable, to the political leaders of the region. They would rather rot in hell than yield the remainder to California. However much of their 7.5 million acre-feet existed, they intended to develop it.

All of the representatives and senators of the Intermountain West, Republicans and Democrats alike, supported the CRSP and looked to Oscar Chapman, secretary of the interior, for support. They got it in 1950. "I am convinced that the plan is the most economical of water in a desert river basin and therefore is in the highest public interest," he said. Echo Park Dam was a sore point, but the secretary seems to have been assuaged by Atomic Energy Commission projections of insufficient electrical power in the Intermountain region—power needed for the development and testing of the hydrogen bomb, a key program of the Truman administration.[15]

Chapman's approval marked a preliminary victory of one Interior Department agency, the Bureau of Reclamation, over another, the National Park Service. Park Service director Newton Drury protested the CRSP because two of the Bureau's proposed dams, Echo Park and Split Mountain, fell within the boundaries of Dinosaur National Monument, a 211,000-acre preserve straddling the Utah-Colorado border. It was bad enough that in 1939 surveyors with the Bureau had constructed an unauthorized road into Echo Park, the hollow where the Green and Yampa rivers combine. No one stopped them because no one was stationed at Dinosaur at the time.

The Park Service couldn't afford a ranger and typically didn't need one there. Though the monument included miles of spectacular canyons, it was known (if it was known at all) for its dinosaur quarry, located at the southwestern boundary far from the deepest canyons. An unlikely place for a controversy, Dinosaur was nonetheless poised in the 1940s to take center stage in a national debate on parks. During World War II, several national parks had been opened to mineral and water development, but overall the park system had escaped undisturbed. Now, in the prosperity of peacetime, director Drury hoped for a much-needed budget hike to add personnel and improve recreation facilities. But the immediate postwar years brought little change. Appropriations remained low, and several park units—including Olympic, Glacier, and Mammoth Cave national parks—faced new threats from loggers and especially dam builders. To national park watchdogs, these threats amounted to a test of the national park idea, and they turned scenic Echo Park into the testing ground.

The opening salvo came from Bernard De Voto, salty expatriate from Utah and an influential columnist. Through his seat on the interior secretary's advisory board, De Voto learned about the Echo Park proposal in 1950. Since he knew Newton Drury couldn't publicly criticize the Bureau of Reclamation, he took it upon himself in a vitriolic piece called "Shall We Let Them Ruin Our National Parks?" "Echo Park Dam," he wrote, "would back water so far that throughout the whole extent of Lodore Canyon the Green River, the tempestuous, pulse-stirring river of John Wesley Powell, would become a mere millpond. The same would happen to Yampa Canyon. . . . Dinosaur National Monument as a scenic spectacle would cease to exist."[16]

De Voto's column, and Drury's forced resignation soon after, helped galvanize the forces of the Wilderness Society, the National Parks and Conservation Association, the Izaak Walton League, and many smaller groups such as the Sierra Club (just beginning its transition into a national organization). They applied their collective pressure on Oscar Chapman to scrap the dams in Dinosaur. The secretary had some room to reconsider because the AEC had downscaled its projected energy needs. Additionally, the Army Corps of Engineers, the Bureau's rival for appropriations, began to question the CRSP's cost effectiveness. Perhaps the most damaging information came from Ulysses S. Grant III, a highly respected retired officer of the Corps, who told Chapman that the dams in Dinosaur were not essential to the project, as the Bureau claimed. He believed a different combination of dams could achieve the same benefits. Disenchanted with the Bureau, the secretary revoked his approval of Echo Park and Split Mountain dams in 1952, before the CRSP got earmarked for funding. The entire project idled until 1954, after the Republicans had finally replaced the Democrats in the White House. Surprisingly, however, the fiscally conservative Dwight Eisenhower decided to support the CRSP, Echo Park Dam and all. Conservationists geared up for the fight of their lives.[17]

The controversy crested in 1954–55, when the House and Senate conducted two sets of hearings on the CRSP. It is worth delving into the hearings because they preview the debate played out at Lake Powell. The contested scenario of a beautiful, useful reservoir in Echo Park would be played out in reality with the flooding of Glen Canyon.

ECHO PARK

Reading the hundreds of pages of congressional testimony, one thing becomes clear: conservationists of the 1950s were not yet radicals (or even environmentalists, a term popularized in the 1960s). They shared with dam builders a pivotal assumption: the rapid buildup of the American West after World War II was predestined and more or less wonderful. In the immediate postwar period, national confidence in technology and technological authority peaked. Abundance and consumption, those great American virtues, were seen as mutually supportive. Conservationists didn't question, much less oppose, the reclamation dream. "It is correct to state that development of the Colorado River is essential and inevitable," said the Izaak Walton League, which publicly endorsed "the basic purposes" of the CRSP.[18]

But while conservationists looked forward to a future of limitless growth, they wanted safeguards. They wanted wildlands and open space for the relaxation and rejuvenation of the West's future urban residents. Preservation was the partner of industrialization. In relation to growth, then, Dinosaur National Monument was appraised higher as a potential recreation area than as a storage reservoir. Dam proponents turned this logic around, saying that the proposed reservoirs provided both goods: utilitarian water *and* recreational water. As Douglas R. Stringfellow, Utah's freshman congressman, said, "We have two resources. We have the scenery resource, and we have the water resource. The development of one makes the other one attainable."[19]

In fact, beauty and recreation were never burning issues to dam proponents. Yet they found themselves arguing on those terms because they wanted to dam a national monument—part of America's very popular system of recreational nature preserves. Conservationists hammered away at the park issue because it struck a chord and because that's all they had at first. It seemed foolish to challenge the Bureau of Reclamation on its own technical turf. Instead, they argued precedence: If the Bureau puts up dams in Dinosaur, what would stop it from damming other parks and monuments, even the Grand Canyon? Echo Park Dam would represent a disastrous first step, the wholesale selling out of the national park system. If the Bureau got its way, Congress would be saying, in effect, We'll protect our parks . . . until the right proposal for development comes along.

In a sense, park advocates had fought this battle before—and lost. In the early 1910s, the city of San Francisco went after the water of the Hetch Hetchy Valley in Yosemite National Park. Though exceptionally beautiful, Hetch Hetchy suffered from proximity and resemblance to the main valley. Few people made the effort to visit this "Little Yosemite," with its waterfalls and verdure. And the way San Francisco portrayed it, the pleasure of a few "nature cranks" hardly measured up to the needs of a growing city of half a million. As for natural beauty, the city commissioned a retouched photograph showing waterfalls reflected in a reservoir, a seeming improvement on loveliness. Dam opponents, led by John Muir, founder of the Sierra Club, refuted this, saying that the storage facility would produce mudflats, snags, and stains. It would destroy a living space. But the larger issue, they believed, was the integrity of the national park idea.[20]

Precedence comes in different forms. The preservationists of Muir's era were trying to set a course for the emerging national park system, which still lacked a managing agency. Conservationists of the 1950s, on the other hand, were trying to sustain a course for the National Park Service, formed in 1916, three years after the loss of Hetch Hetchy. In the well-known language of its enabling legislation, the purpose of the Park Service is to "conserve the scenery and the natural and historic objects and the wild life therein and to provide for the enjoyment of the same in such manner and by such means as will leave them unimpaired for the enjoyment of future generations." Perhaps the key word in this daunting dual mission is *unimpaired*. It means different things to different people at different times. Concerning Dinosaur National Monument, conservationists had one idea, the Bureau of Reclamation had another. The Bureau said, in so many words: Parks are for the enjoyment of people, right? So what good is Dinosaur right now? Hardly anyone goes there. The roads are bad; the rivers are treacherous. A placid, beautiful reservoir would not impair anything. It would permit thousands more Americans to enjoy the monument. What's so wrong with that?

In reply, the director of the Wilderness Society, Howard Zahniser, spoke cautiously: "We like playgrounds. We appreciate the recreational values of reservoirs. In favoring the upper Colorado River project we favor something we believe is going to result in a great many reservoirs where that sort of recreation will be available, but in the national park system as in the wilderness areas our purposes are different."[21]

These purposes had to do with nonmotorized peace and natural quiet. Moving by the power of a river, not a machine, was the best way to experience Dinosaur, conservationists believed. But since they too held that national parks—even the so-called primeval parks—were for people, they carried the burden of proof concerning river running. They had to show it was safe and democratic. Starting in 1953, members of various conservation groups, especially the Sierra Club, began arriving in Vernal, Utah, by the busload. Luckily, they had a guide right in town. Much to the chagrin (and occasional hostility) of his neighbors, Bus Hatch opposed the proposed dams and guided scores of like-minded people down the river. In 1953 alone, Hatch and his family business hosted more than five hundred people, including one group with four youngsters, a disabled adult, and a seventy-six-year-old man. "Children in Boats Run Utah Rapids, Californians Refute Claim That Wild Green River Is Dangerous" read a headline in the *Los Angeles Times*. The next year, the claim busters and the merely curious returned in double the force. The Sierra Club's executive director, David Brower, took a trip with his secretary, who had never before been camping. Brower held her up as living proof of Dinosaur National Monument's existing accessibility. The hazards of river running had been grossly exaggerated, he told Congress. "Without proper precautions you can get into trouble, and not just on a river. Even in a bathtub."[22]

Some locals dismissed such statements as misleading and responded with their own misleading statements. The publisher of the *Vernal Express* reported that more than a dozen people had drowned in the Green River over the previous decade—but offered scant specifics about the fatalities. Several "professional boatmen" in town submitted harrowing letters to William Dawson, their congressional representative. "I almost lost my life along with four others on one trip," read one. "I lived in constant fear last summer while the Sierra Club was on their trip." In fact, these stories were fabricated or taken out of context.[23]

Potshots didn't prevent conservationists from making their point: people *could* visit the Dinosaur canyons; they *hadn't*, that's all. "The value is there," said Joseph Penfold of the Izaak Walton League, "even though as yet untapped, in just exactly the same sense as there is a power value in running water, even though it has not yet been harnessed [in] a turbine."[24] Opponents of the dams claimed that the public had convincingly shown its interest in "harnessing" this latent accessibility. In 1954, with the controversy raging, seventy thousand visitors came to the national monument, up from twelve thousand just two years before. Conservationists noted that Yellowstone National Park received less than ten thousand visitors in its first ten years. Given time, they suggested, Dinosaur would achieve equivalent popularity.

So far, the monument had been neglected—here was something both sides could agree on. Until 1953, the minimal staff lacked even the funds to buy a neoprene raft (costing about a hundred dollars) for river patrols. To locals, this was nothing new. "Since the establishment of the original monument in 1915," wrote one, "citizens have listened to glowing predictions of what was going to be done to develop the area to make it one of the most attractive in the entire Park Service system. After 39 years of waiting for something to happen, the monument is still in such an undeveloped condition that it is embarrassing to direct visitors to the headquarters, which is composed of a few lumber shacks."[25]

Realizing they had an issue to exploit, the congressional proponents of Echo Park Dam promised a phenomenal $21 million appropriation for development of the reservoir. Conservationists couldn't wave around money like that, but they counter-pledged that with the elimination of the dam, they would work to develop the monument and turn it into a moneymaker for the region.

Road paving was a natural starting point. "For canyon country it is nothing short of amazing to discover how complimentary the land is for road construction," remarked conservationist Charles Eggert. He went so far as to imagine a hotel in Echo Park at the river's edge. In 1954, David Brower had suggested the possibility of an expanded boat concession by which about nine hundred people could put-in per day—adding up to seventy thousand tourists per season. Brower conceded, however, that "the head count puts the emphasis on quantity, and is likely to overlook the qualitative experience national parks can and should provide." And in private Brower had begun to doubt this whole line of attack: addressing the side effects of the proposed dams rather than the merits of the dams themselves.[26]

But at least conservationists had altered the terms of the debate. By 1955, dam opponents had placed Dinosaur on the map—not some godforsaken canyon but part of the beloved national park system. They forced the Bureau to acknowledge the beauty of Echo Park. Before, the nicest word dam promoters could muster was "picturesque." A typical early brochure pooh-poohed this "rugged No-Man's land" where only trash fish could survive. But in subsequent brochures the wording softened. The choice was now between (1) what was "virtually a no-man's land—incomparably beautiful though it is"; and (2) a "veritable paradise for millions of Americans who love the out-of-doors."[27]

Roy Despain, an avid outdoorsman, was an unlikely supporter of the latter. In his testimony before Congress, he celebrated the splendor of the Green and the Yampa and regretted that his river trips "and my desire to have my posterity have this experience" would die. However, since thousands more people would enjoy the canyons as reservoirs, Despain believed it "would be selfish and narrow-minded" to oppose the dams. "[Despite] this loss I feel that this project would create more beauty than it would destroy."[28]

Similarly, the Bureau of Reclamation argued that the standing water behind Echo Park Dam would reflect, not diminish, the grandeur of the place. The cliffs would still soar. The Green and the Yampa already "inundated" 3 percent of Dinosaur National Monument; as reservoirs, they would cover only 7 percent more. Yes, but you're missing the point, said conservationists. "The pinyon pines, the Douglas firs, the maples and cottonwoods, the grasses and other flora that line the banks, the green living things that shine in the sun against the rich colors of the cliffs—these would all go. The river, its surge and its sound, the living sculptor of this place, would be silent forever, and all the fascination of its movement and the fun of riding it, quietly gliding through these cathedral corridors of stone. All done in for good."[29] In other words, the singular wonder of Dinosaur would become another pretty lake.

Conservationists summarized their arguments against Echo Park Dam in a 1955 book called *This Is Dinosaur: Echo Park Country and Its Magic Rivers*. Though the book came from the press of Alfred A. Knopf, a prominent conservationist, David Brower of the Sierra Club acted as the ghost publisher. He devised the idea, appointed the editor (his friend, Wallace Stegner), and helped secure the contributors. The book featured chapters on the various resources of Dinosaur—its history, scenery, ecology, geology—framed by essays about the purpose of national parks. A surprising, resounding success, *This Is Dinosaur* led to a new type of environmental publication: coffee-table propaganda. In 1960, Brower launched the influential Exhibit Format Series with Ansel Adams' *This Is the American Earth*, soon to be followed by Eliot Porter's *In Wildness Is the Preservation of the World*, which became something of a missionary tract for the Sixties generation of wilderness activists.

In many important ways, the Echo Park campaign anticipated public relations tools used by future environmentalists—picture books, brochures, filmstrips, direct-mail pieces, and so on. David Brower, perhaps the most innovative and influential American environmentalist of the late twentieth century, also demonstrated the value of well-prepared and well-spoken congressional testimony. In 1954, behind the microphone, he humiliated the Bureau of Reclamation by examining its data with his "ninth-grade arithmetic." Previous criticisms about national parks, natural beauty, and outdoor recreation had put the Bureau on the defensive, but it hadn't yet yielded its position: Echo Park Dam was the "keystone" of the entire CRSP. That key assumption started to crumble when Brower revealed a simple math error by the Bureau. The agency claimed that every alternative dam or combination of alternatives would result in much greater evaporation losses. However, in calculating the projected evaporation for a "high" Glen Canyon Dam, the Bureau forgot to subtract a significant figure. When corrected, the numbers showed that Echo Park's evaporation advantage over the "high" Glen was slight, and thus the tables turned. As historian Mark Harvey says, "Instead of merely publicizing the beauties of Echo Park, [conservationists] could now boast they had met Bureau engineers on their own ground and won a mathematical argument."[30]

True, but by offering an alternative to Echo Park Dam, conservationists were still playing the game. Rather than simply eliminating one large reservoir from the CRSP, they felt obliged to make up for the loss. Stupidly, the Bureau refused the gift. During the second round of hearings in 1955, the defenders of the CRSP came up with other reasons—national defense, for example, or hydropower production—why Echo Park Dam was "indispensable." (The Bureau wasn't willing to admit the primary *political* justification for the dam.) Each time, the newly confident opposition challenged the defense. Changing tactics, the Bureau and its backers argued against the merits of the proposed alternative, the "high" Glen Canyon Dam. Its reservoir would flood Rainbow Bridge National Monument, they said. Conservationists replied that the same situation existed with the planned "low" dam, and the Bureau had already planned on a dike to keep the water from the 160-acre monument. Next the Bureau claimed the sandstone walls might not support a "high" dam. Conservationists asked for hard evidence and got only soft answers. They felt the Bureau was merely being obstinate. The "high" dam was the perfect solution. The West would get the water and power it needed, and America would keep Dinosaur and the national park system intact.

Throughout this debate, Glen Canyon remained an abstraction. No one said anything about its beauty or its recreational values, for the simple reason that it didn't matter. Glen Canyon was lost—that was a given. And who cared, anyway? It wasn't designated. It wasn't a national park or a national monument.

Who cared? Well, among others there was a small group of friends who called themselves the Utah Committee for a Glen Canyon National Park. Though they didn't get a chance to testify in 1954, they submitted a written statement to Congress. Buried in the back of the published proceedings, it accused the "so-called conservationist groups" of misfocusing on Echo Park while "turning their backs on the far more important damage" planned for Glen Canyon. At times, the committee's platform resembled a personal testimony: "Only those who have experienced the majesty of the lonely river, dwarfed by its brilliant surroundings, can fully understand the fanatical devotion of those who have seen the green glens, the incitingly cool, fern-draped pools in the side canyons, and the supreme spectacle of the incredible stone rainbow." While stopping short of questioning the benefits of reclamation, the committee recommended an overhaul of the 1922 Colorado River Compact before any dams were built, especially when Glen Canyon and Rainbow Bridge were at stake. "Let us not allow a costly, destructive, unnecessary dam to destroy their eternal magnificence," the committee concluded.[31]

It's hard to gauge the statement's impact on the "so-called conservationist groups." In late 1955, the magazine of the National Parks and Conservation Association published an appreciation of Glen Canyon by William Thompson, a member who had taken a river trip. "Glen Canyon dam itself might well be dedicated a vast tombstone, marking beneath its mud and water a graveyard of some of the most sublime scenery on the face of the earth," he wrote. "Scarcely more beauty would be destroyed were Zion or Yosemite dammed." But Thompson's do-or-die urgency wasn't shared by Fred Packard, the executive director of the association. In the very same issue, Packard reported on his recent tour of western states, which included a river trip through Glen Canyon. Though impressed by the beauty of the place, he couldn't oppose the dam. To him, Glen Canyon Dam was a done deal.[32]

David Brower had never seen Glen Canyon, but he had heard from Wallace Stegner and others that Dinosaur didn't hold a candle to it. By mid-1955, he had developed deep reservations about the dam—but not yet because of its threat to beauty. Brower was preoccupied with data. The more he studied the plans for the CRSP, the more he suspected that the entire project, like the 1922 compact, was flawed: the Bureau wanted more dams than it needed to regulate the river. Brower wanted to go after Glen Canyon Dam and the CRSP on technical grounds, but he was going out alone. His colleagues urged realistic goals: with the Bureau backpedaling, they should focus on the defeat of Split Mountain and Echo Park dams.

Reluctantly, Brower agreed. In October 1955, the Council of Conservationists offered a deal: they would *support* the CRSP if the Bureau dropped its plans for Dinosaur and agreed to protect Rainbow Bridge. The Bureau accepted, and western congressmen put the CRSP on the fast track (hoping to elude fiscal conservatives who had begun to criticize the CRSP as a massive pork-barrel project). At the last possible moment, David Brower changed his mind and pleaded with the Sierra Club board to oppose the entire CRSP package. They weren't moved.

In early 1956, Congress passed the CRSP legislation, which included two key provisions: no dam or reservoir should be built in any park or monument; and Rainbow Bridge National Monument should be kept from "impairment." Most conservationists hailed the bill as a momentous victory, which in fact it was. Their unlikely coalition saved Dinosaur, reinforced the national park idea, and strengthened their own movement. After standing for decades on the margins of American politics, conservationists could finally claim a significant national victory.

Only with time, as the glory of the doomed canyon became widely known, did conservationists come to rue their victory. They wondered, Could we have defeated this dam, too? Probably not, but who knows? What if we had tried? Second-guessing became more intense when it became clear by the early 1960s that Congress and the Bureau had no intention of honoring their promise to keep Lake Powell out of Rainbow Bridge National Monument. The simplest solution, limiting the height of the reservoir, was never seriously considered. Option two, building a barrier dam below the natural bridge, won approval from the interior secretary in 1960 under pressure from conservationists, but Congress repeatedly and specifically denied appropriations. The Tenth Circuit Court of Appeals would later rule that Congress had effectively negated the provisional language of the CRSP by refusing to act on it.[33]

A depressed David Brower tried to shoulder the blame for all of this; friends feared he might kill himself. Eventually, though, he turned his grief into productive energy and spearheaded a new title for the Exhibit Format Series. Published in 1963, *The Place No One Knew: Glen Canyon on the Colorado River* went on to become the most renowned and influential book ever published on the canyon.

Considering the importance of *The Place No One Knew*, it's worth noting what it's *not*. It's not a denouncement of the CRSP or dam building in general. Not a word or a picture goes to the fabulous canyons of the Gunnison River flooded by the CRSP; nothing remembers Flaming Gorge, Horseshoe, Kingfisher, and Red canyons of the Green River. In 1871, Frederick Dellenbaugh, chronicler of the second Powell expedition, called this "grand series" of canyons "the acme of the romantic and picturesque." Yet Flaming Gorge Dam, which flooded them all, which rose according to the exact same timetable as Glen Canyon Dam, provoked zero regret, zero discord. As Roy Webb observes, this "other 'place no one knew'" has been forgotten. In the Sierra Club files of David Brower, there are boxes and boxes about Echo Park and Glen Canyon, and one lonely folder about Flaming Gorge. It contains a single item: a Bureau of Reclamation "fact sheet."[34]

Though the hulking concrete block at Glen Canyon may have been the obvious Antichrist for western conservationists after the 1960s, it overshadowed the greater cumulative losses caused by small dams, of which hundreds were built in the postwar era. In the late 1950s, John Graves composed a book about a farewell trip down the lovely, historic Brazos River in central Texas. "When someone official dreams up a dam, it generally goes in," the canoeist sadly wrote. "Dams are ipso facto good all by themselves, like mothers and flags. Maybe you save a Dinosaur Monument from time to time, but in-between such salvations you lose ten Brazoses." Ten more places "no one knew."[35]

To be fair, even after the Echo Park debate, conservationists didn't really have the clout—or the conviction—to stage a radical reassessment of dams. *The Place No One Knew* was a step, however, and a generous one. To finance this oversized color publication, Brower ignored the rules of business (a habit that would contribute to his dismissal from the Sierra Club in 1969). First he solicited prominent Club members for sixty thousand dollars in interest-free loans. Next he bumped the publication date up to April 1963, waiving the lucrative holiday shopping season. Last he sent free copies of the twenty-five-dollar book to every member of Congress, every member of the California legislature, and every major newspaper in the land. Profit was immaterial to Brower. He honestly believed that if the right people saw Eliot Porter's magnificent photos of magnificent Glen Canyon, there still might be a chance to stop the reservoir even though the dam was basically complete. Beyond that, he wrote, "the purpose of the Glen Canyon book is to forestall . . . any further scenic-resource disasters resembling the one imminent with the closing of the gates at Glen Canyon dam."[36]

He had a disaster downstream in mind.

RIVAL CROWN JEWELS

On 21 January 1963, the high-pressure gates in the right diversion tunnel of Glen Canyon Dam squeezed shut, marking the effective birth date of Lake Powell, because the river had to rise thirty-four feet to reach the temporary tunnel on the left. That same winter day, Interior Secretary Stewart Udall and Bureau of Reclamation Commissioner Floyd Dominy called a press conference in Washington, D.C. It wasn't, however, to talk about the good news from Glen Canyon—no, the government had more canyons to flood. From the podium, Udall and Dominy unveiled the Pacific Southwest Water Plan, an ambitious, audacious project meant to pacify California and Arizona, who believed there wasn't enough water in the Colorado River for their mutual needs. Under the proposed solution, water from the Sierra Nevada would be stored behind new dams in northern California, then arrive in southern California via new canals. Meanwhile, the Colorado River water Los Angeles would otherwise be using would go to Phoenix and Tucson via more new canals (the Central Arizona Project). Of course, all of this movement of water would require power, and much of that power would come from two "cash register" dams on the Colorado River in the upper and lower Grand Canyon.

Udall had qualms about those last two dams, but he also had unbreakable loyalties to his administration and his home state, Arizona. The presenter by his side had no qualms at all.

Floyd Dominy looms larger than life in the history of water development in the twentieth-century American West. No federal official has been hated as much by environmentalists, with the possible exception of Ronald Reagan's interior secretary, James Watt (the man who was "bored" by the Grand Canyon). But unlike Watt, who embarrassed himself out of office in less than a term, Dominy served under three different presidents, Eisenhower, Kennedy, and Johnson. The commissioner is remembered as one of the most able and ruthless bureaucrats ever to serve in Washington. He presided over the Bureau during its glory years, when, as a semiautonomous agency with a vast appropriation, it reengineered the rivers of the West.[37]

To survive as long as he did, Floyd Dominy had to adjust, at least superficially, to changing administrations and changing public opinion. A good example comes from LBJ's presidency, when the commissioner gave a speech, "Open Spaces for All Americans," before the Outdoor Recreation Congress for the Greater Pacific Northwest. "One of the most important aspects of the Great Society is the preservation of open spaces and to make them readily accessible to our citizens," Dominy began. He expressed alarm that children could now grow up in the city without learning anything about the country. In the East, he warned, time was running out to preserve open space. In the West, however, there was time and room enough to set aside vast new recreational areas. And the Bureau of Reclamation was ready at last to join the cause. For many years, admitted Dominy, "the idea of anyone's traveling to the usually inaccessible dam site in pursuit of pleasure simply did not register."[38]

The veracity of that last statement can be checked against the Bureau's original documentation for the CRSP. *A Natural Menace Becomes a National Resource* included a handful of paragraphs on recreation, and this single, rather lackluster projection: "The many recreational advantages of the upper basin will be more fully enjoyed as they become more accessible through improved transportation." A chart estimating the recreational costs and benefits of various proposed reservoirs was noteworthy for its extremely low dollar figures. For example, the Bureau suggested that $228,800 would cover the construction costs of recreational facilities at the Glen Canyon reservoir, offset by an expected $111,757 in annual returns. (The estimated cost of the dam, meanwhile, was $64 million.) As of 1946, recreation didn't count as a "national resource." Up until the Dinosaur debate, the Bureau merely referred to it as a "bonus." The technocrats would learn better. By 1965 the Interior Department was calling for the expenditure of $16.7 million on the development or improvement of nine marinas at Lake Powell.[39]

"Thus what was an incidental by-product of Reclamation ripened, after a singularly inauspicious start, into a major benefit of the program," continued Dominy in his speech. He lauded the "sparkling new industry" of tourism for "bestowing untold benefits of happiness, health, and relaxation from the rapid pace of today's world." To illustrate the Bureau's commitment to public recreation, the commissioner highlighted recently completed Glen Canyon Dam. Its benefits were manifold, he declared.

> [Glen Canyon Dam] is food for growing America, drinking water for dwellers in an arid country, electric energy to provide the comforts of life and to turn the wheels of industry. It is jobs and paychecks—in the West and across the nation—and it is also taxes for the United States Treasury.
>
> *Most significant of all,* however, it is health and fun and the contentment of contemplating Nature's beauty for thousands who might never experience these thrills of the outdoors if engineers had not inserted between the steep walls of Glen Canyon a mammoth concrete slab to control and clear the erratic river that used to be known as the "Big Red."[40]

Dominy wanted to confront dam opponents on their own turf: beautiful scenery. The commissioner criticized those "professed conservationists" who "want to lock away our scenic wonders and keep people out." He flatly denied that Glen Canyon had been destroyed. "Quite the contrary— the area has been enhanced for public use and enjoyment." Dominy then showed some pictures of scenic Lake Powell. From there, he went on to discuss the reservoirs proposed for the Grand Canyon, "which I expect will rival the beauty of Lake Powell." For those with concerns, Dominy offered these palliatives: None of the inundated areas would be visible from the main rim of Grand Canyon National Park; even at their deepest, the reservoirs would flood but a small vertical distance of the canyon's great depth; and best of all, the water would provide easy access to one of the most beautiful places on earth.

"Open Space for All Americans" marked the beginning of a new public relations campaign by the Bureau of Reclamation-cum-Recreation. The makeover continued the same month, April 1965, when the Government Printing Office released a promotional booklet, *Lake Powell: Jewel of the Colorado*. In it, Dominy offered a concise technical justification for future dams in the Grand Canyon, and a personal testimony of the beauty of Lake Powell. The bulk of the thirty-page tract, however, was devoted to striking color photographs of the reservoir, accompanied by engineered poems:

I sing a song for common man
Desk-numbed and city trapped;
Now free—now hearing clearly
Great chords of healing solitude.

And most striking of all:

To have a deep blue lake
Where no lake was before
Seems to bring man
A little closer to God.

The timing of the publication could not have been more deliberate. The issue of dams in the Grand Canyon was slated for congressional hearings later in the year, and the Bureau's lead opponent, the Sierra Club, had just published a new Exhibit Format book, *Time and the River Flowing: Grand Canyon*. It bore an uncompromising message: no more dams on the Colorado. Under David Brower's leadership, the Club had radicalized—a result, in part, of the loss of Glen Canyon. The epilogue to *Time and the River Flowing* contained a section on the Glen called "Remember These Things Lost." It suggested that the Bureau wanted to do to the Grand what it did to the Glen: obliterate incomparable beauty for kilowatts that could be produced elsewhere. To further highlight the comparison, the Club produced a motion picture on each canyon to be shown on consecutive reels.

Bureau of Reclamation memoranda reveal that *Jewel of the Colorado* was explicitly meant "to combat the corrosive influence" of *Time and the River Flowing* and *The Place No One Knew*. In other words, to counter the claim that its proposed dams were nonessential, the Bureau printed pretty pictures of Lake Powell. This had its own logic: if the public could be counted on to believe the government engineers when they said that dams in the Grand Canyon were necessary, the issue could be simplified into a contest over beauty and recreation—a river versus a reservoir. Thus, for the purpose of public relations, the true purpose of the Glen Canyon reservoir didn't matter. It only mattered that the public got the message (as stated in the official justification for *Jewel of the Colorado*) that "scenic values still remain and in many instances are enhanced by a sparkling blue lake replacing the muddy waters of the undisturbed Colorado." During the Echo Park debate, the only comparable reservoir was Lake Mead, a reservoir surrounded by low, cactus-covered mountains that many people found unattractive. But now, during the Grand Canyon debate, the Bureau could show off Lake Powell, a reservoir surrounded by great billows of orange and red sandstone. It was superbly photogenic.[41]

In 1965, the Government Printing Office ran off sixty-three thousand copies of *Jewel of the Colorado*. Prominent backers of the Pacific Southwest Water Plan, including the Metropolitan Water District of California and the Central Arizona Project, purchased twenty thousand copies. An additional three thousand went to the Bureau's regional offices and visitor centers for public distribution. Floyd Dominy mailed at least seventy-seven gift copies to foreign dignitaries—all of them leaders of agencies responsible for irrigation, hydropower, or water development. Thus bureaucrats in Sudan, Afghanistan, Lebanon, Turkey, and Australia could see for themselves the advantages of a lake in the desert. For the United States, the commissioner's mailing list came to nearly a thousand. For the most important people, those congressmen and senators involved in the pending legislation, Dominy supplied an autographed copy. In the fifty or so thank-you notes that came back, *Jewel of the Colorado* was variously described as "perfectly beautiful," "superb," and "informative."[42]

One congressman, however, threw a fit. John Saylor, a Republican from Pennsylvania, had become a staunch critic of Reclamation during the Echo Park hearings. Now, ten years later, he blasted the glossy booklet as "one of the most pernicious and blatantly illegal lobbying campaigns" he'd ever seen.[43] Since it was, in fact, illegal to use appropriated funds for lobbying, the General Accounting Office and the Justice Department launched preliminary investigations. In defense, the Bureau claimed that its booklet fell under its congressional mandate to provide public information.

Appraising the Bureau's case, the Interior Department's solicitor found no evidence of propagandizing or lobbying—and even if there was, he said, it wouldn't matter because such activities were allowed if requested by a member of Congress. And indeed, Frank Moss, junior senator from Utah, and chairman of the irrigation subcommittee, had written a letter to Dominy in December 1964. "It is alleged that natural beauties are being destroyed," said Moss. "I would like your viewpoint." In February 1965, Dominy responded with a personal statement illustrated by his own photographs of Lake Powell. Impressed, the senator suggested that Dominy publish it as a brochure. What the federal solicitor apparently didn't know was this: the commissioner had made the publication decision much earlier, even before the senator wrote his first letter. Moss may have been aware of the situation. Upon receiving his autographed copy of *Jewel of the Colorado*, he wrote, "I'm happy that I could enter into this little conspiracy to get these things printed out."[44] Legal or ethical or neither, it was a low-budget conspiracy, using only 16,511 tax dollars for printing. Saylor's allegations came to naught.

Maybe it didn't have the weight of *The Place No One Knew*, but Floyd Dominy was very proud of his seventy-five-cent booklet. Some of the photographs came from his own camera; some of the text came from his own pen (the rest from ghost writers). The commissioner took copies to all of his public appearances for maximum visibility. He even approached the Book-of-the-Month Club (which had featured *Time and the River Flowing*) for a review. The club president, Axel G. Rosin, turned him down for business reasons but threw in a critical personal note: "Being an old outdoor man . . . I wince when I see the photograph of, for instance, the outboard motor pulling three beauties on water skis. I can just imagine this scenic beauty of the canyon completely spoiled by the din of the roaring motor and the squealing of hundreds of people when they fall into the water."[45]

Rosin wasn't the sole critic. Alfred G. Etter of Defenders of Wildlife wrote a damning review that criticized the commissioner for using pictures and poetry to sell the religion of reclamation. He questioned man's "Dominyon" when it required the destruction of places like Glen and Grand canyons. "A bible isn't written overnight. The ring is hollow. It is man worshipping man, and, in particular, one man worshipping himself."[46]

When Dominy got hold of Etter's piece, he penned a sarcastic—and dead serious—reply.

I was delighted with your paean of praise for Lake Powell—reservoir and booklet.

It will have a treasured place in my scrapbook of memories for those future days when after the necessary additional dams are built on the Colorado, I can find time to paddle my little canoe up Driftwood Canyon, or Dungeon Canyon, or Forbidding Canyon, or a hundred others. Then I can simply drift gently in the gloom of overhanging cliffs, in splendid solitude and wonder whether it was all worthwhile.

Was it worthwhile, I will ask myself, for Columbus to discover America, or for Lewis and Clark to have paddled up the Missouri?[47]

Dominy could sound so cocksure because he believed he was in the majority. He was with those people who preferred the familiar to the unknown. The same people preferred comfort over simplicity; driving over walking; lakes over rivers; blue over brown. What he forgot, however, is that the majority will sometimes suspend their preferences in favor of their ideals, such as national parks. If the Bureau had wanted to dam another non-familiar, non-designated beauty spot like the Glen, it surely could have done so. But when it proposed to flood the *Grand Canyon* in Grand Canyon *National Park*, it targeted not just a geographic and a political space but two mythic spaces. In American consciousness, the idea of the Grand Canyon was as big as the place. Dam opponents only had to tap into it.

And it was David Brower who did it, employing yet another innovative public relations tactic. In 1966, he authorized a full-page ad on the inside front pages of the *New York Times*, the *Washington Post*, and the *Los Angeles Times* saying, "Now only you can save the Grand Canyon from being flooded . . . for profit." This caught a lot of attention, including that of the Internal Revenue Service, which revoked the Sierra Club's tax-exempt status for engaging in "substantial" efforts to influence legislation. This hasty action by America's most despised federal agency pushed the dam debate from the inside page to the front page. Sierra Club membership skyrocketed. Taking advantage of the moment, Brower helped develop another full-page ad, which asked, "Should we also flood the Sistine Chapel so tourists can get nearer the ceiling?" In the months to follow, the public flooded Congress with hundreds of thousands of letters saying no. Most letter writers didn't know or care about the Pacific Southwest Water Plan. It didn't matter; this was the Grand Canyon. And this was the 1960s, the decade when environmentalism began to seep into American society. Bowing to public opinion, Congress passed a law in 1968 forbidding dams between Lake Powell and Lake Mead.[48]

(Under the revised water plan, electricity for the Central Arizona Project came from coal-fired power plants, one of which was built on the southern shore of Lake Powell, using strip-mined coal from Black Mesa on the Navajo and Hopi reservations. Ironically, the Navajo Generating Station has since been implicated in producing Grand Canyon smog. Nor did the big canyon in fact escape the impacts of dams. In the 1970s and 1980s, it became clear that Glen Canyon Dam had severely altered the downstream ecosystem. Before 1963, the Colorado River in Grand Canyon was warm and silty, with extreme variations in flow depending on the year and season. After 1963, the river was cold and clear, with no seasonal fluctuations but extreme daily fluctuations corresponding to peak electrical demands. Native fish in particular have struggled under this new regime; most are now extinct, endangered, or waiting to be listed. The absence of scouring floods has led to a dramatic increase in riparian wildlife and vegetation, but this controlled environment also favors the tamarisk, a noxious introduced plant. Perhaps most worrisome, the Grand Canyon's beaches and sandbars have not been replenished by incoming sediment. Most have reduced in size; some have disappeared.)

At Grand Canyon, Brower's yes-or-no question was answered, but it refused to go away at Lake Powell. With tourists now in reach of the finger of God, was it worth it? For affirmation, Floyd Dominy could look to his folder of clippings on Lake Powell. In 1965, England's Princess Margaret pronounced the scenery "fabulous and unbelievably beautiful." Likewise, practically every travel article about the new reservoir overflowed with praise. "When man trifles with nature," wrote one visitor in 1968, "the result in esthetic terms is only rarely an improvement. One great exception is Lake Powell." He suggested national park status for the place. Even those who became aware of the environmental controversy had a hard time resisting the spectacle of red rock and blue water. Royce and Dora Knight, who operated a charter plane service out of Page, Arizona, told an anecdote from the 1960s: "One time we went up to Hite to pick up the head of the Sierra Club, Dave Brower. Brower told his son, 'You will not look out of that window at the lake; you will only look inside the plane.' But the kid was on a different plane so he looked out the window all the way and when he landed, he came into the airport building and bought a book on the lake." "I came to bury, not to praise," said a contemporary reporter, quoting Shakespeare. "But looking across the broad expanse of Lake Powell, I realized I had judged in haste." Even the *National Geographic* had little negative to say about the reservoir. It concluded its cover story with the words of river runner Buzz Belknap: "Maybe the dam shouldn't have been built, but it's mighty hard to mourn Glen Canyon now that I've seen Lake Powell." Another observer summed up the feelings of many when he wrote, in verse, "A river disappears / a lake rises / some beauty is lost / a much wider world of beauty is found / a new world of recreation is ours."[49]

As a caveat, it should be said that many who came to Lake Powell to pass judgment had never seen Glen Canyon except in photographs. Comments like "some beauty is lost" reflect their mental projections based on the reservoir. And frankly, Lake Powell was so beautiful it was hard to imagine something *more* beautiful underwater. Those who knew the canyon, however, believed. Gaylord Staveley, a river runner, operated the concession at Hite, Lake Powell's northernmost marina, in the mid-1960s. "It isn't necessary to be making money from Lake Powell, or have hopes of doing so, to pronounce it beautiful," he commented. "It's more difficult to be avid about it, though, if one has known both the lake and the incomparable canyon it covers. Then I think one is entitled to claim a more objective evaluation."[50]

In 1965, river rat Sylvia Tone wrote a sad letter: "Last spring I made the mistake of taking the boat trip on Lake Powell. I was more than depressed, and told my friends Lake Powell was a dead world. Deadness is the only word that describes it. Not a flower or a leaf or a tree or little lizard, and being old emotional and sick at heart, I cried." Boatman Ken Sleight was equally blunt: "As I have witnessed the inundation process in Glen Canyon from the beginning, I can attest and swear that we have been robbed of much beauty, much enchantment. Inundation means destruction. It has been taken away so that we can no longer see it. This is not creation."[51]

But whatever it was—creation or destruction—it was ongoing. Most of the scenes depicted in *Jewel of the Colorado* lay two to four hundred feet below the future high-water mark. In time, the reservoir would look less like a swollen river and more like a sandstone fjord. The lower tributaries would fill to the brim. "The few canyons that will remain are the upstream ones that were not even run-of-the-mill-Glen-Canyon spectacular," said Phil Pennington of the Sierra Club.[52]

He, like nearly everyone else who knew the Glen, considered Clear Creek, a tributary of the lower Escalante River, to be the zenith of spectacular. Two miles from its mouth, the canyon came to its jaw-dropping conclusion by narrowing at the top while widening at the bottom. "The great walls arched toward one another, forming high and almost symmetrical overlapping parabolas. They enclosed about an acre of ground, in which had grown willows, grasses, columbine, and maidenhair fern. The center of this scene was a slim waterfall, no more than a foot in diameter, that fell sixty feet into a deep and foaming pool."[53] This space—a room, really—combined qualities of outdoor and indoor space rarely achieved in architecture, human or nonhuman. The room was called Cathedral in the Desert.

David Brower visited the Cathedral several times during the years of dam construction. He expressed his anguish by taking photographs, some of which appeared in the epilogue to *Time and the River Flowing*. "There would never be anything like it again," he wrote. In 1969, he returned (as ex-director of the Sierra Club) to the half-sunken Cathedral. As arranged by John McPhee, ace reporter for *The New Yorker*, Brower's tour guide was none other than the departing commissioner of the Bureau of Reclamation. It went like this: Dominy got to take Brower on the reservoir, then Brower got to take Dominy down the Grand Canyon. All the while, McPhee took down their ongoing and generally good-humored quarrel. In the Cathedral, however, their voices dropped to whispers. Even with the greenery gone, and the waterfall reduced to ten feet, the place inspired reverence. While they were inside, another boat carrying a middle-aged couple and an older man cruised in. Seeing a government insignia, they pulled over to chat. Honored to meet the commissioner, they presented a compliment: "This lake is beautiful." "Thank you," replied Dominy. Afterward, he tried to appease Brower. "I'm a fair man," he said. "Just to show you how fair I am, I'll say this: When we destroyed Glen Canyon, we destroyed something really beautiful. But we brought in something else." Brower filled in the blank: "Water."[54]

This "unusual companionship" next went to another side canyon of the Escalante River to see Gregory Natural Bridge—or what was left of it. Near its mouth, Fiftymile Creek had gnawed through the neck of an incised meander. The resulting hole grew to measure approximately 175 feet wide and seventy-five high. A striped patina of desert varnish graced the massive structure. Cottonwoods formed a trembling border of green. Natural bridges are uncommon, even on the Colorado Plateau, but lovely Gregory, considering the arid setting, was a rarity: the rock canopy spanned a perennial streamflow.

Gregory Natural Bridge. Note human figure for scale. (Photograph by W. L. Rusho.)

Before Lake Powell, few people had seen the bridge; it wasn't "discovered" until 1940. Between 1949 and 1963, its visitor register accumulated only 150 signatures, most of those in the very last year. Stephen Jett, one who made a "requiem pilgrimage," found that "this massive bridge is, incredibly, eclipsed by the magnificence of its setting. Great cliffs enclosing unbelievable constricted and contorted canyon, strange, twisted rock formations, and great caves and alcoves strain one's credulity." No wonder the

Gregory Natural Bridge on the way under, 1965. (Photograph by Mel Davis.)

bridge became a popular lakeside attraction; it was thrilling to glide beneath the canopy of rock. As the water progressively rose, some chose to backfloat, but one fearless correspondent with *Popular Mechanics* went "blasting through" with only six inches to spare. Utah writer F. A. Barnes recalled a quieter moment:

> I quickly yanked the idling motor into neutral, letting the boat's own momentum carry us on across the dark water. I was entranced by the great squinted eye we were apparently entering, by the bright world beyond the dark one which enfolded us. The last trace of sky disappeared above us and we were under the bridge, under thousands of tons of ancient rock held up only by water-soaked abutments. . . . We reached about the midpoint of the wide span— and I felt the hair on top of my head brush the top of Gregory's opening. I wonder if anyone else bade such an intimate, ultimate farewell to this wondrous span?

The date was October 1968, when the surface of Lake Powell stood at

3,545 feet—155 feet below full pool. Within that remaining vertical distance were hundreds of horizontal miles of canyons with arches, waterfalls, and untold wonders. All doomed. The Cathedral in the Desert would join Gregory Natural Bridge; Clear Creek would become just another run-of-the-mill-spectacular canyon. Caves and beaches that invited boaters one year would be gone the next, replaced by some new sight. Each year, the reservoir was transfigured. When it finally reached capacity (3,700 feet) in June 1980, there were cheers and also laments. "Some experienced boaters shake their heads sadly and say it is a completely different lake," reported one newspaper. The bays had gotten wider, the cliffs had gotten lower. The mouth of Coyote Gulch on the Escalante River, a spot revered by hikers, was flooded. After visiting the ultimate Lake Powell, one photographer said, "For me, the most beautiful areas have been destroyed."[55]

But as Dominy told Brower: "You can lament all you want what we covered up. What we got is beautiful, and it's accessible."

PARADISE—FOR A PRICE

Nowadays, everyone agrees: Lake Powell is the most beautiful reservoir in the world—especially in the early and late hours of the day, when the cliffs glow like embers above the placid blue shore. Visitors go through film as fast as gasoline. "Despite what you may think," wrote one observer, "the sights of Powell are enough to make outdoorsmen of television addicts."[56] The sights include ninety-six side canyons, each with a different character, each with the same amazing contrast of clear water and bare rock. Some open up into watery valleys; others constrict to channels no wider than a boat. Within its tangle of channels, the reservoir boasts some seventy-five arches and bridges. The largest, of course, is Rainbow Bridge.

In addition to sightseeing, fishing has proved its popularity through the years. For those fish that can survive Lake Powell (most species native to the river cannot), the rewards are great. The reservoir acts as a sink for the sediment-borne nutrients of the Colorado and San Juan rivers. Bass, especially, have benefitted. The record striped bass weighed in at forty-eight pounds, eleven ounces. Fish populations go in cycles, and the fishing at Lake Powell varies from good to spectacular. In 1997, anglers were reeling in up to 150 fish per day.

The first lake activity that comes to many people's minds is waterskiing.

With its extremely long main channel, Lake Powell can support water-skiers for as long as they can stand (the world distance record was set here). Better yet, the scenery changes at every turn—more unbelievable cliffs and buttes and distant mountains. "The lake may be one of the most inaccessible areas of the planet served up on a platter—but that platter is velvet smooth, mountain spring water with the desert sun cutting the chill," wrote one enthusiast. "This is water skier's paradise."[57]

In the 1990s, adrenaline lovers turned their eyes from water skis to personal watercraft (PWCs)—Jet Skis and the like. Of the 62,000 boats licensed in Utah in 1993, about 10 to 15 percent fit into that category. Incompatible with wilderness as these loud, fast machines may seem, their riders can still echo frontier rhetoric in celebrating the experience: "Lake Powell is one of the most remote, and most dramatic, cruising grounds in the American West. Its wide-open shores and magnificent canyons give you the feeling that you're cruising straight into the heart of the Old West. . . . We all claimed some open space and opened up our machines. I was riding Kawasaki's 900Zxi, a red-hot Jet Ski that tops out at 57 mph." Lake Powell still attracts wilderness lovers and even provides opportunities for exploration. One avid Lake Powell visitor, Dick Hodgson, recently published *An Explorer's Guide to Lake Powell Country* with "over 720 canyons, coves, inlets and other lake features numbered, named and described, many for the first time." Hodgson, who calls Iowa home, treats his vacations like expeditions. He encourages others to choose a section of the reservoir and probe its crannies, taking detailed notes and systematic photographs.[58]

"I have an idea about Lake Powell," writes Rob Schultheis, a contributor to *Outside* magazine, "that you can use it to get back into the wildest kind of unspoiled canyon country—places that have somehow been missed by the tourists." Schultheis admits he used to dream about a giant explosion at Glen Canyon Dam. "But I have become more realistic with age. . . . Call me an unindicted co-conspirator in a plot against Wild America, but I am beginning to explore the lake, to try to understand it, and even to enjoy it." He tells of a kayaker friend who paddled into gorgeous stretches of side canyons too narrow for any boat. With a little effort, hikers can find similar pristine pockets.[59]

For the majority of people, however, Lake Powell means group time. A houseboat, some friends, and several cases of beer go a long way toward making many people's ideal vacation. This is America's premier houseboating lake, so large and varied that no number of trips can exhaust it. Sunshine is virtually guaranteed, but the occasional rainstorm is no discouragement: the joy of houseboating comes from the juxtaposition of the outdoors and the indoors, the rugged and the refined. Vacationists might waterski in the morning, Jet Ski in the afternoon, take a shower, take a nap, make lasagna, then fish in the twilight to the sound of a favorite CD. Lake Powell fills many niches: it can be a place to explore a new world; a place to escape the ordinary world; and a place to celebrate the things of the consumer world—or all three in one trip. As one travel writer wrote of his houseboat trip, "It's a floating party/exploration/picture taking/bridge playing/unwinding three or four days that are as pleasant as any we've spent anywhere, anytime."[60] Many vacationists consider Powell the greatest spot on earth, bar none. Among their names for it, culled from the travel literature: Fisherman's Paradise, Angler's Paradise, Boater's Paradise, Houseboater's Paradise, Waterskier's Paradise, Water Sportsman's Paradise, Vacationer's Paradise, Recreationist's Paradise.

One more from the list, however, puts a damper on the enthusiasm: Rich Man's Paradise. Although the Bureau of Reclamation introduced the new Glen Canyon as "the place everyone will know," in practice, "everyone" has been an exclusive category.[61] Owning a boat and a vehicle capable of towing it (not to mention the time to get away) is generally a privilege of the upper classes. Even renting a boat requires a deep pocket. In the mid-1990s, a no-frills eighteen-foot machine cost $928 per week. The smallest houseboat, a thirty-six-footer with three beds, cost $675 for the minimum stay of three days, $1,241 for a week.

And don't forget the price at the pump. Houseboaters can expect to spend over five hundred dollars per week on their oversized load, which chugs along at about two miles to the gallon. This helps explain the high consumption of gas at Lake Powell—an estimated five million gallons per year. Remarkably, 20 percent of that fuel comes from one source, the Dangling Rope Marina. This self-contained floating facility in Dangling Rope Canyon is the only service station in the busy eighty-mile stretch of water between Wahweap and Bullfrog. The marina used to be located in Forbidding Canyon, near Rainbow Bridge, where it became the largest waterside gas station west of the Mississippi River and the single most profitable Chevron station anywhere. It moved in 1984 because of traffic congestion. During the summer, the marina's thirty-odd employees keep busy repairing boats, pumping gas, and selling the twin "essentials," ice and beer. Said the manager, "We're as good as any 7-Eleven anywhere."[62]

Consumerism is a major part of the lake experience. As one reporter has observed, "More people are coming to Lake Powell not to escape the comforts of modern living, but to enjoy them." Nothing illustrates this better than the houseboat. The standard rental model comes with beds, toilet, hot water, shower, fridge, stove, and barbecue. An upgrade ($1500 more per week) comes with TV, VCR, more toilets, more showers, more everything. The concessionaire owns over three hundred houseboats but not nearly enough: reservations for the summer fill up a year in advance. The lucky folks have the money to buy their own, which they store at the reservoir (in one of 1,200 private slips) or nearby storage facilities. These pleasure craft can cost as much as a second home. According to one sales representative, some of the top-of-the-line boats come with helicopter landing pads, hot tubs, saunas, hardwood dancing floors, designer furniture, "and of course, multiple air conditioners."[63]

For the relationship between boating and class, I need only look around my hometown. In Provo, Utah, like so many cities in the desert West, boating is popular. You'll even find some lower-income families with a boat parked in the driveway. These families won't go to Lake Powell, however. They'll go to Utah Lake, located right next door in the valley. For whatever reason, the lake has a bad reputation. I grew up (in a well-to-do neighborhood) thinking it was little more than a cesspool. Certainly no self-respecting water-skier would go there. Provo's upper-class boaters might go to one of the mountain reservoirs for a weekend fix, but when it comes to their big summer break, it's time for Powell, a six-hour drive away. If you see a top-end boat outside a house with a three-car garage, you *know* where the people inside go to play.

Granted, not everyone who visits Lake Powell is rich. By taking advantage of reduced off-season rental rates, and/or sharing boating costs among large groups, vacationists can save hundreds, even thousands, of dollars. Some middle-class families simply swallow the expense because their annual trip to Lake Powell is the most important week of their year. Meanwhile, stop-and-go automobile tourists can take a half-day tour to Rainbow Bridge for about sixty dollars per head. The fact remains, however, that no one who visits Lake Powell is poor.

Before the dam, a Glen Canyon river trip wasn't always cheap, but it wasn't necessarily expensive. Some people floated down the Colorado in surplus boats and lived on army rations. Nonprofit groups conducted trips on shoestring budgets. "One of the big differences I've noticed [with Lake

Powell] is that the scout groups and young people's groups have quit coming," said river runner Frank Wright in 1966. "I feel badly about this, but then there are a lot of people who come and enjoy the lake."[64] In terms of recreation, accessibility means numerical democracy but not always representative democracy.

But what incredible numbers! Now hosting close to three million annual visitors, Glen Canyon National Recreation Area (GCNRA) typically ranks among the twenty most popular areas administered by the Park Service. And measured in visitor days (the cumulative amount of time spent by recreationists) it ranks near the very top. In 1994, for example, GCNRA boasted 2.18 million visitor days, while Yellowstone National Park had 1.25 million distributed among 5.4 million people. That is, Yellowstone acted as a drive-through, while Lake Powell acted as a destination. A 1985 survey of 299 boating parties showed that their average stay was a remarkable 4.5 days.[65]

Lake Powell wasn't expected to be this popular. Of all the official forecasts, the most optimistic—and surely it seemed ludicrous at the time—came from Floyd Dominy in 1963: "Personally, I believe Glen Canyon will attract two million-plus visitors a year." It took only fifteen years to prove him right.[66]

The transformation was most remarkable at Rainbow Bridge, once the single most inaccessible unit in the national park system. In the 1920s, Zane Grey wrote confidently that "the tourist, the leisurely traveler, the comfort-loving motorist would never behold it. Only by toil, sweat, endurance and pain could any man look at Nonnezoshe."[67] He could not have been more wrong. By the early 1970s, Lake Powell had risen high enough that boaters could park within sight of the span. Soon it became common to see visitors in swimsuits and thongs, holding a camera or a beer, or a dog on a leash. By the early 1990s, the 160-acre national monument received more than two hundred thousand annual visitors, so many that the Park Service contemplated the possibility of restricted use hours and mandatory shuttle boats.

Growth has been a constant struggle for land managers. Compared to most national parks, the per-capita budget of GCNRA is extremely low. As a partial remedy, Lake Powell's concessionaire recently agreed to set aside five cents from every dollar in revenue toward lakeside improvements. The agreement stipulates, however, that these improvements must benefit the concessionaire as well as the Park Service and the visitor. Thus the money helps pay for new facilities but does nothing for law enforcement or education.[68]

From the concessionaire's perspective, of course, more growth means more profit, more success. Lake Powell is big business. In 1988, Del E. Webb, a major real estate and development corporation, announced the sale of its five marinas and concession rights. The buyer was ARA (now ARAMARK), an international leisure corporation with 120,000 employees in fifty states and five foreign countries. At the time, ARA's revenue totaled approximately four billion dollars, of which $77 million went toward its Lake Powell acquisition. Not a bad price for a piece of paradise, or, as ARA called it, "America's Natural Playground"—a registered trademark.[69]

THE PROBLEM OF RAINBOW BRIDGE

The original concessionaire, Canyon Tours, belonged to Art Greene, a chain-smoking, chain-smiling cowboy. Born in 1895, he grew up on a ranch near the San Juan Mountains of southwestern Colorado. In 1917, when America declared war on Germany and Austria-Hungary, Greene joined the army, but not before marrying his sweetheart, Ethyl Johnson. Two years later, wounded in action, he returned from Europe. Back together, Art and Ethyl started a family and struggled to make ends meet. Art bounced from job to job, including ranching, lumber milling, and carpentry. When World War II arrived, and all of his sons and sons-in-law entered the armed services, he vowed that the Greenes would have better fortunes after this war than the last.[70]

From his cousin, Harry Goulding, owner of the famous Goulding's Trading Post in Monument Valley, Art got the idea of going into the tourist business. In 1943, Art and Ethyl became part owners of the Marble Canyon Trading Post and Lodge, located in the House Rock Valley of Arizona, near Lee's Ferry. Their sons and daughters and in-laws eventually joined them, and by 1949, the Greene family had enough money to start their own business, the Cliff Dwellers Lodge, located a few miles closer to the Colorado River. As noted earlier, about this time Art began guiding tourists up the river to Forbidding Canyon (the access to Rainbow Bridge) using a motorboat called *Tseh Na-ni-ah-go Atin'*, Navajo for "trail to the rock that goes over."

The lodge became a busy spot in the 1950s, thanks to uranium prospectors, river runners, and government surveyors. From one survey team, Greene learned that the Bureau of Reclamation intended to build a dam in Glen Canyon, fifteen miles upstream from Lee's Ferry. Soon after, he and his family started speculating on future lakeside property. Art had some extra money from selling a uranium claim, and in 1953 he applied it to a lease on six sections of barren, trackless Arizona state land. Everyone laughed—but not for long. After GCNRA was established in 1958, the National Park Service had little choice but to grant Greene a concession contract. Part of the family stayed on at the lodge; the rest relocated to the new development, which they called Wahweap. Here the Greenes established a lodge, motel, airfield, trailer village, marina, boat repair shop, and boat tour operation. One of the boats in the new fleet went by *Ethyl G.*, in honor of Greene's late wife. She passed away before seeing the sage-covered mesa above the deep canyon of Wahweap Creek become a bay, before seeing the river become a lake.

Art saw it all, and in 1965, in a reflective mood, he recorded his feelings in a letter. He addressed it to Vaud E. Larson, local representative of the Bureau of Reclamation. "Thought maybe you and your boss Mr. Dominy in Washington, might like to hear from an old river rat, who gave you a pretty good but loseing [*sic*] fight over the building of Glen Canyon Dam," he began.

> From a fellow who perhaps knew and loved Glen Canyon better than any man, a fellow who wanted to share the beauties of Glen Canyon and Rainbow Bridge with the world[.] Glen Canyon is without a doubt the beauty spot of the entire length of the Colorado River. . . .
>
> From a fellow who with a tear in his eye, and a hurt in his heart saw Sentinel Rock, Outlaw Cave, the Incen[d]iary Urn, Music Temple and others slowly covered by Lake Powell.
>
> From a fellow who now sees that where one monument was covered, 10 more were brought into view. Where in the 40s, & 50s, 150 people was considered a good year. Where, now in one week that many people share this beauty with us, where folks can bring their own boats now on beautiful Lake Powell (where very few dared as a river). Where they can enjoy boating, water sports[,] outstanding scenery, and excellent fishing. Where they can enjoy this year about 1,000 miles of the most beautiful shoreline in the world. And highlighted by Rainbow Bridge.

I feel sure Lake Powell is destined to be one of the outstanding, recreation areas in the world.

I wish I had time to tell you of all the people made happy by Glen Canyon, and now by Lake Powell[,] of all the beautiful things that they have written and said. I can recall one judge from New York who said Art, God must have worked over time on this job[;] even he couldn['']t create all this beauty in 6 days. . . .

Yes I am glad I lost that battle. But feel I won the war.[71]

The letter was sincere but a bit disingenuous. In fact, as Greene well knew, many people, including Boy Scouts and geriatrics, had "dared" the river before the dam. And Greene never seriously fought the dam; he had a great deal to profit from it. From all accounts, however, his desire to share the beauty of Glen Canyon and Rainbow Bridge came from his heart. He loved the look in people's eyes when they saw for the first time the rock that went over.

Greene, who died in 1978, would have appreciated a magazine article from the following year. The author, C. William Harrison, an older man, took a trip in the next-generation *Ethyl G.*, a forty-nine-passenger boat. Rainbow Bridge "had long ago, how long I could not remember, become one of the great dreams of my life," he wrote, "an inexpressible, unexplainable longing." When the tour boat rounded the final bend and his dream of stone was revealed, Harrison wept: "In that one small enchanted moment of revelation, I had reached out and touched the latchstring of Eternity."[72]

One of the regular boatmen for the *Ethyl G.* was Ray ("Rotten") Watton. He started his professional career as a carpenter and came to Page to work on the dam. After his employment ended, Watton went to work for Canyon Tours repairing boats and later driving them. In the 1960s, he led many overnight camping trips to remote parts of the reservoir, including Gregory Natural Bridge. "I was gone [on trips] most of the time," he remembered in a 1986 interview. "The lake was just forming and as it formed you could go further and further back into the canyons, so it was always interesting. . . . I always had to watch for submerged trees, logs, and stumps that were being covered by the water. We didn't know where we were going either because we were always exploring." In those early days, Watton piloted twenty-foot boats. They held about a half dozen tourists and lacked a roof or a restroom. Later, as tours to Rainbow Bridge became more popular and profitable, Canyon Tours moved up to thirty-one, then forty-seven, and finally fifty-six-foot luxury boats that accommodated eighty-eight passengers. Watton became a full-time Rainbow Bridge chauffeur, cracking the same jokes over the intercom day after day as he logged the same sixty miles from Wahweap to the national monument. Year by year, he saw the business expand; by the late 1980s, about a hundred thousand people per year came to Rainbow Bridge with the concession, now owned by Del Webb. Looking back, Watton expressed his preference for the days before the boom. "Now you find a complete different class of people," he said. "Back then, people didn't mind getting their feet wet; or if it rained they didn't mind getting wet—they enjoyed the whole thing. Now it's all luxury: people want restrooms on the boat, don't want to get feet wet, don't want any bad weather. It's been a tremendous change in people who come here."

"Those days it was fun," he concluded. "Now it's a job."[73]

Watton was describing one of the trade-offs of Lake Powell. When a beautiful remote place is made accessible to motorized travel, more people will be able to come, with less to prevent them from coming for the "wrong" reasons. Those reasons are surely debatable, but this general point is not: people are less likely to examine their motivations when they don't have to. When it takes no effort to reach Rainbow Bridge, visitors are less inclined to ask themselves, What is my reason for going here? Is it a good reason?

There is a second, related trade-off. Though a variety of beautiful experiences are possible at the easy-to-reach Rainbow Bridge, the experience of walking up Forbidding and Bridge canyons from the river is not among them. A world of experience has been lost, and some people believe that world was inherently richer, among them Edward Abbey: "Lake Powell has transformed what was once a delightful adventure into what is now merely a routine motorized sight-seeing excursion. The loss is great, and immeasurable, and cannot be compensated for by any amount of industrialized mass tourism. You cannot creep from quantity to quality. The two are not commensurable. I have also made the visit to Rainbow Bridge by motorboat and can personally testify that it is a meager, shallow and trivial experience when compared to the hike up the canyon." Abbey had spent a summer in the late 1960s as GCNRA ranger, so he probably saw his share of shallow motorboat tourists. On the other hand, the Rainbow Bridge visitor register contains these and other similar notations from the same period:

A dream finally realized

Waited 25 years for this view

Better than anticipated for 50 years

Lifetime dream fulfilled

Such experiences could hardly be called trivial. By the mid-1970s, however, this kind of expression had become rare in the register. As the reservoir grew up, visitors seemed to treat Rainbow Bridge as a lakeside attraction rather than a special destination, a reason for thanksgiving. Lots of boaters simply recorded the number of times they had boated to the national monument. While some always expressed amazement—"Nearer My God to Thee!"—an increasing minority took the opportunity to complain. Their entries were directed at the National Park Service: "You need a drinking fountain [pop machine, ice, etc.]"; "Need trash cans!"; "Need film stand"; "Need steps to climb over it"; "Give tours to the top"; "Get a guide to tell about it"; "Please put benches under the shade of the bridge"; "Put a Tarzan swing in the middle"; "Let kids fish off boat dock"; "Stock more bass"; "Get a bigger store [at Rainbow Marina]!!!"; "Lower the Beer prices"; "I counted the suggestions and 1004 people want a drinking fountain—with me that's 1005"; "Install a beer fountain."[74]

The 1970s also saw a marked increase in scatological, sexual, and otherwise offensive material in the register (including some very unartistic "drawings"). True, back in the 1950s and 1960s, river-running Boy Scouts left their share of crude remarks, but they seem innocent in comparison. The last page of the last register in the Park Service's collection, dated June 1979, pretty well summed up the change. Over an entire page of entries, someone had scrawled, "Fuck you."

Rainbow Bridge was no longer a place to escape to. When reporter Jim Carrier made a July visit in 1987, the courtesy dock was completely full with houseboats, speedboats, and PWCs. Carrier talked to a man parked illegally in the tour boat spot, impatiently waiting for his family to run up and run back. The man was driving a fifty-foot houseboat equipped with seven ice chests, four parasols, and "chaise lounges galore." As for Rainbow Bridge, located three hundred yards up the canyon, the man said, "I don't need to see it." Carrier may have felt the same after walking up the trail. "It could have been one of the golden arches for all the hubbub," he wrote. "A family was jumping into the water below [the bridge], swimming and shrieking at each leap." One year later, on a hot August day, another reporter watched as a crowd beneath the bridge bellowed dares at cliff divers: "Higher, higher!" Eventually, a park ranger showed up and reminded people

The easy, waterborne access to Rainbow Bridge, 1983. (Photograph by Tom Fridmann.)

that diving and swimming were not only prohibited but offensive to local Navajos, for whom the bridge was sacred.[75]

Back in 1974, tribal members tried to keep such a scene from ever happening. In the district court of Utah, eight Navajos from the Navajo Mountain region and three tribal chapters (similar to provinces) sued the commissioner of the Bureau of Reclamation and the secretary of the interior. For relief, the plaintiffs sought to limit the elevation of Lake Powell to prevent the flooding of sacred sites and Holy People—inseparable in Navajo cosmology—in the vicinity of Rainbow Bridge. At the very least, they wanted the government to establish restrictions on visitation.

The court ruled against the plaintiffs, primarily on the grounds that they had no property interest at Rainbow Bridge National Monument. Though surrounded by tribal land, the bridge itself belonged to the federal government. And even if Navajos could claim the property, wrote Judge Aldon J. Anderson, the "interests of the defendants would clearly outweigh the interests of plaintiffs." Translation: the concerns of a relatively few Indians didn't measure up to the might of the metropolitan American West, which banked on the full operation of the Colorado River plumbing system.[76]

But the Navajos refused to roll over; they took their case to the Tenth Circuit Court of Appeals. In its 1980 decision, the panel of judges rejected Anderson's interpretation that property interest was the determining factor, but still upheld his decision. The court deferred to a golden rule of constitutional law: action that infringes on a religious practice violates the First Amendment unless the government establishes a competing interest of "sufficient magnitude." With the CRSP, said the Tenth Circuit, the government had met its requirement; Glen Canyon Dam had sufficient magnitude. Additionally, the judges wrote, "we do not believe plaintiffs have a constitutional right to have tourists visiting the Bridge act 'in a respectful and appreciative manner.'" Otherwise, Rainbow Bridge would become a "government-managed religious shrine."[77]

The upshot was that the Navajos got nothing. Anger and sadness grew as the reservoir submerged sacred sites and tourists acted up. "They walk on and trample our holy places," complained Floyd Laughter of the Navajo Mountain community. "They bring and throw their trash even on this [upstream] side of Rock-arch. You see, in the beginning, when the area was created and set aside, it was not for the purpose of disposing cans, bottles, and other trash. Rather, it was set apart for the placing of prayers, offerings, and cornpollen. That is what I say. And that is what many of us think."[78]

The situation reached a new climax in August 1995, when a small group of Navajos and "purified" non-Indians from the Page area held a four-day cleansing ceremony at the bridge. The activists, known as Protectors of the Rainbow, were not sanctioned by the Navajo Nation or any local chapter. Without prior notification, they roped off the trail from the dock one morning, and put up homemade signs warning people away. The sing, performed by a medicine man, was "for strength, power and to bring spirituality back to the lives of our people; because the government wants to take this place away; and to cleanse Rainbow Bridge of defilements allowed by the [National Park Service], litter, graffiti, profanity, and immodesty upon our sacred ground." In a press release, the Protectors of the Rainbow additionally listed "12 Points" of protest, all of which dealt with current problems on the reservation:

> Our youth do not know who they are, and they act like they have no relatives.
>
> Power lines criss-cross our land, yet many of our people do not

have electricity.
We are losing our culture.
We are losing our language.
We are losing our land.[79]

For four days, Rainbow Bridge was silent except for the sing. Tour boats halted. Wisely, the Park Service allowed the ceremony to continue without confrontation. In fact, the incident gave GCNRA a golden opportunity to implement some changes in its management of Rainbow Bridge National Monument, changes that had been approved already. GCNRA distributed a new brochure for visitors called "Respect for Tradition." The text likened Rainbow Bridge to a cathedral. It stated that "American Indians consider Rainbow Bridge a sacred religious site. . . . Special prayers are said before passing beneath the Bridge: neglect to say appropriate prayers might bring misfortune or hardship." Trying to promote a "bridge between cultures," the Park Service then asked non-Indian visitors to "respect these long-standing beliefs. *Please do not approach or walk under Rainbow Bridge.*" To make the message more obvious, the agency erected a sign and a shin-high barrier around a viewing area below the bridge.

The new policy made a few upset. "We've been coming here and walking under the bridge since 1974, so you could say this is our religion," said a boater from Arizona. When other longtime lake users rose up in anger, the superintendent of GCNRA clarified his position. "It is absolutely not illegal for you to walk under Rainbow Bridge," he said. "A ranger might ask you if you noticed the sign, but you will not be stopped; you won't get a citation." Attempting to avoid any First Amendment violations, the Park Service calls this policy a "voluntary request." Even so, some visitors resent being requested. One woman told off a ranger: "You say we should do this out of respect for the Indians, but isn't it disrespectful to us? It's reverse discrimination."[80]

Despite its problems, the "Respect for Tradition" campaign has helped alleviate some forms of misbehavior at the national monument. In effect, it has created a buffer between the bridge and the reservoir. That's just what the Park Service wanted. In its 1993 General Management Plan for Rainbow Bridge, it identified an underlying problem: the public viewed Rainbow Bridge "as an extension of the recreational experience at Glen Canyon NRA." Through improved interpretation, the agency hoped to communicate that "Rainbow Bridge is not the same as Glen Canyon [NRA] . . . but a special place."[81]

Well, of course. And what about the flip side of that comment? *Glen Canyon is not the same as Rainbow Bridge, but a profane place.* Isn't that the truth? After all, what if an official brochure admonished boaters to treat Lake Powell with reverence? What if it compared the place to the Sistine Chapel? Wouldn't people shake their heads?

BEACH PARTY!

Lake Foul. Floyd's Void. The Blue Death. These are some of the names that river lovers have given to the reservoir. Many refuse to call it a lake; they insist on Powell Reservoir or "Lake" Powell. To them, the place is more than profane; it is evil. Their enmity runs deep. A friend of a friend of mine—a college student—drove all the way from Oregon just to piss on the face of the dam. He lacked the generosity of Wallace Stegner, the most tender of all dam haters, expressed in a 1966 travel article: "Lake Powell *is* beautiful. It isn't Glen Canyon, but it is something in itself. The contact of deep blue water and uncompromising stone is bizarre and somehow exciting. . . . And yet, vast and beautiful as it is, open now to anyone with a boat or the money to rent one . . . it strikes me, even in my exhilaration, with the consciousness of loss. In gaining the lovely and usable, we have given up the incomparable." Stegner had returned to Glen Canyon to see what the Bureau of Reclamation had done to his favorite section of the Colorado. For him, the best part of the lake trip was boating to the end of the flooded Escalante River, turning off the diesel engine, and going for a walk with friends in silence. "We are not, it seems, water-based in our pleasures; we can't get a thrill out of doing in these marvelous canyons what one can do on any resort lake." But rather than condemning other types of recreation, Stegner proposed a compromise: "Why not throw a boom across the mouth of the Escalante Canyon and hold this one precious arm of Lake Powell for the experiencing of silence? Why not, giving the rest of that enormous water to the motorboats and the waterskiers, keep one limited tributary as a canoe or rowboat wilderness?"[82]

Stegner had been a presidential conservation advisor during Kennedy's first year in office, so his opinion carried some weight in Washington. After Floyd Dominy read Stegner's article, he wrote the author a warm letter. He thought Stegner's suggestion for the Escalante deserved "commendation and serious consideration. In fact, from my own personal viewpoint, I would extend control such as you propose so far as feasible not only to the Escalante arm but to many of the other canyons which have been opened to boat travel by the reservoir."[83]

Dominy said he passed the suggestion along to George Hartzog, director of the National Park Service. The agency had a precedent for motorized/nonmotorized zoning at Yellowstone Lake in Yellowstone National Park. At Lake Powell, however, nothing ever came of the idea except the stated goal in a recent GCNRA General Management Plan to maintain a "semi-primitive" lakeside setting in the Escalante arm ("Visitor Use Zone 9"). This setting is meant to provide the "opportunity to experience solitude, tranquility, quiet." The region surrounding the Escalante River canyon is one of quietest spots in America; ambient noise monitoring has found average decibel levels in the low twenties. (A mosquito's buzz, for comparison, rates about forty decibels.) However, this quiet is reserved for those, like Stegner, who walk away from the water. The increasing popularity of Visitor Use Zone 9 among boaters and jet skiers has compromised GCNRA's management goal for the lakeside setting. Time will tell if the Park Service resurrects the idea of a boom.[84]

Looking back, it may seem strange that Floyd Dominy, Lake Powell's number one fan, would have supported restrictions on its recreational use. But while celebrating the coming of mass recreation in *Jewel of the Colorado*, the commissioner seemed to favor more contemplative forms of play: "You have a front-row seat in an amphitheater of infinity. The bright blue sky deepens slowly to a velvet purple and the stars are brilliant—glittering in that vast immensity above. Orange sandstone cliffs fade to dusky red— then to blackest black. The fire burns low—reflected in the placid lake. There is peace. And a oneness with God." From today's perspective, Dominy's descriptions of peace at Lake Powell seem anachronistic. By 1990, with GCNRA hosting over 2.5 million vacationers per year, peace was all but unobtainable, at least in the summertime. More to the point, it seemed that fewer and fewer people *wanted* restful serenity. Recently, a University of Utah student collected Lake Powell stories from her peers; the most common motifs, she reported, were "naked people," "boat wrecks," "dangerous feats," and "drinking too much." The party crowd often displays a disturbing lack of knowledge of—not to mention respect for—the local environment. One Park Service archaeologist told of an Anasazi dwelling whose beams had been ripped out for a campfire. "We're seeing destruction of all sites within a mile of the shoreline of Lake Powell," she said. "An incredible loss."[85]

Kim, a friend of mine, grew up with Lake Powell. She has seen a lot of changes but not as many as her parents, who have been boating and waterskiing on the reservoir since the very beginning, 1963. More than thirty years later, Kim says, "my parents still wave at everyone who passes us. But people are different than when they came in the Sixties. [The new-comers] come to Powell to show off their expensive toys and to get a tan to show off when they return home. It is no longer a place to 'get away.' All sandy beaches are packed with houseboats, Jet Skis, wave runners, and in some places, motorcycles. You have to fight for your own space and your own right to be there." Stan Jones has lived in Page, Arizona, since the mid-1960s and has witnessed the ascendance of high-speed water sports. He has a great personal stake at Lake Powell, since he makes his living publicizing the reservoir's beauty through articles, booklets, and his well-known map, which he updates regularly. Though "Mr. Lake Powell," as he is known, has no regrets about Glen Canyon, he has mixed feeling about the ongoing changes at the reservoir. He's glad that people love the place, but how they love it concerns him. Compared to the early days, he told me in 1995, recreationists are "truly different." They are toy lovers. Twenty-five years ago, Jones encountered fishermen and families who appreciated primitive camping in pristine country. Some folks water-skied, but even they were a different breed, he contends. For them, thrill wasn't every-thing. Today, however, it's all about "speed and greed." Big boats, big egos. People don't like to share beaches or canyons, says Jones. And they drive like lunatics. On a highway, they would be pulled over and arrested for reckless endangerment. He wishes the Park Service would zone the reservoir's large bays for PWCs and reserve the rest for fishing and explor-atory boating. As it is, Jones and his wife visit the reservoir only in the winter; the tourist season finally grew too mad.[86]

"We recognize the fact that when people come here they come to party, and they go to great lengths to accomplish that end," said a Park Service spokesperson in 1991. "We are not here to tell them how to party or what to do. But we are here to protect the resources and to protect the visitors from harm."[87]

And so, more and more, rangers have been forced to act as cops, par-ticularly during the craziness called Memorial Day. In the early 1990s,

GCNRA personnel referred to this holiday weekend simply as "the event." For three days, tens of thousands of partyers between the ages of sixteen and twenty-five converged on the reservoir "to drink beer, fornicate and fight," as one ranger put it. During the 1992 weekend, rangers made ninety-seven arrests and took reports of 589 additional infractions or crimes, including rape. Almost all of the action occurred on two beaches: Lone Rock near Wahweap Marina in Arizona and Hobie Cat near Bullfrog Marina in Utah. Officials estimated that eighteen thousand people and their vehicles squeezed onto the fifteen-acre Hobie Cat Beach in 1992. Kane County sheriff Max Clark drove by and saw, among other spectacles, "a woman openly engaged in a sex act involving a funnel, a rubber hose and beer." Law enforcement officers were less concerned about sex than drugs, but when they tried to arrest a suspected dealer, they were surrounded by a group of screaming, chanting youth. Fearing for their own safety, the officers abandoned the scene and only dared to return undercover. Though GCNRA brought in extra police from other National Park Service units, it wasn't enough. The rangers conceded the beach to the partyers.[88]

GCNRA officials vowed to "take back" Hobie Cat. They made early preparations for the next year, establishing a temporary "metropolitan-style criminal justice system in Bullfrog—complete with bailiffs, judges, bail bondsman, holding cells and a courtroom—to process scores of lawbreakers."[89] With the increased presence of law enforcers, the 1993 weekend was better, but that's not saying much. *Outside* magazine published these excerpts from the dispatch log of the Bullfrog Subdistrict from a single day of the long weekend:

12:10 a.m.	Drunk minor being transported to Visitor Center.
9:03 a.m.	Gentleman passed out in men's restroom near gas station.
11:50 a.m.	Cliff-diving accident below restaurant at employee swimming cove.
1:05 p.m.	Visitor reports individual threatening with a knife on Hobie Cat Beach.
1:16 p.m.	Gangs from Salt Lake roaming the beach stealing T-shirts at gunpoint.
5:50 p.m.	Hit-and-run jet ski at Bullfrog marina.
5:53 p.m.	Call to Kane County Sheriff; suspected drug activity in A-loop of campground.

6:53 p.m.	Car stopped for suspected DUI; found pound of dope.
7:42 p.m.	Two boat collisions; intoxicated drivers, no injuries.
10:59 p.m.	Fight breaks out over firewood on beach; one visitor hit in face with two-by-four, several teeth missing.[90]

By 1994, however, officials felt they had gained the upper hand. Attendance at "the event" had dropped to eight thousand. Rumors spread that the National Guard would be there the next year. Not true, but GCNRA was ready with one hundred officers at Hobie Cat Beach—where parking was now prohibited. In 1995, only three thousand people showed up. By Lake Powell standards, it was a low-key holiday. The party had moved somewhere else.[91]

But this wasn't the end of the story. In the summer of 1995, when the heavy snowpack of the Rockies had melted, Lake Powell recovered some of its water storage after several years of drought. The rising reservoir covered the Hobie Cat Beach with warm, shallow water. With all of the trash and human waste left over from the previous years of partying, conditions were ideal for fecal coliform bacteria. GCNRA officials promptly closed the area.

LAKE FOUL

Lake Powell has a history of waste problems. In the beginning, boaters dumped their sewage directly into the water, but the growing threat of pollution forced the Park Service to require on-board marine toilets in 1969. However, a 1994 survey found that 32 percent of boaters lacked sanitation devices. As for restrooms, Lake Powell essentially has none beyond the docks. Visitors do it in their boats or on the beaches, of which there are few. But in 1997, GCNRA essentially outlawed the use of nature as a potty. To make life easier, the Park Service installed two new dumping stations in the popular lower section of the reservoir. It will take time, however, for visitors to change their habits and for the reservoir to recover from years of abuse. GCNRA monitors the water quality at over fifty locations and periodically quarantines beaches.[92]

Besides toilet paper, pop cans and rifle shells often dot the campsites and side canyons. The Park Service instituted an "Adopt A Canyon" cleanup program in the 1980s, but the need existed far earlier. "Something must be done to alleviate reservoir litter-bugging," river runner P. T Reilly wrote in 1964. "Bridge Canyon is especially littered but indiscriminate discarding of plastic containers, papers, bottles, tin cans and uncovered toilet areas are in evidence from one end of Glen Canyon to the other."[93] In fact, Glen Canyon and its popular glens (especially Bridge Canyon) had developed a trash problem even before the dam. While the reservoir covered up some of the old unsightliness, it provided a repository for the new. In 1968, the *New York Times* reported on the common sight of bottles and cans bobbing in Lake Powell. "People come out of the city today and just don't know how to treat these places," said superintendent William Briggle. "They're used to dumping their garbage where they are." Fifteen years later, nothing had changed; after a tour of littered beaches, a reporter pronounced that "the throw-away society has reached Lake Powell. We can be thankful that most of the shoreline is vertical stone."[94]

Yet out of sight doesn't mean out of existence: the bottom of Lake Powell is collecting trash. Divers can find, among other things, "an amazing variety of sunglasses." A Phoenix diver-entrepreneur makes "zany lampshades" by gluing the spectacles to paper or fabric. Not surprisingly, the nonplastic relics of antiquity haven't fared as well underwater. In the 1980s, the Submerged Cultural Resources Unit of the National Park Service conducted dives to check on the condition of Glen Canyon's Anasazi ruins. "Pretty devastated" was the summary conclusion.[95]

At its maximum elevation, 3,700 feet, the reservoir hides the ugliness, including the "bathtub ring," or "Dead Zone," a mineral stain (blue-green algae bonded with calcium carbonate) resulting from the contact of water and rock. But the reservoir is rarely full. After topping out in 1980 and again in 1983–84, Lake Powell drastically receded during consecutive years of drought. The programmed outflow from the dam exceeded the natural inflow from the river. The nadir came in early 1993 when Lake Powell stood eighty-eight feet below maximum, about where it stood in 1973. The drawdown wasn't all bad: cliffs and canyon stretches reappeared, looking decent save for the chalk-white stain. At Rainbow Bridge, the "swimming hole" disappeared, replaced by the original flowing streamlet. The drought provided visitors an opportunity to relive their memories of a former Lake Powell, or to see new (old) beauty.

Unfortunately, the low water also uncovered trash. Not just any trash:

used engine batteries, a few at first, then dozens, then scores. Alarmed about possible lead contamination, the Park Service considered the impossible: closing Lake Powell. To the agency's great relief, the lab tests came back negative. The issue then turned to criminal responsibility. Since most of the batteries turned up near Wahweap Marina, the finger pointed at the concessionaire, ARA, which owned some three hundred houseboats, each with a pair of batteries. Asked if his company was involved in illegal dumping, ARA's public-relations officer stated, "Certainly it's not a company policy." Sensing the coming scandal, the concessionaire staged a public good deed by sending trash-collecting divers to the surface of Wahweap Bay. They returned with "200 to 300 batteries, 133 barbecue grills, over 300 deck lawn chairs, miles of rope, tons of plastic trash cans and even fire ovens."[96]

This was enough to catch the attention of Arizona's Attorney General's Office, which launched an investigation. It found that ARA (and a subsidiary of the former concessionaire, Del Webb) had used the reservoir as "an underwater landfill." More than a hundred truckloads of trash and a thousand batteries had been dumped near Lake Powell's five marinas between 1981 and 1990. In 1993, the state fined the concessionaire $1.3 million, the largest environmental penalty ever assessed in Arizona. In a separate action, the Interior Department scolded the Park Service for negligent law enforcement. Since then, the agency has conducted periodic underwater trash sweeps—just another part of managing America's Natural Playground.[97]

SQUAWFISH MEMORIES

Despite the trash, and the crowds, and the rowdies, an impressive number of people still love Lake Powell. Magazine and newspaper coverage from the 1990s includes such titles as "Paradise at Powell"; "Made for Fun— Lake Powell"; "Surreal Lake Powell Is Out of this World"; "Getting Away from It All"; and (no joke) "Lake Powell, A Grand Canyon with Water." Indeed, for those who like the combination of rugged beauty and modern luxury—and who wouldn't?—the reservoir has earned the title "Heaven on Water."

Frankly, for most people it's impossible to dislike the place. In 1995, a *New York Times* travel writer came with a skeptical eye, aware of the conflicts surrounding the dam and reservoir. But in no time she relented: "From the bow of a 36-foot houseboat, cruising through clear blue water thriving with bass, trout and pike, drifting past a geologic calendar of red rock, muddy shale, pink or white sandstone and limestone, we found it hard to be sorry the lake is here."[98]

By the same token, it's easy for the beneficiaries of the dam to accept at face value the familiar justification for Lake Powell. They may use themselves as evidence that gaining a lot of accessibility makes up for losing a little beauty. But they are wrong—on lexical if not moral grounds. The choice of verb is crucial. No matter how popular, Lake Powell cannot *make up for* Glen Canyon, because, very simply, it's not an equivalent place. Likewise, the reservoir's accessibility and the lost canyon's beauty do not cancel out one another. Even if they could be expressed as equivalents, they couldn't supply the answer to the incessant question: Was Lake Powell worth it? There can be no answer because there are still more variables out there, including some that are independent of human experience.

Before the dam, every May, June, or July, a certain population of Colorado squawfish (*Ptychocheilus lucius*) would swim to the mouth of the San Juan River in Glen Canyon. Some fish came from downstream, others from the Green or upper Colorado. When they reached the silty San Juan, something in their brains—or something in the water—told them to make a turn.

Colorado squawfish sport a white belly and a pale green back with silver on the sides. In the early twentieth century, people often referred to this long, slender species of minnow as "white salmon" or "Colorado River salmon." After he and his brother floated down the river in 1911, Ellsworth Kolb wrote, "These salmon were old friends of ours, being found from one end to the other of the Colorado, and on all its tributaries. They sometimes weigh twenty-five or thirty pounds, and are common at twenty pounds; being stockily built fish, with large, flat heads. They are not gamey, but afford a lot of meat with a very satisfying flavour."[99] Historical photographs indicate the fish could reach lengths up to six feet and weigh up to a hundred pounds. Of the eight fish species native to Glen Canyon, they swam at the top of the food chain, the king of the Colorado. Their oversized lips fronted a mouth with no teeth. Their prey—fish, insects, sometimes even small birds and mammals—was shredded on the way to the stomach by incisors in the throat.

Now extinct in the Grand Canyon, the squawfish has been federally listed as an endangered species. The healthiest populations exist in the Green and upper Colorado, where spawning runs of over 250 miles have been recorded. After reaching the designated genesis zone—a freshly deposited gravel or cobble bar—the female squawfish releases up to seventy-five thousand sticky eggs, while the male contributes his milky sperm mixture. In less than a week, the fertilized eggs enter the larval stage, let go of the cobbles, and float downstream to their nursery habitat. The luckiest of the one-third-inch larvae get captured in the safety of backwaters, which often form at the mouths of secondary stream channels.

The San Juan canyon was an excellent spawning stretch but probably an inferior nursery. Before being dammed in the 1960s, the river was extremely changeable; it would rage for a month or so in late spring, then drop to a trickle in fall and winter. Furthermore, with its steep gradient and narrow canyon, the San Juan didn't have space to spread out and form many large, stable backwater areas. The Colorado River in Glen Canyon, however, was more spacious and mellow. It fell at an average rate of about two feet per mile, compared to the San Juan's seven. The different personalities of the two rivers worked to the advantage of the squawfish. The San Juan's babies became Glen Canyon's adults.

Today, Lake Powell floods the lower eighty miles of the San Juan. The river's relic squawfish are isolated, dying. Without continuous human intervention, this population will probably become extinct. Squawfish can live up to forty years, so it's possible, at the time of this writing, that a few ancient individuals remain who have memories—if there's such a thing as fish memories—of growing up in the Glen.[100]

For animals that didn't live in water, the loss of canyon habitat was more sudden and traumatic. Bill Greene, son of Art Greene, remembered that "rattlesnakes and scorpions were all around; I called [Lake Powell] 'Scorpion Acres' for awhile. When the water came up and made islands, you had to be very careful because all the insects and snakes and game of any kind would go toward the center to keep from drowning. Pretty soon you'd get out and find nothing but hundreds of scorpions and snakes on the islands. Lots of animals were trapped and drowned. [We] saved a few cows, but it wasn't fun getting them in the boat."[101] In April 1963, when Lake Powell was rising about one foot per day, volunteers from Page, Arizona, staged a public rescue of a stranded cow. For some two weeks, the unbranded brown-and-white range animal had been stranded on a ledge above the water. Boaters deposited hay on the ledge to keep the cow from starving. Finally, the volunteers lassoed the terrified animal and very slowly coaxed her onto a wooden plank leading to a flat-bottomed boat. She was eventually turned loose on the north shore of the reservoir. The general manager of the Arizona Society for the Prevention of Cruelty to Animals drove all the way from Phoenix to take part in the rescue.

The indigenous fauna fared much worse. They had nowhere else to go. Animals, like humans, congregate near water. Thus, in its first few vertical feet, Lake Powell destroyed not only an entire historical region but an entire habitat. Next it destroyed a hidden habitat: those stretches of side canyons above unscalable pour-offs. Stan Jones, that indefatigable explorer of Lake Powell, visited many of these stretches as soon as the rising reservoir allowed access. "Nobody had ever been there; no four-footed animal had ever been. They were of access only to lizards and birds. They were absolutely teeming aviaries. They had all kinds of birds in them. The birds were so used to having those areas all to themselves that as I would walk up the canyons, they would actually dive at me, like birds will do at other unwanted birds. . . . This was an absolute haven for them. There was nothing to fear." Perhaps two hundred bird species lost some or all of their habitat to the deluge. This was one of the prices of Lake Powell, yet it seldom gets emphasized. The lives of animals—and the river itself, a kind of life force—languish in a discussion that hinges on recreation and aesthetics (or, alternatively, politics and money). Natural beauty is a human property, but the natural world is not. It's unfair to the Colorado and the creatures who lived with it to explain away their losses with the addition of Lake Powell. To them, the reservoir gave nothing.[102]

For people and other life, the Glen was unique, irreplaceable. The same adjectives apply to the reservoir, however. Each place is (or was) a kind of paradise. It would be best to begin the debate with this compassionate recognition, but that's hard for dam haters who have never spent time at Lake Powell, or for lake lovers who have never learned about Glen Canyon. Indeed, for those who grew up boating on Powell—two generations and counting—the reservoir might as well have been there forever. I've actually encountered teenagers in Utah who believed Lake Powell was a natural lake. As Richard Shelton wrote in a poem about Glen Canyon, "We will move over the water / with such speed we will forget / even what we have never known." The problem is, there's little incentive to examine the past when the present feels so good, as so much of the travel literature betrays:

"Camp No. 2 at the end of Desolation Canyon, Lake Powell, 5/26/88." (Photograph by Mark Klett.)

Motoring into Cottonwood Canyon late one afternoon, the land suddenly opened up, and the rounded, voluptuous, solemn walls fell back to reveal a grass and sagebrush valley held in the rock's loose embrace. [My companion] spoke into the intercom, and suddenly a John Philip Sousa march blared from the bridge speakers. We placed the hailer microphone over a speaker, and instantly Sousa filled the canyon with his simple, robust patriotism. An echo of the headlong exuberance, the powerful lust which settled the West and built the Glen Canyon Dam, bounded back. It felt embarrassingly good to be alive.

Lust and exuberance—is this the best historical explanation for the dam? Maybe not, but it sounds pretty believable from the bow of a houseboat.[103]

DRAIN THIS?

David Brower, still active at eighty-three, came to the University of Utah in 1995 to "debate" Floyd Dominy about Glen Canyon Dam. The exchange created little heat but lots of jokes, perhaps because these living legends knew they couldn't—and weren't supposed to—change each other's mind. Yet despite the light mood, the ex-director of the Sierra Club projected an insistent passion, as if his work wasn't done. Dominy, looking unbelievably young, seemed happily retired, at ease with himself and his place in history. "I make no apologies," he said. "I'm proud of my career; it was justified. We need to develop resources." The ex-commissioner was at his best talking about dam projects and dam requirements, water compacts and water control. When he got on a roll, he sounded like a narrator for an old Bureau of Reclamation filmstrip. His opening statement summarized the 1922 Colorado River Compact, the CRSP, and Glen Canyon Dam's relationship to both.

Brower followed with a rambling, anecdotal statement. "I started building dams at age six," he said. "I most enjoyed destroying them. I got over the habit of dam building. Floyd's built some good ones, a few bad ones too. He's made a mistake or two, but so have I." Brower talked about his role in the defeat of Echo Park Dam, and his regret about Glen Canyon Dam. "Although it's done all sorts of beautiful things for the [CRSP] project, it was *totally unnecessary*." He explained: If the Colorado River Compact were revised to reflect the actual discharge of the Colorado River and to allow interbasin leasing of water rights, the function of Glen Canyon Dam could be served by Hoover Dam. Lake Mead (slightly larger than Lake Powell, but rarely used to capacity) would regulate the river and store unused Upper Basin water, which the Lower Basin would use at a price. At present, the Upper Basin has nothing to gain and lots to lose by letting its unused water run downstream. Brower expressed his disbelief at such a "ridiculous" system. Change it, he said, and drain Lake Powell.

Dominy just shook his head.[104]

But Brower was serious. Two weeks later, he convinced the Sierra Club board to ratify a motion to decommission the dam. (Or, to interpret it another way, the board kowtowed to its legendary leader of old). This was a step away from the Club's conservatism of the 1980s and a breach of its bottom-up decision-making policy. For Brower, however, this was a peak of personal satisfaction, a kind of glorified penance. "I've turned from regret to restoration," he wrote in *Sierra*, announcing the Club's new campaign, "Let the River Run Through It." Unlike some environmentalists, he didn't dream of dynamite blasts. He simply wanted to reopen the diversion tunnels, keeping the dam "as a tourist attraction, like the Pyramids, with passersby wondering how humanity ever built it, and why." Defending his proposal, Brower touted a recent Bureau of Reclamation study showing that 8 percent of the Colorado River disappeared at Lake Powell through evaporation or percolation. Considering the going (and projected) price of water in the metropolitan West, this missing water represents millions, even billions of dollars. According to Brower, the highest economic use of the river would be to let it run free in Glen Canyon. The lost energy revenue could, he claimed, be offset by energy conservation measures. More to the point, "The sooner we begin, the sooner lost paradises will begin to recover— Cathedral in the Desert, Music Temple, Hidden Passage, Dove Canyon, Little Arch, Dungeon, and a hundred others. . . . In time, Glen Canyon will reassert itself, through the action of wind and water. And we will know what Alexander Pope knew: 'And finer forms are in the quarry / Than ever Angelo evoked.' Once again, for all our time, the river can run through it."[105] The article ended on that poetic note, before Brower could get to the immense technical complexities of draining Lake Powell. Suffice it to say his plan is semicredible, semiludicrous. Glen Canyon Dam may be necessary on paper only, but that paper is a set of treaties, laws, and legal precedents governing the use of the Colorado River, the most intensively litigated river in the world. It might be possible to reform the "Law of the River" to make the dam obsolete. However, it would require the combined initiative of citizens, politicians, and bureaucrats, and some heroic cooperation over water rights, historically one of the most contentious issues in the American West. At the same time, it would probably require a reform of the way westerners use water—limiting growth and getting by on less.

So far, there's little movement in that direction. Take the example of Washington County, Utah, located in the southwest corner of the state, in the low desert where Joshua trees grow. Called "Utah's Dixie" for its mild climate, the county has attracted lots of outmigrating Californians and retirees. In 1980, 26,000 people lived here; in 1990, 49,000; and by 1997, 73,000, with no end in sight. All of these people (and the nine golf courses) rely on the itsy-bitsy Virgin River. Quail Creek Reservoir, completed in 1984, is expected to maintain the county through 2005, at which point a new dam, Sand Hollow, will delay the crisis ten more years. Ultimately, the county must either find new water or halt new growth. In 1997, well aware of that choice, the Washington County Water Conservation District began requesting rights-of-way for a 120-mile pipeline from Lake Powell. If this project goes through, draining Lake Powell will become all the more problematic. David Brower may be right that the reservoir was "unnecessary" in 1963, but over time, even an unnecessary project can *become* necessary as developments build up around it. Thus, while Brower's 1996 proposal was probably premature, his sense of urgency had some merit.[106]

Some ecologists share this urgency. Dave Wegner was the lead scientist for the Bureau of Reclamation's Glen Canyon Environmental Studies (GCES). Instituted in 1982 in response to a lawsuit by the Environmental Defense Fund, GCES was meant to quantify what Grand Canyon river runners had said for years: the dam had changed the downstream ecosystem. The resulting environmental impact statement (EIS), a model of thoroughness, was published in 1995, and its recommendations led to a change in the operation of Glen Canyon Dam. In 1996, the government pledged to reduce daily fluctuations and to conduct periodic flood releases meant to churn up sediment from the riverbed. The goal is to stay the destruction of beaches and native fish habitat. However, the new flow regime will do little to restore pre-dam conditions, the goal of some scientists. In the long run, endangered fish like the razorback sucker and humpback chub may still go extinct. (One possible solution: add sediment to the river at Lee's Ferry via a pipeline slurry.)

Then there's Wegner's idea. Why spend millions of dollars to mitigate the *effects* of a dam when you could spend millions of dollars to remove the *cause*, and get a canyon back to boot? In 1996, frustrated with the Bureau's handling of GCES, Wegner resigned and announced his support for the Sierra Club. He added San Juan and Flaming Gorge dams—two more CRSP projects with disastrous effects on native fish—as worthy candidates for elimination. Razing dams "is the only way you're ever going to restore these ecosystems," he said.[107]

But other scientists questioned the very idea of restoration. They emphasized that the regimented river in Grand Canyon has led to an increase in riparian growth, which in turn has favored endangered and threatened species such as the bald eagle and peregrine falcon. "These species are using the modified conformation of the ecosystem to their advantage," said ecologist Larry Stevens. "We've had gains in biodiversity and habitat that really should be considered when thinking about river restoration." Then there's the problem of sediment. Opening up the dam's diversion tunnels would introduce lots of it, to be sure, but the accumulated sediment beneath Lake Powell contains concentrations of heavy metals and toxins from the leaking of motorboats and the leaching of farms and uranium tailings.[108]

Wegner characterized this more as a potential threat, another reason to drain the reservoir now. There's a window of opportunity, he said, to restore both the Glen and the Grand. In 1997, he joined the recently formed Glen Canyon Institute of Salt Lake City to initiate a privately funded "Citizen's Environmental Assessment" on eliminating Lake Powell. Such a document would have no legal standing, but the hope is that it would prod the Bureau of Reclamation to conduct a more thorough EIS. Originally a cadre of former river runners, the Institute rode the wave created by the Sierra Club, the nation's foremost environmental organization. "We are talking about the largest, most important restoration project in human history," gushed Adam Werbach, the Club's new president. "At my age, 24, I have never had the chance to see Glen Canyon, but I hope my children will."[109]

In their initial excitement, activists like Werbach seemingly forgot that every EIS contains a section on socioeconomic impacts. These are not insignificant when it comes to Lake Powell. Consider, for example, the Navajo Generating Station, located on the Navajo Reservation not far from Lake Powell. In addition to ash, this power station emits prodigious clouds of steam. The steam comes from water, of course, which comes from a pipeline connected to the reservoir. Designed to utilize a constant clearwater flow, the plant would need some reengineering to survive the return of the river. It might simply close. That's a frightening prospect to the Navajo Nation, which already suffers from chronic high unemployment. About 1,200 tribal members work at the plant. Many of them live in Page, Arizona, within sight of Glen Canyon Dam.

Page's non-Indian population likewise fears the future according to the Sierra Club but more in relation to the service industry. According to 1997 figures from the Utah Travel Council, Lake Powell generates $455 million per year in tourist revenue. Without this cash inflow, gas-and-motel towns like Page (population 8,200) would undoubtedly wilt, and surrounding counties and states would lose a substantial tax base. "You could replace houseboat recreation with river recreation—canoeing, rafting, hiking—in a heartbeat," responded Dave Wegner. Locals laughed: what kind of replacement is that? Boaters spend a lot more money than hikers or rafters.

And they spend it happily, because Lake Powell is famously fun. Each year, over four hundred thousand boats cruise the reservoir, and the owners of those boats (and the associated repair shops, gas stations, and marinas) wouldn't surrender without a fight. Bumper stickers in Page expressed defiance: "HEY, SIERRA CLUB, DRAIN THIS."[110]

"It would be an insult to the world to drain Lake Powell," said Verna Stoddard, business manager of the Lake Powell Yacht Club. Tourists come all the way from Japan and Germany to marvel at this lake. Would they, she implied, prefer taking pictures of a muddy river working its way through a sterile mudflat? Well, who knows? Such an enormous restoration project— unprecedented in the world—might well become an attraction in itself. Provided, that is, that tourists could accept the pace of the project. Speaking anthropocentrically, draining Lake Powell is an irrational form of de-layed gratification. It means a long, slow, even tedious transition between a beautiful reservoir and a re-beautified canyon, as springtime floods and summertime storms (and workers with high-pressure hoses?) work on the mountains of muck. Environmental restoration defies human time. "Two, three decades," promised Brower, but his optimism seemed unfounded. "Aesthetically, oh, dear God, it would be a stinking, ugly mess," said a spokes-person for the Page Chamber of Commerce. Why, locals asked, would you willfully destroy the most beautiful place in the world? Utah representative Chris Cannon concurred. He made some suggestions "roughly as stupid" as draining Lake Powell: "return Mount Rushmore to its pristine state"; "remove the Statue of Liberty and reclaim Liberty Island"; and while you're at it, "remove the Golden Gate from San Francisco Bay."[111]

In short, the opposition's response to David Brower fed from amuse-ment and annoyed disbelief—and more than a trace of fear. High-ranking Republican James Hansen even deemed it necessary to convene congres-sional hearings on draining Lake Powell. Words like *kooky* and *bizarre* showed up regularly in opinion statements. "If Glen Canyon was not needed and Lake Mead could do the job, why was that dam built?" asked Ted Stewart, director of the Utah Department of Natural Resources. "I hate to have a knee-jerk reaction, but this looks like another example of a group of elitists trying to take away recreational opportunities from the common folk."[112]

It's worth noting, however, that in his *Sierra* article Brower never men-tioned the recreational use of Lake Powell. To him, it's peripheral to the real issues: the loss of a wild river in Grand Canyon, and the loss of wild beauty in Glen Canyon. These losses literally pain him and other canyoneers. It's fair to call it religious pain. "The core reason to drain Lake Powell," read one letter to the editor, "is a spiritual reason. . . . Lake Powell has dammed Glen Canyon, which is the spiritual heart of the Colorado River. . . . Recreation is important, but boats trailing water skiers are a trivial reason to keep Lake Powell when there is a powerful spirit of peace and wisdom from our Mother Earth to be gained." The author, a man from Alpine, Utah, spoke of draining in terms of "repentance."[113]

Most members of the pro-lake camp don't appreciate—perhaps can't fathom—the depth of this "spiritual" feeling. But misunderstanding cuts both ways: anti-dam activists generally fail to appreciate the importance of Lake Powell to others. Because the sin of the dam is to them self-evident, they do not accept the love that others profess for the reservoir. They do not respect the recreation that goes on there. Stories about drunken teenage miscreants confirm their suspicions about the kind of people attracted to a dammed river.

But 2.5 million people is a lot of people; they come for a lot of reasons. One of these is routinely overlooked, perhaps because it doesn't fit the standard definition of "outdoor recreation": family time, loved ones using a houseboat on Lake Powell as a means of being together. No one would mistake it for a wilderness experience, or even a nature experience, but houseboating with family can have its own deep meaning. As one visitor said, echoing a thousand voices, "Our days houseboating on Lake Powell were perhaps the best family vacation any of us had ever had." Who knows whether people like this understand the purpose of Glen Canyon Dam. Who knows whether they pause to consider the consequences of beauty made accessible. But this much is clear: to them, Lake Powell matters.[114]

In Utah, many large families (common because of the Mormon emphasis on children) share the expense of an annual vacation or reunion at Lake Powell. "We've been every year except one," said Julie Grow of Salt Lake City. "We've tried to substitute other places like Flaming Gorge [Reservoir], Yellowstone, California beaches and Disneyland for a vacation alternative, but nothing measures up to Lake Powell for kids and adults." The Grow family has started many Lake Powell traditions. "We've photographically measured the water level at 'Big Toe' every year," she said. "And we laugh as we ride through 'Screwdriver Bay,' the place we dropped a set of screwdrivers in the water. We affectionately attach our own names to the lake landmarks."[115] Several families from my neighborhood in northern Utah go to Lake Powell religiously. "Sacred family time" is a phrase that crops up in conversation. For these folks, and many more, Lake Powell provides the setting for some of life's best moments.

My best empirical evidence for this comes from an unusual source: the obituary page. An obituary is a daunting work of literature, a summation of a human life in a paragraph or two. Everything matters in a death notice; authors include only the most pertinent, most cherished details. Thus it means a great deal when the departed or their family mention places, whether they be houses or cities or rivers or reservoirs. Using the electronic archive of the *Deseret News* (a Salt Lake City paper), I found twenty-seven obituaries from the years 1990 to 1995 that mention Lake Powell. The number is not insignificant, considering that the first generation of Lake Powell recreationists is probably still within its life expectancy range.

Perhaps most striking about these obituaries is the connection made by survivors between the reservoir, the departed, and their kin:

He loved to play cards with his friends and his greatest joy was boating on Lake Powell with his many friends and family.

Jim's favorite time of the year was the annual family outing to Lake Powell where he could explore what nature has to offer.

He loved to wrestle with his kids, take them to Lake Powell, snow ski with them, fish with them and even take them to work with him.

His motto was 'Work Hard! Play Hard!' and he shared his zest for living with his family and friends while boating and water-skiing at Lake Powell, cheering for the Utah Jazz, four-wheeling, snow-skiing, hang-gliding and scuba diving.

Jim lived for his family, he loved to enjoy bowling and water skiing at Lake Powell with them.

The greatest love of his life was time spent with his family skiing, visiting Lake Powell, supporting his children in their various activities and just being together.

Beloved husband, father, and grandfather was taken from us suddenly at Lake Powell, doing what he loved best.

[He] was a loving husband, father and grandfather. He loved to spend time with his family, especially on his boat at Lake Powell.

I wait for my adorable husband of 15 years. . . . We have grown and shared so many happy times on our boat at Flaming Gorge and Lake Powell.

He was an accomplished musician and enjoyed boating at Lake Powell with his wife Valerie.

He loved trips to Lake Powell with his family and friends.

Susie lived for her family and enjoyed years of fun at Bear Lake and Lake Powell with her family and close friends.

Someone I know told me about a friend of hers whose daughter died in an accident on Lake Powell. After sending a note of condolence, she received a reply—a thank-you form letter—that discussed the loss and also the place where it happened. Before this accident, the mother wrote, the lake had been a sanctuary for her family. It still was, more than ever.

AFTERWORD

We waste too much time on arguments about nothing. It happened, we are what became of it. There is no Eden to save, not now, not in 1492. True, we could have done better—but then everything is like a love affair, every-thing could have been done better.

—Charles Bowden

I collect postcards. Of the eighty-odd scenes of Lake Powell in my collection, the prettiest are the work of photographer Gary Ladd, who lives in Page, Arizona, in a house overlooking the dam. Ladd has put together a picture book about Lake Powell. In his excellent preface, he writes: "Whatever your knowledge of Glen Canyon and Lake Powell, don't underestimate them. Glen Canyon was a treasure. It still is."[1]

Ladd's attitude about Lake Powell has evolved. First the place revolted him. He literally felt sick when he was there. Looking at any lake scene, he'd immediately imagine what lay underwater. He never took large-format images of Lake Powell, not particularly out of spite but because it never occurred to him that a reservoir—especially this one—was worthy of serious photography. Later, as he warmed up to the place, he looked at Lake Powell as a means of access to fabulous, almost pristine places. At last, though he seemed a bit ashamed to admit it when I talked to him in 1995, he came to believe that Lake Powell itself was "fabulous." Now he loves the reservoir and regrets it too.

The photographer feels a kinship with those who mourn Glen Canyon, for he sees a "second wave of loss" going on. Those places spared by the lake, those exquisite canyon stretches above the high-water mark, are finally being discovered and trampled by visitors. "Something truly fantastic is being changed forever," Ladd says. He's ready to quit some of his old haunts, having watched enough of their incremental deterioration. Gary wishes he'd arrived ten or fifteen years earlier, in the early days of the reservoir. The pain of loss would be greater, but so too the memories.

Another resident of Page, Joan Staveley, remembers Glen Canyon before the dam. She saw it with her father, river runner Norman Nevills. When asked about Lake Powell, Staveley smiles and immediately responds, "What a marvelous opportunity for people to see beauty!" People including herself. She fondly remembers the reservoir's first few months, when side canyons once inconvenient or inaccessible became easy to reach. She could hardly wait for the water to rise into places like Hidden Passage and Mystery Canyon. This was the best Lake Powell, she says. It still looked like a river, but you could zoom up the glens, where the amazing places—Labyrinth Canyon, Lake Canyon, Cathedral in the Desert, and more—were intact. But it didn't last long. After May 1964, says Staveley, all the best stuff disappeared.[2]

Some memories will always break her heart: the Cathedral, Music Temple, "Lincoln's Bathtub" near Rainbow Bridge, the six-fingered Anasazi handprint in Twilight Canyon. Nevertheless, she says, "I don't lament the 'loss' of Glen Canyon. You know, a lot of Glen Canyon was boring; not everything was scenic. People don't like to admit that now. But I'll tell you, one of the great losses was the San Juan [River]. The Colorado was like a ponderous patriarch, slow and smooth. The San Juan was the kid, full of joy and impudence. A living river." In her memory, she separates the canyon and the reservoir: different worlds, both splendid in their individual ways.

Yet despite her relative freedom from nostalgia, Staveley laments contemporary loss. One of the hardest things, she says, has been watching Lake Powell be discovered by so many people. She always loved the Escalante arm of the reservoir—until the year before, 1994. It finally got too crazy, too crowded. She won't go back, she says, except perhaps in the off-season. Then she laughs: "Maybe I'm in the wrong business!" Joan Staveley works for the Chamber of Commerce.

Change is happening throughout the canyon country—the tourists are coming. Take a look at these visitation figures from Arches National Park:

1950	15,726
1960	71,597
1970	178,484
1980	290,519
1985	363,464

The junction of the San Juan (left) and Colorado rivers in Glen Canyon, March 1963, days before Lake Powell silenced them. (Photograph by A. E. Turner.)

1990	620,719
1995	859,374

Arches' gateway community, Moab, was transformed in the 1980s and 1990s. The former "Uranium Capital of the World" suddenly became the "Mountain Biking Capital of the World." A boom-and-bust energy economy gave way to an out-of-control tourist economy. Motels sprung up faster than morning glory. Meanwhile, away from town, on the public lands, un-authorized campsites proliferated—as did fecal bacteria in nearby washes. Hikers and bikers trampled the fragile desert soil and beat parallel ruts into "hidden" canyons. In response, federal land managers made plans for new outhouses, new restrictions, new permit systems—always lagging a step behind.[3]

In 1994, returning to southeastern Utah after a considerable absence, Page Stegner was surprised and disgusted:

I cross the bridge over the Colorado River into . . . Moab? I don't recognize it. Maybe I never really noticed it before. The town seems to have multiplied. I don't remember all those T-shirt and gift shops, western-wear stores, antique and collectible galleries, Indian-crafts outlets, artisan co-ops, deli/bakeries, bookstores, ORV rentals, bike rentals, rafting companies, helicopter tours, realtors. I count seven realtors. . . .

In other words, Moab has been "discovered."[4]

As if to prove it, in the early 1990s Nike unveiled a new cross-training shoe: Air Mowabb. What is it about this place? Why would millions of people drive hundreds of miles to be here? Is it because, as Edward Abbey said, it's the most beautiful place on earth? Because the biking is extreme? Yes—but I think there's more. Many visitors—many Germans, retired Americans, footloose twenty-somethings, environmentalists with *Desert Solitaire* in their backpack, and others—come for what the country represents: the last of what's good about the American West. More than any other region in the Lower Forty-Eight, this slickrock terrain *looks* pristine whether it is or not.

"All the photos in all the books on all the coffee tables, what they're telling people is not the truth," says one Park Service employee. "They're telling people that it's okay out here, and it's not okay out here. The place is being pulverized and lost."[5]

This urgent—if slightly alarmist—message is gaining attention, but it faces some stiff competition from the purveyors of "okay." For example, after visiting Moab and environs in 1994, a *Washington Post* travel writer promised, "If [visitors] come, they will find a rugged, untamed, unspoiled and still partially unexplored wilderness that, if they choose to plunge into the heart of it, could test their mettle." Amazing but true: people still write this stuff. The lure of the imagined primitive West seems only to grow as America grows. As one Utah essayist has written, "Our very culture—environmentally aware, travel crazy—is on the make for great places." The millions of people who search for (and often find) paradise not-yet-lost—people who experience moments of bliss on jeep trails, at overlooks, in slot canyons—are contributing unintentionally to the deterioration of the canyonlands.[6]

Are there solutions? Yes—well, at least ameliorations. Enhanced public awareness about the ecology of the canyonlands would no doubt help. So would a little self-imposed poverty on the part of visitors. Above all, however, I would like to see a reevaluation of paradise. From my heart, I urge visitors to look beyond the undiscovered, to resist the impulse that privileges the "natural" over the "unnatural"; the pristine over the tainted; southern Utah over the rest of the state; wilderness over home; Glen Canyon over Lake Powell.

Granted, this impulse is not altogether bad; there *is* something wrong with Lake Powell, the cities we call home, and modernity in general. Conversely, Glen Canyon, though by no means untouched, *was* perfect—perfect at being itself—and deserves to be remembered as such. It should not have been dammed. Its remnants should be cherished and protected.

Yet the discoverer's impulse becomes self-defeating if pursued single-mindedly. In literature, it makes for rich expressions of rapture and regret, but only rarely of wisdom. Looking back on the twentieth century and the literature of the canyon country, I detect an ongoing shift from stories predominantly about discovery to stories predominantly about loss. On this spectrum, Glen Canyon occupies the crucial middle position. But I suspect the stories on either side of the dam are really segments of the same connected narrative, one that ends in frustration:

> Now it is all gone. There are no more rivers for me to run or mountains for me to escape to. Like so many others who loved the River, I consider myself as a frustrated conservationist, thinking of the good days when the canyon country was clean, lonely and waiting for the tourists to discover it.[7]

The word *nostalgia* dates to 1688, when Johannes Hofer defended his medical thesis on a common but previously unnamed affliction. Perhaps the most prominent victims were young Swiss soldiers and mercenaries. After leaving the Alps, they became lethargic, depressed, even suicidal. Reminders of home, like the sound of cowbells, provoked uncontrollable weeping. Many of the sick wasted away and died.

According to the fashion of the time, Hofer gave the disease a classical name. He combined two Greek words, *nostos* (to return home) and *algos* (pain). In other words, homesickness. For treatment he recommended leeches, purges, and emetics.

To ward off the disease, officials in the Swiss army forbade their men to sing or even whistle Alpine tunes. Even so, soldiers continued to succumb. In reality, they suffered from tuberculosis, meningitis, and any number of infections—in addition to being homesick. But in the days before bacteriology, nostalgia explained it all. The surest cure was to go home, of course, but one Russian general proved the utility of terror. In 1733, at the onset of a foreign campaign, he announced that the first man to come down with homesickness would be buried alive. The punishment, carried out the very next day, prevented any more outbreaks.[8]

By the twentieth century, doctors had all but dismissed nostalgia as a disease. It was reclassified as a mental ailment and finally a social expression. Today, to quote the *Oxford English Dictionary*, the word refers to "regret or sorrowful longing for the conditions of a past age; regretful or wistful memory or recall of an earlier time." As it was transformed from the pathological to the emotional, nostalgia lost much of its connection to the physical world. Instead of a longing for a place, it became a longing for a time, or simply the longing itself. Commonly associated with childhood, modern nostalgia covets the irretrievable. Unlike a homeland, which can be revisited, childhood, once lived, is forever out of reach.

But there's another kind of nostalgia, one in which the object of desire was lost through willful action rather than inevitable expiration. Anthropologist Renato Rosaldo calls this "imperialist nostalgia": "where people mourn the passing of what they themselves have transformed." Tourism embodies this paradox, of course. Undiscovered places have great power, but once discovered, they lose it. Discovery anticipates loss.

Rosaldo continues: "Nostalgia is a particularly appropriate emotion to invoke in attempting to establish one's innocence and at the same time talk about what one has destroyed."[9] People do this all the time; it's not always as deliberate or sinister as it sounds. Who, for example, doesn't disparage tourists and the developments associated with them? Yet who doesn't play tourist sometimes? Recognizing our complicity in loss may not kill the longing, but it makes it easier to navigate, easier to move through. It may even lead to a change in the way we live so that we destroy less of what we love. I admit, though, that this idealism directed at the future is powerless to alter the past. If I dwell on the dam at Glen Canyon, it's because it's unavoidable; it came before my time. Thus I know I am innocent, and I hate the fact. Sometimes I envy the destroyers, for at least they could have seen the place.

I wonder: Is it possible to feel homesick for the Glen?

Until recently, I considered the canyonlands my true home, even though I have never lived there. Images of slickrock adorned my walls and haunted my dreams. Whenever I became obviously depressed, my mother suggested it was time for another trip. She was right. Exploring new canyons, I felt I was recapturing some of the enhanced awareness that must have characterized childhood. My energy, my optimism returned. Between these camping trips, I studied topographic maps, biding my time. I couldn't bear the thought of never going back.

What is it about this place? I could mention some of its natural features— its exposed rock, its arches and bridges, its island mountains and sunken oases. The fact that three great rivers (the Green, the Colorado, the San Juan) follow the path of paradox through the core of this high-country desert. To the uniqueness of this environment, add the rare qualities born of the relationship between *people* and place. Foremost is that of spaciousness. Southern Utah, with its combination of confines and expanses, canyons and mesas, affords a dual sense of distance and intimacy. There is mystery and disclosure: a visible part to every landscape, and the part always hidden—behind the intervening cliff, beyond the next bend, below the last mesa. Every outlook has possibilities. In the full glory of three dimensions, the canyon country makes the world feel big as few places do.

Accessory to this spaciousness is the sense—or illusion—of remoteness. Because the canyon country shelters so much space, it tends to conceal the presence of people and their marks. Land managers have a term for this: topographic screening. The canyon country has it in spades. Furthermore, it truly is a good distance (measured in miles and obstacles) from America's centers of population. Though this distance has effectively shrunk in the second half of the twentieth century with the improvement of highways and the urbanization of the interior West, remoteness remains— barely—one of the unifying characteristics of the country.

"Speaking as a tourist, I have always thought of it as a landscape where almost everyone else was, like myself, in transit: where no one really put down roots and was forever on the move," wrote the eminent geographer J. B. Jackson in 1960. "I have thought of it as a landscape where a special relationship—tenuous and fleeting but nonetheless real—prevailed between the enormous emptiness and the people who passed through it."[10]

In fact, some people have put down roots. Navajos probably wouldn't use that metaphor, but they have their own understanding of their long-term relationship with the southern edge of canyon country, now a part of their homeland. Southern Utes and Southern Paiutes have separate claims to large parts of the country. As for the Mormon settlers, they and their descendants have continuously inhabited the region's perimeters for more than a century now. They have stayed despite the odds: unlike the main body of Mormons in northern Utah, the slickrock pioneers failed to make the desert bloom. Indeed, judged against what Euro-Americans have made of most of the continent, the material accomplishments of the Mormons in southern Utah seem small. But rather than belittle these people and their labor, it should be possible to honor their communities while celebrating the obstinacy of the land.

Even today, at the close of the twentieth century, after the work of dams and roads, the canyon country retains some of its solitude. In 1996, *Car & Driver* hired a Geographic Information System specialist to find "The Loneliest Place in the Lower 48 States." Using the magazine's criteria—distance from settlement, distance from pavement—she came up with the exact coordinates: 37°24′49.5″ N, 111°16′47.03″ W. Translated, that's thirty miles southeast of Escalante, Utah. Predictably, the editors sent a team (two men equipped with a $37,000 Range Rover, a global positioning calculator, and a sense of humor) to attempt to drive there. They failed: the last four miles they had to walk.

This land repels as well as attracts. Over the twentieth century, however, the attraction has grown while the repulsion, the remoteness, has diminished—and with it something of the spirit of the country. A valuable outlook has become expendable with each step in accessibility: humility. The recognition that the land exists for its own reasons apart from people. The recognition that people belong in this slickrock desert, but only in small numbers.

Fortunately, due to environmental and legal constraints, the canyon country will never fill with residents (though certain towns like Moab will continue to grow). But it seems ready to fill another way—with visitors. At this point, the land's remoteness is less a characteristic than a choice. Wallace Stegner once wrote of "the special human mark, the special record of human passage. *It is simply the deliberate and chosen refusal to make any marks at all.*"[11] He wrote those words in defense of wilderness, but I think they also apply to the spirit of the canyon country. This "spirit" I speak of is not "timeless" or "natural" the way wilderness sometimes claims to be. I speak of what J. B. Jackson alluded to—that special *historical* relationship between people (visitors *and* residents) and terrestrial space. That, along with many nonhuman things in the canyon country, deserves our care.

Many people who know and love the canyonlands are terrified: the secret's out, the place is lost. At times, I'm terrified, too, but I try to temper my fear of "others" discovering my home state with this simple observation: in some way, they too must love this land. Then I try to forget that ugly cliché, "loving it to death," because even if it describes reality (and it does), it fails as a metaphor. Maybe this will sound sentimental, but I don't believe in too much love. I don't believe in love that destroys. If there's anything the world needs for its problems, it is greater, more expansive love.

Terry Tempest Williams has hinted that "the canyons of southern Utah are giving birth to a Coyote Clan—hundreds, maybe even thousands, of individuals who are quietly subversive on behalf of the land." Perhaps this is what T. H. Watkins means when he writes about his "baptism by discovery" in the wildlands of southern Utah; or Gary Nabhan and Caroline Wilson when they say, "A sense of discovery can still be kindled here, even though the canyon country was first 'discovered' by humans twelve thousand years ago." Or even Abbey: "Here you may yet find the elemental freedom to breathe deep of unpoisoned air, to experiment with solitude and stillness, to gaze through a hundred miles of untrammeled atmosphere, across redrock canyons, beyond blue mesas, toward the snow-covered peaks of the most distant mountains—to make the discovery of the self in its proud sufficiency which is not isolation but an irreplaceable part of the mystery of the whole."[12] My memory turns to the many friendly people I've met at campgrounds and scenic pull-outs in southern Utah, the look in their eyes, their exclamations: "This is unbelievable! This is fantastic!" I return their smiles. There is something about this country that invites awareness of the natural world and its sustaining kinship. Some people speak of the canyonlands as a "charismatic" landscape: it takes no effort to be awestruck, to fall in love. "Uh-huh," I say to my new friends, "there's something unique about this place." But, I want to add, it's not unique in isolation. Viewed with open eyes and an open heart, many, many landscapes may testify to the wonder of the world. It need not be the wild or the visually spectacular, someplace worthy of a fine-art print. It need not be faraway. It need not be here.

A few years ago, about the time I started this book, I realized, to my chagrin, that I knew more about a submerged canyon in southern Utah than my birthplace in northern Utah. Here was home, but I never took it seriously. Since that time, however, I've paid more attention to Utah Valley and have finally begun to recognize its sacredness. Now I ask, why didn't I fall in love with the world here? Did I take my valley for granted? Did I assume this place could not be lost?

"We need to give some time to the arts of cherishing the things we adore, before they simply vanish," writes William Kittredge. "Maybe it will be like learning a skill: how to live in paradise."[13]

The destruction of Glen Canyon is done; there's no way around it. And with so many *existing* places in danger, perhaps it's wasted energy to burn a candle for the Glen. Or maybe that's called vision. Sometimes it's hard to distinguish between useless mourning and productive grief. Personally, I worry more about the future of Lake Powell than Glen Canyon because the canyon can only get better. According to precedent, it will resurrect. In the recent geologic past (the last ten million years or so), a series of stupendous lava dams have plugged the Colorado River in Grand Canyon; each time, the river worked through and resumed its business of carrying silt to the sea. Glen Canyon Dam, too, is an aberrance. Time and gravity conspire against it. Someday, when the world is not much older, the song of the river will again echo between walls of sandstone. Wind and rain will uncover the classic desert varnish beneath the cheap white stain left by the reservoir. Flash floods, one at a time, will clear the glens of muck and debris. Cottonwoods will take root. Beavers will recolonize.

When? The Bureau of Reclamation gives the reservoir something like a half-millennium life expectancy. Or sometime in the new century, who knows, people may assist the river in defeating its obstacle. If it happens, I suspect it will be a public decision, not a fiat by a few environmentalists.

In the West, and also the East, aging and destructive dams are coming under intense new scrutiny. Removing dams—especially small ones—isn't crazy. The science is there. Increasingly, the political and moral will is there. The will for Americans to live differently with their history of environmental iniquities: expiating, not merely regretting the past. Many people say restoration is the call of the twenty-first century. Certain shackled rivers wait to prove them right.

However, the Colorado in Glen Canyon is probably not the place to start. Restoration is a relatively new science; it would be wisest to work up to a dam this size. Besides, the ecological benefits of draining Lake Powell are less obvious than, say, those of removing Flaming Gorge Dam. With Flaming Gorge (and minor Fontenelle Dam) gone, the *entire* Green River system would be more or less naturally regulated. It would be a true haven for native fish, a living river.

But the Green River and Flaming Gorge lack what they've always lacked compared to the Colorado in the Glen: human sentiment. People care about Glen Canyon like no other drowned place. At the same time, people care about Lake Powell like no other reservoir. If it were drained, we'd replace one group of mourners with another.

Through human or nonhuman agency, however it happens, the full restoration of Glen Canyon will take more than a lifetime—more than my lifetime, anyway. I'd like to say I'm above self-pity, but no. I cry for the river and I cry for what it might have taught me. That means, I suppose, I long for nostalgia. I mourn a missing possibility: something never realized, like a love affair that fell apart before it started. Left with speculations more than certainties, I can only think to tell a story.

It's 1930. There's a sixteen-year-old boy in Los Angeles, high school diploma in hand. He's free: Everett Ruess departs for a solo trip to Yosemite and the Monterey peninsula. In Carmel, he introduces himself to Edward Weston and spends a few days at the photographer's place. Everett wants to be an artist; he carries printmaking supplies in his fifty-pound pack. Penniless, happy, he plans to wander next year, too. Maybe Arizona. He's heard of Monument Valley. Eyes wide open, he watched the screen version of Zane Grey's *The Vanishing American*, filmed on location among the canyons and mesas.

With his parents' permission—how could they stop him?—Ruess walks and hitchhikes as far Kayenta, Arizona, where he calls on traders John and Louisa Wetherill, who give him information on routes and trails. This country is everything he hoped for. "Here I am at last on what was, ten years ago, the final frontier," Everett writes to a friend. He announces his intention to discover some prehistoric ruins in Monument Valley. "Don't laugh. Maybe you thought they were all discovered, but such is not the case. Most of the country is untouched." It's Navajo country. At first, Everett considers the "Navvies" filthy and dishonest. He isn't bashful, however, about using their hogans for shelter, or even firewood.[14]

Painting and exploring, he makes his way to the San Juan River in Utah with a newly bought burro. Everett calls him Everett, "to remind me of the kind of person I used to be." Just two months gone, the teenage vagabond feels different. He signs his letters with a "euphonic and distinctive" name,

Lan Rameau. After his correspondents in California gently mock his appellation, he changes it to Evert Rulan. The boy and the burro and a stray Navajo sheepdog called Curly go on to Canyon de Chelly, Grand Canyon, then Zion, then Grand Canyon again, where Evert runs into a Fox film crew shooting scenes for *The Rainbow Trail*, based on the Zane Grey novel. At the rim, he meets another adolescent on the loose. They talk, and Evert gives him his first good meal in a very long time. Whenever Evert runs out of supplies (every couple of weeks), he tries to find temporary work. "I make it a rule not to be concerned about filthy lucre until after I'm broke," he says. Usually something materializes, whether it's cutting hay, chopping wood, or loading watermelons. Evert hates to wire for money—it's during the Depression—but occasionally he must. He tries to placate Mom and Dad by showing them his budget:

Rent	nothing
Electricity	"
Gas for heat and cooking	"
Telephone	"
Retirement assessment	"
Savings	"
Running burro, oats, etc.	.25
Food	$10 to $20
Magazine, newspapers	nothing
Burro insurance	"
Doctor bills	"

"My whole life is roughly mapped out," Evert tells his only sibling, an older brother with a job. There will be "a year or two in the open, working hard on my art. Then I shall wish for city life again, and to see old friends if they still exist." He'll obtain a studio and exhibition space, earn some money. "Then I am going to lead a very civilized life, getting plenty of good music, having many new experiences in reading, and having social experience. I shall find new, worthwhile friends, meanwhile continuing with art, and perhaps poetry. After having lived intensely in the city for a while (it may not be in Hollywood), I feel that I must go to some foreign country." But ultimately, "before physical deterioration obtrudes, I shall go on some last wilderness trip, to a place I have known and loved. I shall not return."

His 1931 trip goes on for ten months. Evert hitchhikes home in time for Christmas and becomes Everett Ruess again. Only in name: his thoughts return immediately to the red rock canyons. Everett's father, a Unitarian minister with two Harvard degrees, thinks the boy should go to college. His mother and mentor, Stella, just tries to understand. By April, the teenager is gone.

Everett makes his way from the Salt River near Phoenix to Mesa Verde in Colorado. At times on this arduous seven-month trek, he feels purposeless, or maybe just lonely. His dog, Curly, has run away following an intemperate beating. Wanting for reading material, the boy asks his parents to mail him copies of *Magic Mountain* and *The Brothers Karamazov*. He wishes they could send a phonograph, too. To relieve his melancholia, Everett sometimes tries to play Brahms or Beethoven in his head. Usually, though, he needs only to reopen his eyes. "The country is fiercely, overpoweringly beautiful," he writes.

Ruess returns in the fall and enrolls at UCLA. "I had some terrific experiences in the wilderness since I wrote you last—overpowering, overwhelming," he tells a friend, trying to catch up. "But then I am always being overwhelmed. I require it to sustain life." As a student, Everett has a hard time with assignments, but he writes an essay for himself about the malevolence of work.

During the holiday break, Everett tramps around northern California, stopping to see the Weston family. When classes resume in January 1933, he can't take the routine. He earns three D's. "I'm glad it's over," Everett says with a tone of finality. "College was a valuable episode, but I didn't let it get a strangle hold on me." His parents aren't sure: they fear he's courting a nervous breakdown. They approve when Everett leaves for the Sierra; leaving always improves his spirits. "Time and the need of time have ceased entirely," he writes from the mountains. "A gentle, dreamy haze fills my soul, the rustling of the aspens lulls my sense, and the surpassing beauty and perfection of everything fills me with quiet joy and a deep pervading love for my world."

Everett can sense his life plan accelerating, condensing. In the fall, he moves to a "mean hovel" on Polk Street in San Francisco. He knocks on the door of Ansel Adams. They chat, trade prints. He makes friends with Maynard Dixon, another devotee of the Southwest, and his wife, the photographer Dorothea Lange. In the city, he also finds like-minded people his own age. Excited, Everett keeps late hours talking politics and philosophy. Whenever he can, he trades his work for tickets to the symphony or opera. As an afterthought, he wonders how to pay his rent. "I have been living a life of wild extravagance and utter penury, with an undercurrent of starvation and an overture of magnificent music," he boasts. There's also a girl.

Yet after half a year—time enough for a failed romance—Everett is ready to leave. "I have been having some interesting and valuable experiences here in San Francisco," he writes. "I cherish them, for I know that there will never be another period in my life like this." There's no question where Everett will go. His brother drives him as far as Kayenta and says goodbye in April 1934. Goodbye, welcome home. "Once more I am drunk with the lust of life and adventure and unbearable beauty," Everett writes from the red rock canyons. He's living his childhood dream. He writes his parents for a copy of *Don Quixote*. In letters to friends (not parents), Ruess recounts his adventures and near-death misadventures. He climbs a cliff, almost falls. Stings from a hive of bees leave his eyes swollen shut for three days straight. Yet another time, a wild bull charges him twice. "One way and another, I have been flirting pretty heavily with Death, the old clown," Everett remarks nonchalantly. "This time in my wanderings I have had more reckless self-confidence than ever before. I have gone my way regardless of everything but beauty." He calls beauty his god.

As he continues his journey—to Monument Valley, Rainbow Bridge, and beyond—he rants about "beauty that is inconceivable," yet his letters take on a world-weary tone. Everett senses his futility: "I am condemned to feel the withering fire of beauty pouring into me. I am condemned to the need of putting this fire outside myself and spreading it somewhere, somehow, and I am torn by the knowledge that what I have felt cannot be given to another." Though he constantly longs for "intelligent companionship," he's lost his faith in human empathy. He believes that "he who has looked long on naked beauty may never return to the world, and though he should try, he will find its occupation empty and vain, and human intercourse purposeless and futile. Alone and lost, he must die on the altar of beauty."

Now twenty, Everett has come to prefer the company of Indians—"childlike and simple and friendly." The affection is mutual but probably not for the same reasons. Decades later, an elderly Navajo man named Tahonnie will recall this encounter:

> We bedded the sheep down for the night, and the young man, known to us as Everett, entered our camp. We did not know him and we were all very afraid. He gave us no warning. . . . When he arrived, we were singing songs and he suddenly appeared across the fire from us. We stopped singing. We looked at him and at one

another. We thought he was crazy. He did not speak to us, only smiled and nodded his head. He talked to his dog and two [burros]. After a while, he sat down next to the fire. He pulled tobacco from his pouch and rolled cigarettes. He began to sing Anglo songs that we did not know. It was very funny, and he smiled at us.[15]

Henceforth, the Navajos in the area make reference to the "crazy but wonderful white boy." Truth be told, Everett feels almost at home among the Indians. At least he feels increasingly removed from his own culture, particularly its emphases on material wealth and security. He reserves his harshest words for the Indian traders, whom he characterizes as exploiters. The traders, meanwhile, believe correctly that Everett pushes his burros too hard. A reckless boy but likable. No matter how much he broods inside, he retains his outgoing, even brazenly affable demeanor. One acquaintance will remember him as a "strange kid" who loved the "Navajos and everybody, loved animals, burros, dogs, kids, and everything."

With his new burro, Cockleburr, Everett climbs Navajo Mountain, a sacred peak of the Navajo people. Looking north, he gains his first view of Glen Canyon and the canyonlands of Utah, "as rough and impenetrable a territory as I have ever seen. Thousands of domes and towers of sandstone lift their rounded pink tops from blue and purple shadows. To the east, great canyons seam the desert, cutting vermilion gashes through the gray-green of the sage-topped mesas." He decides he must go there.

After a working stint, a trip to the Hopi Mesas, and a return visit to Grand Canyon, Everett wanders north into Utah, stopping at Bryce Canyon. In typical fashion, he makes himself known to the park ranger, a local man, and spends a few days at his house in Tropic with his nine children. It feels great to be part of a family again. Everett goes to church and a community dance. It's Utah, so people ask him about his religion. "Pantheistic hedonist," he replies, laughingly. He's having great fun. "If I had stayed any longer I would have fallen in love with a Mormon girl," he confides to his brother, "but I think it's a good thing I didn't. I've become a little too different from most of the rest of the world." He takes his two burros (the new one, Chocolate, has been renamed Chocolatero) eastward to Escalante. He meets practically the whole town, including a few visiting Navajos who had crossed Glen Canyon to trade. Everett has a meal with them; he converses, best as he can, in their language. Later, he shoots the breeze with some local boys. They hunt for arrowheads (Everett's childhood passion) and go to a picture show: *Death Takes a Holiday*.

It would be easy to stay here too, but Everett has other intentions. On a crisp November morning, with the cottonwoods dropping gold, he bids farewell to his new friends and heads southeast, where no one lives. Meanwhile, going a different direction, the postman carries two upbeat letters to Ruess's family in California. He says he won't see another post office for a month, maybe two.

As to when I shall visit civilization, it will not be soon, I think. I have not tired of the wilderness; rather I enjoy its beauty and the vagrant life I lead, more keenly all the time. I prefer the saddle to the streetcar and star-sprinkled sky to a roof, the obscure and difficult trail, leading into the unknown, to any paved highway, and the deep peace of the wild to the discontent bred by cities. Do you blame me then for staying here, where I feel that I belong and am one with the world around me?

Ruess travels the old Hole in the Rock road (just another trail to him) about fifty miles, at which point the roadbed—the bench between the Straight Cliffs and the canyons of the Escalante—shrinks and starts to break apart. Here the wanderer meets two shepherds with whom he stays two nights, telling jokes, talking geography. He likes the sound of the canyons nearby. So, after one more goodbye, he enters the earth by way of an obscure stock trail.

As he moves slowly downstream, toward the Escalante River, his passageway moves from perfection to something more. A rivulet flows beneath a canopy of branches, then breaks away in bends that undercut the slickrock so deeply that the vaulting walls conceal the sky. A natural window connects a pair of these meanders with the beauty of emptiness. When Everett encounters paintings by a long-vanished people, white on red, he senses kindred spirits. He adds his mark to the panel. Placing his knife to the canyon's skin, he cuts four letters—his new name, his last word.

Three months later, having heard nothing through the mail, Everett's parents send an anxious note to the postmaster in Escalante. She alerts her husband, a county commissioner, who organizes a search committee. Everyone in town expresses concern for the friendly stranger from California. In early March, searchers enter Davis Gulch and find Everett's burros enclosed in a brush fence (constructed by ranchers, who use the canyon for spring pasture). Downstream, the men find size nine bootprints and an inscription, "NEMO 1934," but no sign of the boy or his belongings—his bedroll, food, art equipment, and diary. After combing the canyon, and checking the country above, the volunteers return to Escalante discouraged. A second search, conducted soon after, also ends in failure. Undaunted, the county commissioner enlists the financial aid of the Associated Civic Clubs of Southern Utah. "*No one* gets lost in southern Utah," its president declares. The third time around, searchers find no new clues but one more inscription.

Nemo: Latin for "no one." Stella Ruess thinks it may refer to a story in the *Odyssey*. Later, her husband decides it must come from Jules Verne's *Twenty Thousand Leagues under the Sea,* a book Everett read several times. The protagonist, Captain Nemo, abandons the confusion of the world in favor of solitude and freedom beneath the waves.

In 1935, the *Salt Lake Tribune* sponsors an expedition to northeastern Arizona to investigate the theory that Everett crossed the river to join some Navajo friends. John Wetherill doesn't believe it for a minute; if any white boy were living among the Indians, he'd know about it. Lacking for leads, the *Tribune*'s reporter, John Upton Terrell, seeks out a medicine man, Natani, and one of his wives, a noted seer (whose name the reporter neglects to record). Together the Navajos perform a ceremony. As soon as their sing begins, rain begins to fall. Afterward, under a clearing night sky, Terrell's guide, an Anglo, interprets:

[Medicine man]: Go to the forks of the rivers.
[Interpreter]: He lives there?
[Medicine man]: He was there. Close by he made a camp. You will find the fire.
[Interpreter]: Have you seen him? (He meant in a vision.)
[Medicine man]: He has gone away from there.
[Interpreter]: He's dead.
[Medicine man]: He has gone away and does not mean to come back. . . .
[Seer]: He (Ruess) has given himself to our gods. He has taken us in his arms and wished to come among us.
[Interpreter]: Does she say he came into the Navajo country?
[Medicine man]: She says he did not. He went away there where he camped.[16]

Lake Powell visitors walk through Everett Ruess's place of disappearance, 1967. The reservoir now extends to the base of the natural window. (Photograph by Mel Davis.)

Later, Terrell meets a Navajo–Paiute named Dougeye, who says he met Everett in Escalante last fall. Terrell offers him money to lead the way to Davis Gulch. Dougeye accepts, reluctantly; like most Navajos, he fears the dead, even the possibly dead. Dougeye proves to be an excellent guide, however. He knows where to cross the San Juan River and the Colorado, and he knows the location of springs. In Glen Canyon, he shows Terrell a petroglyph panel that was chalked by an archaeologist. "Grave hunter," he says. "Get lost, too. We find three days. Not lost. Crazy."

The party eventually reaches the Escalante River, then Davis Gulch, where the ashes from Ruess's fire remain. Dougeye examines the area and concludes, "White boy come in, not go out." Terrell concludes that "Everett Ruess was murdered in the vicinity of Davis canyon. His valuable outfit was stolen. He never reached the Colorado river."[17]

As late as 1938, however, Stella and Christopher Ruess believe that Everett, or whatever he may call himself, still exists in the Southwest, somewhere. Through the grapevine, they hear of several brown-haired, young, artistic types living in small towns in southeastern Utah and southwestern Colorado. On a long shot, the Ruesses mail these men news clippings about Everett, and a confidential letter:

> We are not interested in urging him to come home, unless he should so desire. We are not interested in telling the world he is found. We feel that he has a right to live his own life to his own ends in his own individual way. He is no doubt getting in his experiences more education for his future work. He may become a nature writer like Thoreau or Burroughs, illustrating his own writings. . . . If Everett so prefers, we could all meet at some agreed place in Colorado or Utah—Everett may not want to come here, but prefer to maintain his new identity there. We have much to tell him and he to tell us. You may show him this letter if you know him and if you are not he. Tell him we often see him in our dreams.[18]

The leads prove false. In 1948, Stella Ruess, age sixty-eight, treks to Davis Gulch with a bouquet of wildflowers—an act of acceptance, a kind of goodbye.

By this time, Everett, like the subject of any good mystery, has attracted attention. A portion of the wanderer's correspondence has been serialized and later reprinted as a booklet. It's superseded in 1983 by a complete edition of the letters, accompanied by a discussion of various theories: murder by cattle rustlers or renegade Navajos; a fall from a cliff; a planned disappearance; suicide; drowning; anemia. All conjecture—nothing conclusive has been found, nothing proved. Frankly, people prefer it that way. Ruess is now a canyon country cult figure. His admirers include Wallace Stegner and that other regional cult figure, Edward Abbey. One academic has called Everett Ruess "a preeminent performance artist" whose last word "is by a certain standard the most successful bit of nature writing ever attempted by an American. The Word can come no closer to the utterly wild." Fittingly, the Southern Utah Wilderness Alliance adopted one of Ruess's block prints for its logo—a silhouette of two burros and a man on the trail.[19]

The world of Ruess, like Ruess himself, is lost. His erstwhile home, Los Angeles, has been dedicated to development; his destination, Davis Gulch, has been flooded by Lake Powell. Today in the West, when changes like these seem commonplace, people could use Ruess's inspiration—if not his example.

Everett Ruess went to wild places for no other reason but to be there. He shunned consumerism, sought nothing but beauty.

From a different perspective, however, Ruess was one more explorer in search of paradise. A visitor who preferred romance over history; there over here; leaving over staying.

Those are adolescent preferences, and for that it's easy to excuse Everett. If the wanderer had stayed a while longer in the world, he might have changed. That, of course, would have been our loss, for we wouldn't have his story. Ruess is especially compelling because he took a familiar narrative (the youth who travels far for wisdom) to a remote, unfamiliar conclusion. This is the one who never came back. His story fades away without family or home, without a past or a certain future. That's why, for all his vital beauty, Everett Ruess makes a poor role model for people in southern Utah. If the canyon country of the future means to be sane, its visitors and inhabitants need a story—or rather, diverse, connected stories—in which they don't have to leave home to find sacred ground, a story in which they never have to forsake the world to become one with it.

Nevertheless, Everett Ruess will always be worth remembering for the love that burned through his hubris. He possessed an inspiring sense of wonder, that rare and most sane ability to see beauty in everything and everybody. When I remember Everett, I think about the boy who tried to learn Navajo, who laughed and flirted with Mormons he barely knew. Then I think about the boy who could have been me who surrendered to the canyons.

Beneath the slack surface of the Davis Gulch inlet, the flooded home of NEMO, water flows. Slowly. The submarine current must stratify according to density. But at last, in the turbid darkness, the creek unites with the sunken Escalante. From here, like everywhere, the water knows the way. Weeks, even months, may pass, but the water will find the Colorado's drift; it will find the dam, where, after falling through a turbine, it will reenter the light and reflect the red walls of the Glen. This happens every day. The reservoir changes. The river moves.

AN OUTLINE HISTORY OF GLEN CANYON
BEFORE THE DAM

As near as anyone can tell, the Glen Canyon region has been continuously occupied for the last nine thousand years. Most centuries have been pretty quiet, however. The earliest peoples, the Archaic, were hunter-gatherers who used the country in small, highly mobile groups. It wasn't until near the beginning of the Christian calendar that the Archaic people north of the Colorado River turned to farming. South of the river, meanwhile, the ancestors of the Anasazi people made this transition centuries before, during the Basketmaker II period.

Archaeologists divide Anasazi history into five cultural periods: Basketmaker II (1200 B.C. to A.D. 500), Basketmaker III (A.D. 500–750), Pueblo I (A.D. 750–900), Pueblo II (A.D. 900–1150), and Pueblo III (A.D. 1150–1350). The famous cliff ruins of Mesa Verde date from the last period, the twilight of the Anasazi. It was during the period of greatest florescence, Pueblo II, that Glen Canyon was colonized. For whatever reasons, hundreds of "backwoods Anasazi" migrated to this hinterland from the main population centers to the south and east. Apparently the canyon was a transition zone between the cultural influences of the Mesa Verde region in present-day Colorado and the Kayenta region in present-day Arizona. North of the river, the Anasazi presence ended altogether, with the exception of the Escalante River and the Kaiparowits Plateau. The northland belonged to the Fremont people, whose history remains dim. It seems they preceded the Anasazi in their occupation of the Glen Canyon region and left before the Anasazi cleared out around 1300.

There are no great apartment-house ruins in the Glen Canyon region, but there is ubiquitous evidence of small-scale farming. Probably the most common structural relic is the storage bin—a rock-and-mortar cubbyhole for dried corn. In addition to maize, the Anasazi planted squash and beans. They supplemented their crop diet with animals such as deer and rabbits, and plants such as the prickly pear cactus, which they domesticated. In terms of agriculture, the Pueblo II benefitted from their place in climatic history. Centuries of aggradation (the accumulation of sediment) had turned the canyons into planter boxes, a condition that lasted until the twelfth century, when a cycle of drought and degradation—gully erosion—began. But even before, it should be said, this land was never lush. "In Pueblo II time the Anasazi actually specialized in gardening in 'marginal' areas," explains Jesse D. Jennings, director of the Glen Canyon Salvage Project, and "by understanding water and its conservation and use (and the idiosyncrasies of their crops), extended their domain into areas where neither then nor now is gardening truly feasible."[1]

Some of the specializations were truly grand. At the Little Rincon (an abandoned meander) in upper Glen Canyon, some Pueblo III overachievers built a dam in a small, steep wash. This masonry-lined catch basin filled with springwater, which emptied through an adjustable gate into a slab-lined tunnel and then into a canal. Farther down the canyon, at Beaver Creek, archaeologists uncovered a system of irrigation ditches lined with river cobbles.

Only a few southern tributaries—Moqui Canyon, Lake Canyon, and Navajo Creek in particular—bear witness to long-term, intensive agriculture, but the Anasazi roamed throughout the region. They created an extensive trail system over the slickrock, as indicated by the ubiquitous hand- and footholds on the walls of Glen Canyon. It seems the farming skills of these people were exceeded only by their rock-climbing prowess. Following some of these trails, twentieth-century daredevils have found Anasazi ruins and rock art in unlikely places. At a remote site in a gloomy slot canyon, David Roberts wrote, "The glorious logic of Chaco Canyon or Mesa Verde was utterly absent here. One had the sense not of the proud inheritors of a bold civilization, but of furtive hermits, marginal mystics, outlaws and rebels."[2]

Mystics or not, these people knew when to leave. They evacuated Glen Canyon about the same time their parent populations left the Colorado Plateau for regions south. A great decades-long drought precipitated the exodus, but there may have been other factors, such as war. No one knows for sure.

The next four centuries of Glen Canyon's history are poorly understood. Human activity seems to have been limited to hunting and gathering. Bands of Utes claimed the country north of the Glen, while Southern

Paiutes claimed the south. The Hopis, probable descendants of the Anasazi, paid ceremonial visits to the Navajo Mountain region just south of the canyon. As for the Navajos, they migrated to the Anasazi homeland around the fourteenth or fifteenth century, but stayed west and south of the Glen Canyon region until the 1800s. The Navajo economy had two foci: agriculture learned from the Pueblo peoples, and livestock bred from Spanish stock.

Though the Spanish had entered New Mexico by 1600, they didn't get to southern Utah until much later. The first well-orchestrated *entrada* occurred in 1776, when Fray Francisco Atanasio Domínguez and Fray Silvestre Vélez de Escalante and eight others went looking for a route from Santa Fe to the mission in Monterey, California. With the help of many different native guides, these Catholic fathers made their way up the western slope of the Rockies, crossed the Green River in eastern Utah, and rested in Utah Valley at the foot of the Wasatch Mountains, where they preached to a friendly audience of Utes. Afterward, the party turned south, following the general route of modern I–15. A little north of present-day Cedar City, Utah, the fathers decided to forgo California. It was October, cold and snowy, and their food was low. Not everyone in the group supported the decision, however, so they cast lots. Fortune—or God—agreed with the fathers: it was time to go home. Continuing south, the group dropped from the Great Basin to the low desert of southwestern Utah, where Paiutes told them of a river crossing to the east.

Getting to the Colorado River, however, was anything but easy. Crossing Arizona north of the Grand Canyon, the group repeatedly became lost in the jumble of canyons and mesas. The weather was bad, then the food ran out, forcing the men to kill a horse. Half-starved, they reached the mouth of the Paria River on October 26. Here the Colorado River exited Glen Canyon and flowed in the open for a few hundred yards before dropping into Marble Canyon. It was a perfect place for a ford—except the water was wide, swift, and cold. When the two best swimmers barely got across with their lives, Domínguez and Escalante went to Plan B: they tried to build a boat. It didn't work. The fathers looked glumly around them—the Vermillion Cliffs on one side, the Echo Cliffs on the other. They named the place Salsipuedes—"get out if you can." That night they ate horse again.

After extensive looking and worrying, they devised a route by which they could scale the 1,700-foot cliffs. Once on top, they set out in search of a better ford. One night they camped in the canyon of Wahweap Creek directly below present-day Wahweap Marina on Lake Powell. After navigating across several more arroyos, the group found a way to the river down a relatively gentle slickrock slope (for the animals, the men carved steps). At the bottom, they found a wide, shallow river and crossed with ease at five in the afternoon of November 7, their voices and muskets raised high in praise for God. On the south side of the river, they picked up an Indian trail and eventually found their way to the Hopi Mesas, where they obtained food. From here to Santa Fe, the road was familiar and easy.

In his journal/report submitted to the King of Spain, Fray Escalante gave a nicely detailed account of the five-month journey and an appraisal of Glen Canyon: "In all that we saw around here no settlement can be established along [the river's] banks, nor can one go one good day's march downstream or upstream along either side with the hope of [the river's] waters being of service to the people and horse herd, because, besides the terrain being bad, the river flows through a very deep gorge. Everything else adjacent to the ford consists of very tall cliffs and precipices."[3]

Domínguez and Escalante had named the ford La Purísima Concepción de la Virgen Santísima; it would later be known as El Vado de los Padres and finally its English equivalent, the Crossing of the Fathers. Though very well known to native peoples of the region, it represented to the Spanish the first crossing of the canyons of the Colorado River (nearly six hundred miles in all, from Moab to Lake Mead). Between 1776 and 1848, the ford was used occasionally as part of a caravan route from New Mexico to California, both of which became Mexican territory in 1821. At that point, the crossing was superseded by the Old Spanish Trail, which avoided the Glen Canyon region altogether by crossing the Colorado at present-day Moab, Utah, and the Green at present-day Green River, Utah. The only people with reason to actually enter the canyons were fur trappers, though the extent of this enterprise remains hazy. French trapper Denis Julien carved his inscription in Cataract Canyon with the date 1836.

Despite these preliminary *entradas*, Glen Canyon was officially "Unknown" on American maps when Mexico ceded the Southwest to the United States in 1848. It took a while for the government to fill in the blank spot. Lieutenant Joseph C. Ives poked around the lower Grand Canyon in 1858, and Captain John Macomb poked around the upper Colorado River in Utah in 1859, but the canyon system as a whole was not understood until John Wesley Powell led a hardscrabble group of nine strangers down the Green and Colorado in 1869. Considering the rumors of waterfalls and impassable rapids, not a few believed Powell was floating to his death. He tried his best: his round-bottomed boats were woefully inadequate for a shallow, rocky river; one crashed and sunk a few weeks into the trip; the other three sprung leaks. The men were forced to portage most rapids—exhausting, time-consuming work.

After the punishment of Cataract Canyon, Powell and his men took delight in the next 170 miles: the Glen, the longest stretch of calm water they would encounter. They spent two whole days relaxing at an alcove they called Music Temple. But the calm preceded the storm: after Glen Canyon, Powell and his edgy, malnourished men faced the Grand Canyon. Tempers grew sour; the scant supply of flour turned moldy. Three men opted to climb out rather than continue. They made it to the top only to be killed by Southern Paiutes.

When the remaining party exited the Grand Canyon, they were weary, famished, and famous. Capitalizing on the notoriety, Powell worked to secure funding for a second expedition. Constant trouble on the 1869 trip had left precious little time for science. The second time around, in 1872, things went more smoothly. Powell even left the trip twice to conduct other business. In Glen Canyon, the party cached a boat near the mouth of the Dirty Devil River to be used at the end of a future reconnaissance of the territory around the Unknown Mountains (later named the Henrys, after Joseph Henry, director of the Smithsonian Institution, a sponsor of the expedition). Powell's men also stopped at Crossing of the Fathers, where Jacob Hamblin, a Mormon scout, had sent two packers with supplies. The river expedition ended for the year a few days later at the mouth of the Paria River, where another remarkable Mormon, John D. Lee, had settled with two of his wives.

Lee and Hamblin figured prominently in the Mormon colonization of southwestern Utah. Today, Lee is most famous as a participant in the Mountain Meadows Massacre, while Hamblin is most famous as a peacemaker. This "buckskin apostle" forded Glen Canyon many times at the Crossing of the Fathers to proselytize, trade, and negotiate with Navajos. In the mid-1800s, the time when Mormons expanded south and east, the Navajos expanded north and west. The result was friction and occasional violence. The town of Kanab, the base of operations for the Powell Survey, had to be evacuated after raids by Navajos. Both sides lost lives. Finally, in 1870, Hamblin and Powell brokered a peace treaty at Fort Defiance, Arizona. This cleared the way for the Mormons to settle the headwaters of the Little Colorado River. Lee's Ferry opened for business in 1873 and remained the all-important link between southwestern Utah and northern Arizona for nearly six decades.

Strangely, when the Mormons decided to colonize the San Juan country in southeastern Utah in the late 1870s, the vanguard group didn't use Lee's Ferry. It opted instead to cross Glen Canyon right in the middle at an ad hoc crossing called Hole in the Rock. The name fairly well described the precipitous descent to the river, beyond which was the roughest country anyone had ever seen. A trip supposed to last weeks dragged on for six months as the party picked and blasted a road that ended at a townsite they called Bluff. For roughly the next year, the Hole in the Rock Trail remained the town's access to the outside world. Wagons went up as well as down until a better crossing was located at Halls Creek. While the Hole in the Rock expedition is justly celebrated as a heroic epic in pioneering, it's right to remember, as Gary Topping says, that it was also "one of the most unnecessary and ill-advised epics in American history."[4]

After the Mormons claimed the San Juan country, they almost lost it. Fierce resource competition came from two sides: Navajo and Paiute graziers and out-of-state cattle barons. "Few range regions can boast a more varied or more exciting past," writes historian Charles Peterson.[5] Hoping to stay alive, the town of Bluff converted from an agricultural to a livestock economy in 1886 with the formation of the Bluff Pool. The Pool grazed cattle in the drainages of White Canyon and Lake Canyon, both of which empty into Glen Canyon. Al Scorup, an elected member of the National Cowboy Hall of Fame, later assumed control of this range. At his business peak in the early twentieth century, he presided over some two million acres: the vast triangle between the Colorado, the San Juan, and the Abajo Mountains. Meanwhile, north of Glen Canyon, cattlemen from Escalante and Boulder sent thousands of animals into the canyons of the Escalante River.

Glen Canyon had its share of outlaws and rustlers, too, who employed various river fords. Their favorite was Dandy Crossing, named by prospector Cass Hite in 1883. On a hint from Hashkeneinii, a Navajo headman, Hite discovered that the bars of the Colorado River contained significant—if exceedingly fine-grained—deposits of gold. In a matter of months, after the news spread, Hite had company.

The first phase of the Glen Canyon "gold rush" lasted about seven years. Thereafter, attention shifted from the Colorado River to the San Juan River. In 1892, the United States axed off a portion of the Navajo Reservation for the sake of the prospectors in the so-called Bluff excitement. Most of the mining activity took place between the mouth of Grand Gulch and the Big Bend of the San Juan, all of which now lies beneath Lake Powell.

Perhaps a thousand men—apparently no women—participated in both phases of the mini-boom. To reach their claims, they used scows, rafts, flat-bottomed boats, skiffs, rowboats, paddlewheelers, and sailboats. Eventually, the one-man gasoline powerboat became the favored means of transportation. As for mining technology, people tried everything: panning, sluicing, hydraulic mining, dredging. In Glen Canyon, the biggest obstacle was getting water onto the land. The river fell at such a low gradient that most of the gold-bearing bars lay nearly flat; gravity-powered water diversions seldom worked. Water wheels were used to good effect at Good Hope Bar and Olympia Bar, but the simplest invention proved to be the best: a hand-operated sluice box equipped with fine carpet to catch placer gold. "The energy and ingenuity the prospectors displayed is astonishing," wrote Jesse D. Jennings.

> Everywhere one sees evidence of their presence; initials in an Indian ruin far up canyon, abandoned equipment amid ragged pits on a gravel bar, a crumbling shack or deep cut steps slanting up the cliffs from a gravel terrace all testify of their detailed search as well as their blasted hopes. The distances from supply bases, the lack of local population, and the roughness of the country itself—all made the herculean but hitherto unsung efforts of these men the more remarkable.[6]

But these men were thinking small. No one was bold enough (or rich enough, or dumb enough) to attempt the comprehensive development of the canyon's mineral resources—no one, that is, until Robert Brewster Stanton. Considering his résumé, it all made sense. Stanton first visited Glen Canyon in 1889 as the lead engineer in a railroad survey. It's hard to believe today, but the Denver, Colorado Canyon & Pacific Railroad Company meant to do exactly what its name implied: build a railroad from the Rockies to the sea via the canyons of the Colorado River. The initial survey was, however, an unqualified disaster. Three boats sank in Cataract Canyon; three men, including the company president, drowned in Marble Canyon. Solemn but determined, Stanton started over, this time with better equipment—including life jackets. Wishing to avoid Cataract Canyon, he transported his boats overland from Green River, Utah, to Dandy Crossing, where he met Cass Hite and inspected the various gold mining operations.[7]

The second time around, the survey went almost smoothly, and Stanton came away utterly convinced of the feasibility of the railroad. He even read a paper to that effect before the American Society of Civil Engineers. A tougher audience was his investors; they lost interest. But Stanton didn't need the railroad as an excuse to return to the Colorado River. He had seen enough gold mining in Glen Canyon to know he could do it better.

Touting the canyon as "nature's sluice box," Stanton secured good funding for a venture he called the Hoskaninni Company. In 1898, he sent crews to stake Glen Canyon from end to end, wrapping around preexisting claims if need be. With one continuous 170-mile claim, Stanton would face less paperwork for his grand idea: recovering all of the river's gold with a long line of massive dredges. First he needed a successful trial run. For the initial dredge, Stanton chose a location about forty miles downstream from Hite, where the river was smooth and straight. Construction began in late 1899, with a workforce of seventy-five men, including fifteen carpenters. It took sixteen twenty-horse teams to haul the parts from Green River, Utah, the nearest railhead. The supply train followed a new road built between Mount Pennell and Mount Hillers of the Henry Mountains. The 180-ton double-decker dredge cost at least a hundred thousand dollars, perhaps even double that.

Dredging began in March 1901. A month later, Stanton reported a net profit of thirty dollars. To his dismay, most of the placer gold left the dredge with the waste water. The ore was simply too fine. After eight or nine months of negligible returns, the operation shut down. The Hoskaninni Company went bankrupt. Though the dredge later sold for $1,100, it never ran again. It remained beached at Mile 121.5 until the reservoir submerged it.[8]

Where there's one fool, there are bound to be more. A few years after Stanton, one Charles H. Spencer rustled up enough money for another big gold operation, this one based at Lee's Ferry. Spencer made one unsuccessful attempt at dredging a gravel bar but saved his greatest effort for recovering gold from the Chinle formation, a soft shale located at the base of the sandstone cliffs. He and his underpaid crew installed high-powered hoses and an amalgamator, both of which required coal power. Unfortunately, the nearest available coal deposit was in Warm Creek, twenty-eight miles upstream. To get to the canyon, Spencer paid for the construction of a switchback mule trail up the cliffs that Domínguez and Escalante had named Salsipuedes. Hoping to improve transportation even further, his company bought, disassembled, transported, then reassembled a three-thousand-dollar paddlewheel steamboat. At ninety-two feet, the *Charles H. Spencer* was the second largest craft ever to float in Glen Canyon. Like the even larger Stanton Dredge, its service was short: five trips in all. It drew too much water and used too much of the fuel it was supposed to be transporting. More to the point, the coal was not needed, for the amalgamating process failed to recover the microscopic gold particles. By 1912, Spencer had lost too much of other people's money, and he left.[9]

About the time the mining era ended, the era of exploration-as-leisure began. The early highpoint came in 1909 with the discovery of Rainbow Bridge in a side canyon of Glen Canyon. Teddy Roosevelt, Zane Grey, and Charles Bernheimer helped popularize the bridge through articles and books. Glen Canyon, too, was getting more exposure. Frederick Dellenbaugh, the youngest member of the second Powell expedition, published *The Romance of the Colorado River* in 1902 and *A Canyon Voyage* in 1908. Brothers and partners-in-photography Ellsworth and Emery Kolb replicated Powell's river run in 1911 and published *Through the Grand Canyon from Wyoming to Mexico* (1914). Julius Stone, president of the failed Hoskaninni Company, floated down the river in 1909 for pleasure and eventually wrote *Canyon Country: The Romance of a Drop of Water and a Grain of Sand* (1932). Charles Eddy carried a pet bear cub on his boat; he described his trip in *The World's Most Dangerous River* (1929). By the 1920s, these and other writings created enough interest that local guide David Dexter Rust was receiving a couple of requests per year for trips down Glen Canyon. It was in the 1940s, however, that Norman Nevills managed first to make a full-time business out of river running. For navigation, Nevills had the luxury of using detailed U.S. Geological Survey river maps, the result of extensive surveying in 1921–22.[10]

In the 1950s, uranium prospectors floated and flew all over Glen Canyon. Despite hundreds of claims, no major mines resulted. At the mouth of White Canyon, however, a corporate-funded uranium mill went up. The adjacent Hite ferry, built by Arthur Chaffin in 1946, experienced a sharp increase in traffic. It never really let up. When uranium fever subsided in the late 1950s, miners were almost immediately replaced by private and commercial river runners, who arrived *en masse* during the construction of Glen Canyon Dam (1956–63).

Recreationists shared the river with members of the Glen Canyon Salvage Project, who raced to document the canyon's cultural and biological resources. The University of Utah, one of the participating institutions, subcontracted the historical work to a young professor, C. Gregory Crampton. He received a pittance of twenty-five thousand dollars for supplies and transportation, and absolutely nothing for salary. He went to the river for the love of it and persuaded some students to accompany him as volunteers. Unlike the main archaeological component of the salvage project, Crampton and company finished their job—that is, they scratched the surface everywhere—before the deadline of water arrived. In four historical sourcebooks, Crampton documented sites of mining claims, stock trails, rock inscriptions, and all the rest. Few stretches of river in the West have ever received such detailed historical work, and few deserved it as much. Glen Canyon had more history than all of the other canyons of the Colorado River put together. In the Bureau of Reclamation's own magazine, Crampton published an outline history, which concluded that "far from being an isolated region remote from the currents of human activity, Glen Canyon has been the very center of a historical panorama including Spanish Padres, Mormon scouts, Government explorers, prospectors, outlaws, trappers, and tourists."[11]

But, of course, Glen Canyon itself always *was* isolated and remote. That's the contradiction that makes its history so intriguing—a periphery that acted like a center.

ACKNOWLEDGMENTS

First and foremost: Thank God for Mom and Dad! Without really knowing what I was up to, they always gave support—financial and otherwise. Credit also goes to friends and siblings, especially Lin and Rachel, for their inspiration and encouragement.

At Utah State University, my blessings to the Honors Program; the College of Humanities, Arts and Social Sciences; the History Department, including Carolyn and Sally; Anne, Barb, Clyde, David, Ona, and everyone else at the *Western Historical Quarterly;* and four fine professors: Mark Brunson, Tom Lyon, Ross Peterson, Jack Schmidt.

While researching, I enjoyed the hospitality of Roxanne and Nolan Clark, Shawna and Virgil Clark, Karen and David Davidson, and Linda and Jim Kindred.

Hats off to archivists and librarians everywhere, particularly the dedicated, underpaid staff of the Utah State Historical Society, my one-time second home. At the Bureau of Reclamation, Ginger Reeve radiated helpfulness and cheer. Kudos to Gary Topping, author of his own Glen Canyon book, for his uncommon generosity with his files.

Love to Vijaya for her tea and conversation, remedies for the loneliness of writing.

In 1997, after a winter of words, I made a river run with the Four Corners School of Outdoor Education. My appreciation to the school, the New Lands Foundation, and the Southern Utah Wilderness Alliance for sponsoring this enlivening trip.

For their comments on individual chapters, thanks to Tom Alexander, Dan Flores, Ed Geary, Mark Harvey, Jay Haymond, Hal Rothman, and my splendid family. David Sewell improved the final product. Nonetheless, the flaws and excesses (and virtues?) are mine. If I were doing it again, I'd do it differently, because, in fact, writing this book changed me.

NOTES

PREFACE

1. Jean Duffy, "The Land That Was Found Too Late," *Salt Lake Tribune Home Magazine,* 17 March 1963.

2. John McPhee, *Encounters with the Archdruid* (New York: Farrar, Straus and Giroux, 1971), 158–59.

3. Abbey quoted in Christopher Manes, *Green Rage: Radical Environmentalism and the Unmaking of Civilization* (Boston: Little, Brown and Company, 1991), 6. For more on environmentalists and the dam, see Charles Bowden, *Blue Desert* (Tucson: University of Arizona Press, 1986), 87–98; and Katrine E. Barber, "Wisecracking Glen Canyon Dam: Revisioning Environmentalist Mythology," in *Change in the American West: Exploring the Human Dimension,* ed. Stephen Tchud (Reno: University of Nevada Press, 1996), 127–43.

The two most powerful books about Glen Canyon remain Edward Abbey, *Desert Solitaire: A Season in the Wilderness* (New York: McGraw-Hill, 1968), 151–95; and Eliot Porter, *The Place No One Knew: Glen Canyon on the Colorado* (San Francisco: Sierra Club, 1963; rev. ed., Salt Lake City: Gibbs Smith, 1988). Other titles from the canon include Edward Abbey, *Beyond the Wall: Essays from the Outside* (New York: Holt, Rinehart and Winston, 1984), 95–103; F. A. Barnes, *Canyon Country Arches and Bridges* (Moab, Utah: Canyon Country Publications, 1987), 258–61, 404–5; Bruce Berger, *There Was a River* (Tucson: University of Arizona Press, 1994); David Brower et al., "Remember These Things Lost," in *Time and the River Flowing: Grand Canyon,* by François Leydet (San Francisco: Sierra Club, 1964), 157–75; C. Gregory Crampton, *Ghosts of Glen Canyon: History beneath Lake Powell,* rev. ed. (Salt Lake City: Cricket Productions, 1994); Charles Eggert, "Forbidden Passage," *Sierra Club Bulletin* 43 (November 1958): 44–52; Colin Fletcher, *River: One Man's Journey down the Colorado, Source to Sea* (New York: Alfred A. Knopf, 1997): 252–58; Frank L. Griffin, Jr., "Visit to a Drowning Canyon," *Audubon* 68 (January-February 1966): 27–32; Steven Hannon, *Glen Canyon: A Novel* (Denver: Kokopelli Books, 1997); Philip Hyde, *A Glen Canyon Portfolio* (Flagstaff, Ariz.: Northland Press, 1979); idem, "A Lament for Glen Canyon," *Living Wilderness* 44 (September 1980): 21–23; Eleanor Inskip, ed., *The Colorado River through Glen Canyon before Lake Powell: Historic Photo Journal, 1872 to 1964* (Moab, Utah: Inskip Ink, 1995); Bruce M. Kilgore, "Silent

River," *Sierra Club Bulletin* 48 (April–May 1963): 6–7; Gary Ladd, *Lake Powell: A Photographic Essay of Glen Canyon National Recreation Area* (Santa Barbara, Calif.: Companion Press, 1994); Katie Lee, *All My Rivers Are Gone: A Journey of Discovery through Glen Canyon* (Boulder, Colo.: Johnson Books, 1998); Katie Lee et al., "People on the River," and E. Tad Nichols, "Glen Canyon As It Was: A Photographic Record," *Journal of Arizona History* 17 (Spring 1976): 39–56, 57–68; Ellen Meloy, *Raven's Exile: A Season on the Green River* (New York: Henry Holt and Company, 1994), 85–97; Eliot Porter, "The Exploration of Glen Canyon," in *Place No One Knew*, rev. ed., 6–7; idem, "Lament for a Lost Eden," *American Heritage* 20 (October 1969): 60–61; P. T. Reilly, "The Lost World of Glen Canyon," *Utah Historical Quarterly* 63 (Spring 1995): 122–34; Terry Russell and Renny Russell, *On the Loose* (San Francisco: Sierra Club, 1967), 91–105; Richard Shelton, "Glen Canyon on the Colorado," in *The Forgotten Language: Contemporary Poets and Nature*, ed. Christopher Merrill (Salt Lake City: Gibbs Smith, 1991), 132–35; Vaughn Short, *Raging River, Lonely Trail: Tales Told by the Campfire's Glow* (Tucson: Two Horses Press, [ca. 1978]), 39–43, 66–69, 103–6; Elizabeth Sprang, *Good-bye River* (1979; reprint, Las Cruces, N.Mex.: Kiva Press, 1992); Gaylord Staveley, *Broken Waters Sing: Rediscovering Two Great Rivers of the West* (Boston: Little, Brown and Company 1971), 135–40; Wallace Stegner, *The Sound of Mountain Water* (Garden City, N.Y.: Doubleday and Company, 1969), 121–36; John Telford and William Smart, *Lake Powell: A Different Light* (Salt Lake City: Gibbs Smith, 1994); Ann Weiler Walka, "Lake Powell: A Canyon Transformed," *Plateau* 65, no. 2 (1994); Stanley L. Welsh, *Water, Stone, Sky: A Pictorial Essay on Lake Powell* (Provo, Utah: Brigham Young University Press, 1974); and Adam Werbach, *Act Now, Apologize Later* (New York: HarperCollins, 1997), 186–200. Also see the special issue of *The Canyon Country Zephyr* (Moab, Utah), April–May 1997.

4. See especially Mark W. T. Harvey, "Echo Park, Glen Canyon, and the Postwar Wilderness Movement," *Pacific Historical Review* 60 (February 1991): 43–67; idem, *A Symbol of Wilderness: Echo Park and the American Conservation Movement* (Albuquerque: University of New Mexico Press, 1994); Russell Martin, *A Story That Stands Like a Dam: Glen Canyon and the Struggle for the Soul of the West* (New York: Henry Holt and Company, 1989); Roderick Nash, *Wilderness and the American Mind*, 3d ed. (New Haven: Yale University Press, 1982), 209–20; Hal K. Rothman, *The Greening of America? Environmentalism in the United States since 1945* (Fort Worth, Tex.: Harcourt Brace, 1998), 33–48, 74–79.

5. Daniel P. Beard, "Dams Aren't Forever," *New York Times*, 6 October 1997, A–17. Also see *High Country News*, 10 November 1997, a special issue devoted to the proposal to drain Lake Powell. On the movement to remove certain dams, see Marc Reisner, "Deconstructing the Age of Dams," *High Country News*, 27 October 1997, 1, 8–11; and Patrick Joseph, "The Battle of the Dams," *Smithsonian* 29 (November 1998): 48–61. On the artificial flood, see George Sibley, "Glen Canyon: Using a Dam to Heal a River," *High Country News*, 22 July 1996, 1, 8–12; and Michael P. Collier, Robert H. Webb, and Edmund D. Andrews, "Experimental Flooding in Grand Canyon," *Scientific American* 276 (January 1997): 82–89.

On the history of reclamation, start with Marc Reisner, *Cadillac Desert: The American West and Its Disappearing Water* (New York: Viking, 1986); and idem, "The Fight for Reclamation," *High Country News*, 20 March 1995. Meanwhile, outside the United States, the reclamation dream lives on. See Patrick McCully, *Silenced Rivers: The Ecology and Politics of Large Dams* (London: Zed Books, 1996).

6. John Wesley Powell et al., *Exploration of the Colorado River of the West and Its Tributaries, Explored in 1869, 1870, 1871, and 1872* (Washington, D.C.: Government Printing Office, 1875), 72.

7. Ibid., 55.

8. Charles Bowden, *Stone Canyons of the Colorado Plateau* (New York: Harry N. Abrams, 1996), 125.

9. William Kittredge, *Who Owns the West?* (San Francisco: Mercury House, 1996), 159.

10. Rick Bass, "Future Loss: A Logan Canyon Reverie," *Salt Lake City Magazine* 7 (September-October 1996): 46–58, quotation from p. 47.

11. Phil Miller, "Provo's Chant: We're No. 2, We're No. 2 . . . ," *Salt Lake Tribune*, 22 November 1997, D-1, 5.

12. Patricia Nelson Limerick, "Uneasy Thoughts from Uneasy Places," in *Arrested Rivers* by Chuck Forsman et al. (Niwot: University Press of Colorado, 1994), 42–43.

13. "Goldwater Regrets Dam," *Phoenix Gazette*, 1 September 1976. Also see Goldwater's memoir, *Delightful Journey down the Green and Colorado Rivers* (Tempe: Arizona Historical Foundation, 1970).

PART 1. THE ROAD TO DISCOVERY

1. Marshall, "Last Outposts of the Frontier," carton 2, folder 36, Robert Marshall Papers, Bancroft Library, University of California, Berkeley; Robert Marshall and Althea Dobbins, "Largest Roadless Areas in the United States," *The Living Wilderness* 2 (November 1936): 11–13. For background, see James M. Glover, "Romance, Recreation, and Wilderness: Influences on the Life and Work of Bob Marshall," *Environmental History Review* 14 (Winter 1990): 23–39.

2. Dave Foreman and Howie Wolke, *The Big Outside: A Descriptive Inventory of the Big Wilderness Areas of the U.S.* (Tucson: Ned Ludd Books, 1989), 12, 230.

3. U.S. Department of the Interior, Bureau of Land Management, *Wilderness Inventory Handbook* (Washington, D.C.: Government Printing Office, 1978), 5–6.

4. For background, see U.S. Department of the Interior, *Report to Congress on R.S. 2477: The History and Management of R.S. 2477 Rights-of-Way Claims on Federal and Other Lands* (April 1993).

5. David E. Miller, *Hole in the Rock: An Epic in the Colonization of the Great American West*, 2d ed. (Salt Lake City: University of Utah Press, 1966), 197.

6. Ibid., 104.

7. Elizabeth Decker, ibid., 197; Miller, ibid., ix.

8. See Richard H. Jackson, "Utah's Harsh Lands, Hearth of Greatness," *Utah Historical Quarterly* 49 (Winter 1981): 4–25; and Lynn A. Rosenvall, "Defunct Mormon Settlements: 1830–1930," in *The Mormon Role in the Settlement of the West,* ed. Richard H. Jackson (Provo, Utah: Brigham Young University Press, 1978), 51–74.

9. Automobile figures come from John A. Jakle, *The Tourist: Travel in Twentieth-Century North America* (Lincoln: University of Nebraska Press, 1985), 121. On western tourism, see Earl Pomeroy's dated but masterful *In Search of the Golden West: The Tourist in Western America* (New York: Alfred A. Knopf, 1957); and Hal K. Rothman, *Devil's Bargains: Tourism in the Twentieth-Century American West* (Lawrence: University Press of Kansas, 1998).

10. Clarence Dutton, *Tertiary History of the Grand Cañon District,* U.S. Geological Survey Monograph 2 (Washington, D.C.: Government Printing Office, 1882), 57; F. S. Dellenbaugh, "A New Valley of Wonders," *Scribner's Magazine* 35 (January 1904): 1–18, quotation from p. 1.

11. Angus M. Woodbury, "A History of Southern Utah and Its National Parks," *Utah Historical Quarterly* 7 (July–October 1944): 111–209, Snow quoted p. 187. I have extensively mined this excellent account.

12. H. Lorenzo Reid, *Brigham Young's Dixie of the Desert: Exploration and Settlement* (Zion National Park: Zion Natural History Association, 1964), 226–27; Woodbury, "History of Southern Utah," 189. For a nice glimpse of growing up in Zion Canyon, see J. L. Crawford, *Zion Album: A Nostalgic History of Zion Canyon* (Springdale, Utah: Zion Natural History Association, 1986). For background on regional tourism and tourism boosters, see C. Gregory Crampton, *Land of Living Rock; The Grand Canyon Country and the High Plateaus: Utah Arizona, Nevada* (New York: Alfred A. Knopf, 1972), 201–29.

13. Woodbury, "History of Southern Utah," 200.

14. Ida Chidester and Eleanor Bruhn, *"Golden Nuggets of Pioneer Days": A History of Garfield County* (Panguitch, Utah: Garfield County Press, 1949), 291; Nick Scrattish, "The Modern Discovery, Popularization, and Early Development of Bryce Canyon, Utah," *Utah Historical Quarterly* 49 (Fall 1981): 348–62, quotation from p. 358. Ruby's Inn, the contemporary resort outside of Bryce Canyon National Park, takes its name from Ruby Syrett.

15. Douglas D. Alder and Karl F. Brooks, *History of Washington County: From Isolation to Destination* (Salt Lake City: Utah State Historical Society, 1996), 221.

16. "The Great Natural Bridges of Utah," *National Geographic* 18 (March 1907): 199–204, quotation from p. 204. For general background on the monument, go to *Utah: A Guide to the State* (New York: Hastings House, 1941), 501–7. On area archaeology, see Fred M. Blackburn and Ray A. Williamson, *Cowboys and Cave Dwellers: Basketmaker Archaeology in Utah's Grand Gulch* (Santa Fe: School of American Research Press, 1997); and Winston Hurst, "Colonizing the

Dead: Early Archaeology in Western San Juan County," *Blue Mountain Shadows* 17 (Summer 1996): 2–13.

17. Zeke Johnson, "Zeke: A Story of Mountain and Desert," manuscript, copy at Utah State Historical Society Library, Salt Lake City (original at Special Collections, Marriott Library, University of Utah).

18. Gary Topping, *Glen Canyon and the San Juan Country* (Moscow: University of Idaho Press, 1997), 261.

19. Johnson to Frank Pinkley, 16 November 1924, Record Group 79 (National Park Service), Entry 7 (Central Classified Files), Natural Bridges National Monument box, National Archives II, College Park, Md.; Philip Johnston, "Utah's Great Natural Bridges," *Touring Topics [Westways]* (September 1929): 12–16, quotation from p. 16.

20. Johnson to A. E. Demaray, 24 August 1929; Johnson to A. E. Demaray, 18 March 1931; and Arno Cammerer to A. E. Demaray, 27 August 1929, Record Group 79.

21. See Jonathan Scott Thow, "Capitol Reef: The Forgotten National Park" (master's thesis, Utah State University, 1986); and Bradford J. Frye, "From Barrier to Crossroads: An Administrative History of Capitol Reef National Park" (master's thesis, Eastern Washington University, 1995). These are the best available sources on the history of Wayne Wonderland, and I have relied on them heavily.

22. *Richfield Reaper*, 25 September 1930, quoted in Thow, "Capitol Reef," 37.

23. J. E. Broaddus, "Wayne Wonderland," *Salt Lake City Municipal Record* 19 (July 1930): 3–7, quotation from p. 4.

24. Robert Sterling Yard, "The New Zion National Park, Rainbow of the Desert" (The National Parks Association, 1919 pamphlet), 25, copy at Utah State Historical Society Library. A later expression of the same idea—that rural Utahns need help to "discover" the beauty around them—is Joseph Wood Krutch, "Undiscovered Country," in *The Desert Year* (New York: William Sloane Associates, 1952), 239–53.

25. Jesse L. Nusbaum, "Certain Aspects of the Proposed Escalante National Monument in Southeastern Utah," *Region Three Quarterly* 1 (October 1939): 27–30, quotation from p. 27, copy at Lee Library, Brigham Young University, Provo, Utah; Charles Kelly, "Proposed Escalante National Monument," *Desert* 4 (February 1941): 20–22.

26. Meeting minutes, 9 June 1936, Escalante National Monument file, State Planning Board: Parks and Recreation records (1935–41), series 01171, box 1, Utah State Archives, Salt Lake City; "Resolutions," 9 June 1936, Escalante National Monument file.

27. The standard account remains Elmo R. Richardson, "Federal Park Policy in Utah: The Escalante National Monument Controversy of 1935–1940," *Utah Historical Quarterly* 33 (Spring 1965): 109–33.

28. Frye, "From Barrier to Crossroads," 120; D. Elden Beck, "Capitol Reef

National Monument," *Utah Magazine* 2 (March 1938): 6, 15, 20, quotation from p. 6.

29. Thow, "Capitol Reef," 47–48.

30. "Who Said 'Last Frontier'?" *Saturday Evening Post* 211 (24 December 1938): 24.

31. Richard Thruelsen, "Tourists' New Frontier," *Saturday Evening Post* 234 (2 September 1961): 30–31, 49, 51–52, quotation from p. 52.

32. Michael B. Husband, "'History's Greatest Metal Hunt': The Uranium Boom on the Colorado Plateau," *Journal of the West* 21 (October 1982): 17–23, quotation from p. 19. I have altered the punctuation slightly.

33. Perrin Stryker, "The Great Uranium Rush," *Fortune* 50 (August 1954), 89–93, 148–58, quotation from p. 89. For overviews, see Raye C. Ringholz, *Uranium Frenzy: Boom and Bust on the Colorado Plateau* (New York: W. W. Norton and Company, 1989); Gary L. Shumway, "Uranium Mining on the Colorado Plateau," in *San Juan County, Utah: People Resources, and History*, ed. Allan Kent Powell (Salt Lake City: Utah State Historical Society, 1983), 265–98; and Arthur R. Gómez, *Quest for the Golden Circle: The Four Corners and the Metropolitan West, 1945–1970* (Albuquerque: University of New Mexico Press, 1994), 17–30.

34. "Uranium Rush: 1956," *True West* 3 (June 1956): 4–7, 34–35, quotation from p. 5; Kevin Fernlund, "Mining the Atom: The Cold War Comes to the Colorado Plateau, 1948–1958," *New Mexico Historical Review* 69 (October 1994): 345–56, quotation from p. 350; Harry Kursh, *How to Prospect for Uranium* (Greenwich, Conn.: Fawcett Publications, 1955), 3.

35. See Peter H. Eichstaedt, *If You Poison Us: Uranium and Native Americans* (Santa Fe: Red Crane Books, 1994).

36. See Richard A. Firmage, *A History of Grand County* (Salt Lake City: Utah State Historical Society, 1996), 298–335; and Ringholz, *Uranium Frenzy*.

37. Robert S. McPherson, *A History of San Juan County: In the Palm of Time* (Salt Lake City: Utah State Historical Society Library, 1995), 259; Herbert H. Lang, "Uranium Also Had Its 'Forty-Niners,'" *Journal of the West* 1, no. 2 (October 1962): 161–69, quotation from p. 165. Also see Darroll P. Young, "Economic Impact of the Uranium Industry in San Juan County," *Blue Mountain Shadows* 16 (Winter 1995/96): 3–40. Employment figures came from Bureau of Economic and Business Research, University of Utah, *An Economic Study of the Proposed Canyonlands National Park and Related Recreational Resources*, March 1962, 67; assessment figures came from A. K. Powell, *San Juan County*, 260.

38. Neilson B. O'Rear, *Summary and Chronology of the Domestic Uranium Program, 1946–1966*, Atomic Energy Commission, Grand Junction Office, May 1966, DOE Collection, printed materials 81.133, Museum of Western Colorado Library, Grand Junction; "Summary, U.S. Atomic Energy Commission Access Roads Program," Grand Junction Projects Office, Department of Energy, Grand Junction, Colo.

39. This paragraph draws from Jay M. Haymond, "San Juan County Roads: Arteries to Natural Resources and Survival," in A. K. Powell, *San Juan County*,

227–39; McPherson, *History of San Juan County,* 251–55; and Charles A. Rasor, "Access Roads: Before and After," speech given 12 May 1956 to the Uranium Ore Producers Association at Grand Junction, Colorado, copy at the Museum of Western Colorado Library.

40. Information from a series of AEC Access Road Program maps in the Uranium Mines Development Corporation file, DOE Map Collection, 1987.72, map drawer 9, Museum of Western Colorado Library.

41. Mark Turner, "This, That & the Other," *Moab Times-Independent,* 22 March 1956, quoted in Ringholz, *Uranium Frenzy,* 270.

42. Joyce Rockwood Muench, "Land of the Sleeping Rainbow," *Arizona Highways* 33 (June 1957): 10–29, quotation from p. 29.

43. Editorial note, *Desert* 26 (April 1963): 5.

44. See, for example, Ray and Virginia Gardner, "Land of the Standing Rocks," *Arizona Highways* 26 (May 1950): 16–23. Also see Jared Farmer, "Naming La Gorce Arch," *Journal of the Southwest* 38 (Spring 1996): 95–111.

45. "Travel Editors—The Park's Great," *Deseret News* (Salt Lake City), 10 May 1965, B-1, B-10. For more flavor of the era, try Jack Breed, "Roaming the West's Fantastic Four Corners," *National Geographic* 101 (June 1952): 705–42; Neil M. Clark, "Valley of Mystery," *Saturday Evening Post* 222 (25 March 1950): 40, 66, 69–70, 72; Nell Merbarger, "Discovering Fable Valley," *Desert* 22 (March 1959): 4–9; W. Robert Moore, "Cities of Stone in Utah's Canyonland," *National Geographic* 121 (May 1962): 652–77; or Weldon D. Woodson, "Exploring the Needles," *American Forests* 64 (April 1958): 30–31, 56–57.

46. "See You in . . . Moab," advertisement, *Desert* 27 (April 1964): 19; "Scenic San Juan County, America's Newest Scenic Wonderland," San Juan County Commission, ca. 1960; "Welcome to Spectacular San Juan County, Utah," Monticello Chamber of Commerce, ca. 1960, Utah State Historical Society Library.

47. Kent Frost Jeep Tours, brochure, 1962, Utah State Historical Society Library.

48. J. N. Macomb, *Report on the Exploring Expedition from Santa Fé, New Mexico, to the Junction of the Grand and Green River of the Great Colorado of the West, in 1859* (Washington, D.C.: Government Printing Office, 1876), 6, 94.

49. Jean Simmons, "Wonderful Light In Canyons Seen," *Dallas Morning News,* 1 August 1965, D-6; Neal Ashby, "An Easterner's Impression of Canyonlands," *American Forests* 71 (August 1965): 24–25, 54–55, quotation from p. 55; Fred Baker, "Land of the Roughriders," *Denver Post Empire Magazine,* 31 July 1966, 8–10.

50. Senate Committee on Interior and Insular Affairs, *Hearings . . . on S. 2387,* 87th Cong., 2d session, 1962, Part 1, 16–21; Part 2, 317.

51. Thomas G. Smith, "The Canyonlands National Park Controversy, 1961–64," *Utah Historical Quarterly* 59 (Summer 1991): 216–42, quotation from p. 233.

52. Gómez, *Golden Circle,* 147; Ashby, "Easterner's Impression," 55.

53. Raymond W. Taylor and Samuel W. Taylor, *Uranium Fever; or, No Talk Under $1 Million* (New York: Macmillan Company), 257. On the road projects, see L. F. Wylie, "Roads to Scenic Treasures," *Reclamation Era* 44 (August 1958): 57–59.

54. Dick Carter, "Bridge at Glen Canyon," *Arizona Highways* 35 (August 1959): 1–3.

55. "Giant Recreational Area in Our Back Yard," *Salt Lake Tribune,* 23 February 1959.

56. Don Howard, "Thar's Tourist Gold in Them Thar Hills," *Salt Lake Tribune,* 25 June 1961; James Eden, "Lake Powell," in *Trends in Travel and Recreation in Utah,* proceedings of the Third Annual Utah Travel Institute, 1 February 1964, copy in Ward Roylance Papers, Utah State Historical Society Library. In fact, Glen Canyon didn't record one million visitors until 1973.

57. Harry E. Fuller, "Test Looms for Utah Road Plans," *Salt Lake Tribune,* 18 January 1966.

58. "U.S. Approves Fund for Glen Dam Road," *Salt Lake Tribune,* 17 September 1966.

59. Report of Utah State Park and Recreation Commission, 1959, 7, copy at Utah State Archives. For background, see Gómez, *Golden Circle,* 119–48.

60. U.S. Department of the Interior, National Park Service, *A Survey of the Recreational Resources of the Colorado River Basin* (Washington, D.C.: Government Printing Office, 1950), 203.

61. Utah State Department of Highways for the State Road Commission of Utah, "Access Roads for the Golden Circle, America's Newest Playground," booklet, 1966, copy at Marriott Library, University of Utah, Salt Lake City.

62. See Utah State Department of Highways, "Utah State Route 95: Utah's First Priority for Utilization of Federal Lands," application portfolio, Special Collections, Marriott Library, University of Utah. Also see John V. Young, "Utah's Land of Standing Rocks," *Sage* 1 (Fall–Winter 1966): 9–14; and *Blue Mountain Shadows* 12 (Summer 1993), special issue on rivers and roads.

63. The passage of the act (86 Stat. 1311) followed public hearings; see U.S. Congress, House, *Hearings . . . on H.R. 15073 and Related Bills,* 92d Cong., 2d session, 1972.

64. See M. Guy Bishop, "The Paper Power Plant: Utah's Kaiparowits Project and the Politics of Environmentalism," *Journal of the West* 35 (July 1996): 26–35.

65. Chamber of Commerce quoted in Edward Abbey and Philip Hyde, *Slickrock: Endangered Canyon of the Southwest* (New York: Sierra Club and Charles Scribner's Sons, 1971), 55; Reid, letter to the editor, *Salt Lake Tribune,* 28 May 1975.

66. McClellan, statement, *Hearings on H.R. 15073,* 96.

67. Joseph M. Bauman, Jr., "Burr Trail," in Allan Kent Powell, ed., *Utah History Encyclopedia* (Salt Lake City: University of Utah Press, 1994), 63–64; Lenora Hall LeFevre, *The Boulder Country and Its People: A History of the People of Boulder and the Surrounding Country, One Hundred Years, 1872–1973* (Springville, Utah: Art City Publishing, 1973), 254. For background history, I

also relied on the docket for *Sierra Club et al. v. Donald P. Hodel et al.*, civil case 87-C-0120G, U.S. District Court, Salt Lake City.

68. "Few Changes Needed to Pave Road," *Salt Lake Tribune*, 12 June 1984, B-1, 3; Charles Seldin, "Senate Gives Preliminary Nod to Paving of Burr Trail," *Salt Lake Tribune*, 25 January 1985, A-5. I have relied on the *Tribune*'s extensive coverage of the Burr Trail between 1984 and 1988.

69. SUWA, Burr Trail poster, no date, copy in author's possession.

70. *San Juan Record* (Monticello, Utah), September 1940, quoted in Norma Perkins Young, *Anchored Lariats on the San Juan Frontier* (Provo, Utah: Community Press, 1985), 311; Wallace Stegner, *The Gathering of Zion: The Story of the Mormon Trail* (New York: McGraw Hill, 1964), 2.

71. Black, statement, *Hearings on H.R. 15073*, 79; testimony of Margie Lee Spencer, 21 February 1987, *Sierra Club v. Hodel*.

72. LeFevre, *Boulder Country*, 83.

73. Nethella Griffin, "Boulder Country," typescript, 1938, Utah State Historical Society Library.

74. Clarence Dutton, *Report on the Geology of the High Plateaus of Utah* (Washington, D.C.: Government Printing Office, 1880), 284, 287; *Utah: A Guide to the State*, 340.

75. Edward A. Geary, *The Proper Edge of the Sky: The High Plateau Country of Utah* (Salt Lake City: University of Utah Press, 1992), 136–37.

76. Matthew Brown, "A Town in Turmoil," *Salt Lake Tribune*, 3 September 1996, B-1, B-6.

77. "Dandy Crossing," box 311, fd. 18, Otis Marston Papers, Huntington Library, San Marino, Calif.

78. For an introduction to gold mining in Glen Canyon, see C. Gregory Crampton, *Standing Up Country: The Canyon Lands of Utah and Arizona* (New York: Alfred A. Knopf, 1964), 124–28. For background on Cass Hite, see Martin Clark Powell, "A Study and Historical Analysis of the Document 'The Trail of Hosteen Pish La Ki for Sixty Snows'" (master's thesis, University of Redlands, California, 1963); and Topping, *Glen Canyon*, 120–25.

79. Barbara Ekker, interview by Lisa A. Fisher, 18 April 1984, transcript, Hite Oral History Program, Utah State Historical Society Library. Also see C. Gregory Crampton, "Historical Sites in Cataract and Narrow Canyons, and in Glen Canyon to California Bar," *University of Utah Anthropological Papers* 72 (August 1964).

80. Richard Sprang, interviewed by Lisa Fisher, July 1984 (transcript titled "Recorded Reminiscences of Hite"), Hite Oral History Program.

81. "Uranium Rush Too Hectic for Colorful Utah Pioneer," *Grand Junction (Colo.) Daily Sentinel*, 15 May 1955, 16.

82. Sprang, "Recorded Reminiscences of Hite."

83. Jana Mellis, "White Canyon: The Uranium Years," *Blue Mountain Shadows* 16 (Winter 1995/96): 62–78, quotation from p. 77 (ellipsis in the original). A marina called Hite was later built a few miles upstream from the old Dandy Crossing.

84. Arth and Della Chaffin to Richard Sprang, 16 January 1966, copy in "Comments by Richard W. Sprang regarding *Chaffin vs. U.S.*," manuscript file, Utah State Historical Society Library.

85. This and the subsequent quotations come from William Rice's transcript, on deposit at the Utah State Historical Society Library.

86. Abbey and Hyde, *Slickrock*, 18–31.

PART 2. EXPLORATION AND THRILL

1. Frances Gillmor and Louisa Wade Wetherill, *Traders to the Navajo: The Story of the Wetherills of Kayenta* (Boston: Houghton Mifflin, 1934), 194. Also see Mary Apolline Comfort, *Rainbow to Yesterday: The John and Louisa Wetherill Story* (New York: Vantage Press, 1980). Unfortunately, neither book is particularly strict with facts. For a background on trading in Navajo country, see Frank McNitt, *The Indian Traders* (Norman: University of Oklahoma Press, 1962).

2. I borrow (and simplify) this idea from Mircea Eliade, *The Sacred and the Profane: The Nature of Religion* (New York: Harcourt, Brace, 1959). For a related study, see John F. Sears, *Sacred Places: American Tourist Attractions in the Nineteenth Century* (New York: Oxford University Press, 1989). Readers interested in the racial and gendered implications of tourism might want to consult Mary Louise Pratt, *Imperial Eyes: Travel Writing and Transculturation* (London: Routledge, 1992).

3. Topping, *Glen Canyon*, 210. For an overview of pre-twentieth century exploration in the canyonlands, see, in addition to Topping's fine book, Herbert E. Gregory, "Scientific Exploration in Southern Utah," *American Journal of Science* 243 (October 1945): 427–549; and Crampton, *Standing Up Country*, 65–76.

4. The literature on Turner and the frontier is too vast for even a cursory listing here. Beginners might want to start with Patricia Nelson Limerick, *The Legacy of Conquest: The Unbroken Past of the American West* (New York: W. W. Norton and Company, 1987), and Gerald D. Nash, *Creating the West: Historical Interpretations, 1890–1990* (Albuquerque: University of New Mexico Press, 1991). On the primitive West in popular culture, see, among many other works, Robert G. Athearn, *The Mythic West in Twentieth-Century America* (Lawrence: University Press of Kansas, 1986). Finally, Kerwin Klein, "Frontier Products: Tourism, Consumerism, and the Southwestern Public Lands, 1890–1990," *Pacific Historical Review* 62 (February 1993): 39–71, offers an interesting (if severely overintellectualized) take on many of this section's themes.

5. See, for starters, William Cronon, "The Trouble with Wilderness; or, Getting Back to the Wrong Nature," in Cronon, ed., *Uncommon Ground: Toward Reinventing Nature* (New York: W. W. Norton and Company, 1995), 69–90; David M. Wrobel, *The End of American Exceptionalism: Frontier Anxiety from the Old West to the New Deal* (Lawrence: University Press of Kansas, 1993), 86–97; and R. Nash, *Wilderness and the American Mind*, 141–60.

6. From Lee Clark Mitchell, *Witnesses to a Vanishing America: The Nineteenth-Century Response* (Princeton: Princeton University Press, 1981), 8.

7. For background on Wetherill and the Antiquities Act, see Hal K. Rothman, *Preserving Different Pasts: The American National Monuments* (Urbana: University of Illinois Press, 1989).

8. *Times* quoted in "Utah's Three Famous Natural Bridge Wonders," *The Inter-Mountain Republican* (Salt Lake City), 27 September 1908, copy in H. L. A. Culmer scrapbook, Utah State Historical Society Library; W. H. Hopkins, "The Augusta Natural Bridge," *Municipal Record* (Salt Lake City), copy with no date located in the "Natural Bridges" clipping file at the Utah State Historical Society Library.

9. Charles Kelly, "Chief Hoskaninni," *Utah Historical Quarterly* 21 (July 1953): 219–26, quotation from p. 221. Also see Robert S. McPherson, *The Northern Navajo Frontier, 1860–1900: Expansion through Adversity* (Albuquerque: University of New Mexico Press, 1988); and Mary Shepardson and Blowden Hammond, *The Navajo Mountain Community: Social Organization and Kinship Terminology* (Berkeley: University of California Press, 1970), 25–42.

10. For background on the San Juan Paiutes, see Pamela A. Bunte and Robert J. Franklin, *From the Sands to the Mountain: Change and Persistence in a Southern Paiute Community* (Lincoln: University of Nebraska Press, 1987); McPherson, *History of San Juan County*, 145–69; and Topping, *Glen Canyon*, 29–39.

11. Hal K. Rothman, "Ruins, Reputations, and Regulation: Byron Cummings, William B. Douglass, John Wetherill, and the Summer of 1909," *Journal of the Southwest* 35 (Autumn 1993): 318–40.

12. See Stephen Jett, "The Great 'Race' to 'Discover' Rainbow Natural Bridge in 1909," *Kiva* 58, no. 1 (1992): 3–66, an exhaustive (and exhausting) article with a near-comprehensive bibliography.

13. William Douglass, "The Discovery of Rainbow Natural Bridge," *Our Public Lands* 5 (April–May–June 1955): 8–9, 14–15, quotation from p. 14 (ellipsis in the original).

14. Mark Twain, *The Innocents Abroad; or, the New Pilgrim's Progress* (1869), opening lines of Chapter 26.

15. Theodore Roosevelt, "Across the Navajo Desert," *The Outlook* 105 (11 October 1913): 309–17.

16. Theodore Roosevelt, foreword to *A Book-Lover's Holidays in the Open* (New York: Charles Scribner's Sons, 1916), vii–x. For a revealing discussion of Roosevelt and masculinity, see Gail Bederman, *Manliness & Civilization: A Cultural History of Gender and Race in the United States, 1880–1917* (Chicago: University of Chicago Press, 1995), 170–215.

17. Hilda Wetherill, "The Trading Post: Letters from a Primitive Land," *Atlantic Monthly* 142 (September 1928): 289–300, quotation 289; Roosevelt, *Book-Lover's Holidays*.

18. Zane Grey, "What the Desert Means to Me," *The American Magazine*

98 (November 1924): 5–8, 72–78, quotation from p. 7; Michael Bell, *Primitivism* (London: Methuen, 1972), 80; "My Own Life," in *Zane Grey, The Man and His Work: An Autobiographical Sketch, Critical Appreciations, & Bibliography* (New York: Harper and Brothers Publishers, 1928), 4.

19. Zane Grey, "Nonnezoshe," in *Tales of Lonely Trails* (New York: Harper and Brothers, 1922). The essay originally appeared in *Recreation* 52 (February 1915): 63–67.

20. See Zane Grey, *The Rainbow Trail* (New York: Harper and Brothers, 1915).

21. Charles Bernheimer, *Rainbow Bridge: Circling Navajo Mountain and Explorations in the "Bad Lands" of Southern Utah and Northern Arizona* (Garden City, N.Y.: Doubleday, Page and Co., 1924), 1; Herbert E. Gregory, *The Navajo Country: A Geographic and Hydrographic Reconnaissance of Parts of Arizona, New Mexico, and Utah*, USGS Water Supply Paper 380 (Washington, D.C.: Government Printing Office, 1916), 44–45; Bernheimer, *Rainbow Bridge*, 3.

22. Harvey Leake and Gary Topping, "The Bernheimer Expeditions in Forbidding Canyon," *Utah Historical Quarterly* 55 (Spring 1987): 137–66, quotation from p. 139; "Huge Animal Footprints Uncovered: Sixty Years' Old Business Man Plunges Into Arizona Wilds and Makes Discovery," unknown newspaper, ca. 1924, box 319, Otis Marston Papers, Huntington Library, San Marino, Calif.

23. "Not in darkest Africa!" advertisement, *Country Life* (June 1925): 128.

24. Topping, *Glen Canyon*, 175, 177; Winifred Hawkridge Dixon, *Westward Hoboes: Ups and Downs of Frontier Motoring* (New York: Charles Scribner's Sons, 1930), 263.

25. Zane Grey, "Down into the Desert," *Ladies' Home Journal* (January 1924): 8–9, 40, 43–44, 46.

26. Candence C. Kant, *Zane Grey's Arizona* (Flagstaff, Ariz.: Northland Press, 1984), 20, 27.

27. John Stewart MacClary, "Reserved," Wetherill register, 13 November 1930, box 250, fd. 14, Marston Papers.

28. John Stewart MacClary, "Shortcut to Rainbow Bridge," *Desert* 2 (May 1939): 3–6.

29. Enos A. Mills, *Your National Parks* (Boston: Houghton Mifflin Company, 1917), xiii–xiv, 239.

30. On the Rainbow Trail, see Gladwell Richardson, *Navajo Trader*, ed. Philip Reed Rulon (Tucson: University of Arizona Press, 1986), and Maurice Kildare, "Builders to the Rainbow," *Frontier Times* 40 (June–July 1966): 14–17, 48–52, though neither account is particularly trustworthy. Over the years the road was straightened and shortened to less than eighty miles.

31. Hulbert Burroughs, "Navajos Call it Nat-sis-an," *Desert* 1 (August 1938): 10–12, 32, quotation from p. 11; "Rainbow Bridge," brochure, ca. 1930, copy in Special Collections, Lee Library, Brigham Young University, Provo, Utah (italics in original); Rupert Larson, "Rainbow Bridge and the Navajo Country: An Examiner Motorlogue," *Los Angeles Examiner*, Automotive Section, 24 May 1925,

1, 6; Larson, "Wonders of Rainbow Natural Bridge in Navajo Mountain Country Revealed By Franklin Scout," *Hollywood Daily Citizen*, 27 May 1925, copy in the Otis Marston Papers.

32. On the history of the lodge, see G. Richardson, *Navajo Trader*; "Guest Book of Rainbow Lodge," *Arizona Highways* 22 (June 1946): 26–29; Shepardson and Hammond, *The Navajo Mountain Community*, 34–35.

33. Pomeroy, *In Search of the Golden West*, 158. On attitudes toward the desert, also see Patricia Nelson Limerick, *Desert Passages: Encounters with the American Desert* (Albuquerque: University of New Mexico Press, 1985). On the social climate of the age, see, among other titles, T. J. Jackson Lears, *No Place of Grace: Antimodernism and the Transformation of American Culture, 1880–1920* (New York: Pantheon Books, 1981); R. Nash, *Wilderness and the American Mind*, 141–60; Peter J. Schmitt, *Back to Nature: The Arcadian Myth in Urban America* (New York: Oxford University Press, 1969); and Alan Trachtenberg, *The Incorporation of America: Culture and Society in the Gilded Age* (New York: Hill and Wang, 1982). On the region's native peoples in American culture, see Leah Dilworth, *Imagining Indians in the Southwest: Persistent Visions of a Primitive Past* (Washington, D.C.: Smithsonian Institution Press, 1996); and Brian W. Dippie, *The Vanishing American: White Attitudes and U.S. Indian Policy* (Middletown, Conn.: Wesleyan University Press, 1982), 284–92.

34. See Marta Weigle, "From Desert to Disney World: The Santa Fe Railway and the Fred Harvey Company Display the Indian Southwest," *Journal of Anthropological Research* 45 (Spring 1989): 115–37; Marta Weigle and Barbara A. Babcock, eds., *The Great Southwest of the Fred Harvey Company and the Santa Fe Railway* (Phoenix: Heard Museum, 1996); and T. C. McLuhan, *Dream Tracks: The Railroad and the American Indian* (New York: Harry N. Abrams, 1985).

35. Armsby, untitled travelogue, Record Group 79 (National Park Service), Entry 7 (Central Classified Files), Natural Bridges National Monument file, National Archives II, College Park, Md.; "Raymond Armsby Installs Bronze Plaque to Guide Who First Took Whites to Rainbow Bridge," unidentified San Francisco newspaper, ca. 1928, fd. 9, Rainbow Bridge Collection, Special Collections, Cline Library, Northern Arizona University, Flagstaff.

36. Wetherill to Arno B. Cammerer, 28 January 1924, fd. 8, Rainbow Bridge Collection. In 1974, near the end of his very long life, Jim Mike was honored by the National Park Service with a small plaque (positioned below the Jo Mora piece), a "Chief Joseph Robe" (by Pendleton Woolen Mills), and a fifty dollar "guide fee." See Zeke Scher, "The Man Who Discovered Rainbow Bridge," *Denver Post Empire Magazine*, 9 December 1973, 14–19; idem, "The Return of Jim Mike," *Empire Magazine*, 11 August 1974, 8–11.

37. "Raymond Armsby Installs Bronze Plaque."

38. "Expedition Honors Indian Who Led Way to Largest Natural Bridge on Earth," reel 5, Otis Marston Papers. No photograph of Nasja Begay seems to exist. Zane Grey's "Nonnezoshe," *Recreation* 52 (February 1915): 63–67, prominently features a picture of the author and a dark-skinned man with earrings

identified as Nasja Begay. However, a copy of the article in box 319, fd. 11, of the Marston Papers bears this handwritten inscription: "This picture is a publisher's mistake. My apologies to our friend, the real Nas Ta Bega. [signed] Zane Grey."

39. Bunte and Franklin, *From the Sands to the Mountain*, 127.

40. Indian Detours brochure, 1929, quoted in D. H. Thomas, *The Southwestern Indian Detours: The Story of the Fred Harvey/Santa Fe Railway Experiment in "Detourism"* (Phoenix: Hunter Publishing Co., 1978), 233–34.

41. Melinda Elliott, *Great Excavations: Tales of Early Southwestern Archaeology, 1888–1939* (Santa Fe: School of American Research Press, 1995), 190, 195.

42. Ansel Hall, "Wanted: 10 Explorers," *California Monthly* 30 (May 1933): 49–50; Andrew L. Christenson, "The Last of the Great Expeditions: The Rainbow Bridge/Monument Valley Expedition, 1933–38," *Plateau* 58, no. 4 (November 1987), 30.

43. Ford Motor Company, *Adventure Bound! With the Rainbow Bridge–Monument Valley Expedition*, 1936, video copy seen by the author at the John Wesley Powell Museum, Page, Ariz.; "With the Rainbow Bridge–Monument Valley Expedition," *Ford News* (March 1936): 47–48.

44. "Huge Wild West Region Suggested for a Park," *New York Times*, 8 July 1934, sec. 10, 22; Ansel Hall, "Exploring the Navajo Country," *American Forests* 42 (August 1936): 382, italics in original.

45. JohniLou Duncan quoted in Topping, *Glen Canyon*, 236.

46. Watson Smith, "Ansel Franklin Hall, 1894–1962," *American Antiquity* 29 (October 1963): 228–29; *Rainbow Bridge–Monument Valley, Explorers Camp, 1933–1949*, a bound folder of articles, brochures, reports, and correspondence located in the Bancroft Library, University of California, Berkeley.

47. Frederick Jackson Turner, "The West and American Ideals," in John Mack Faragher, ed., *Rereading Frederick Jackson Turner: "The Significance of the Frontier in American History" and Other Essays* (New York: Henry Holt and Company, 1994), 143.

48. Edward T. Hall, *West of the Thirties: Discoveries Among the Navajo and Hopi* (New York: Doubleday, 1994), xxiv, xxx.

49. Clyde Kluckhohn, *To the Foot of the Rainbow: A Tale of Twenty-Five Hundred Miles of Wandering on Horseback through the Southwest Enchanted Land* (New York: Century Company, 1927), 252.

50. Clyde Kluckhohn, *Beyond the Rainbow* (Boston: Christopher Publishing House, 1933), 17.

51. Ibid., 204.

52. Richard White, *It's Your Misfortune and None of My Own: A History of the American West* (Norman: University of Oklahoma Press, 1991), 616. The magazine article in question was Neil M. Judd, "Beyond the Clay Hills: An Account of the National Geographic Society's Reconnaissance of a Previously Unexplored Section in Utah," *National Geographic* 45 (March 1924): 275–302. On the *Geographic*'s treatment of foreign cultures, see Catherine A. Lutz and Jane L. Collins, *Reading National Geographic* (Chicago: University of Chicago Press, 1993).

53. Kluckhohn, *Beyond the Rainbow,* 122; Irvin S. Cobb, "Testifying, O Lord, as to Rainbow Bridge," *Arizona Highways* 16 (July 1940): 4–12, 32–34, quotation from p. 12.

54. *Utah: A Guide to the State* (New York: Hastings House, 1941), 508.

55. Robert Frothingham, "Rainbow Bridge," *Country Life* 48 (June 1925): 35–39; Will H. Robinson, *Under Turquoise Skies* (New York: Macmillan Company, 1928); Hoffman Birney, *Roads to Roam* (Philadelphia: Penn Publishing Company, 1930); register entry quoted in W. D. Sayle, *A Trip to the Rainbow Arch* (self-published, 1920), copy in Special Collections, Lee Library, Brigham Young University, Provo, Utah.

56. Zeke Scher, "The Man Who Discovered Rainbow Bridge," *Denver Post Empire Magazine,* 9 December 1973, 14–19, quotation from p. 19; Karl W. Luckert, *Navajo Mountain and Rainbow Bridge Religion* (Flagstaff: Museum of Northern Arizona Press, 1977), 46 (with editorial additions slightly altered). Also see Stephen C. Jett, "Testimony of the Sacredness of Rainbow Natural Bridge to Puebloans, Navajos, and Paiutes," *Plateau* 45 (Spring 1973): 133–42. For a good introduction to the rich relationship between traditional Navajo beliefs and local landscapes, see Klara Bonsack Kelley and Harris Francis, *Navajo Sacred Places* (Bloomington: Indiana University Press, 1994).

57. Luckert, *Navajo Mountain,* 20. The picture identified as "Echo Canyon" on p. 12 of Luckert's book is a different, upstream alcove, not the true Echo Camp.

58. Ibid., 147.

59. Tasker's entry appears in the original Rainbow Bridge notebook register, located (along with the official registers of later years) in the archives of Glen Canyon National Recreation Area, Page, Ariz.

60. Willard D. Morgan, "Over and Under the Rainbow: A Photographing Adventure to the Rainbow Natural Bridge," *Photo-Era Magazine* 67 (September 1931): 115–21.

61. In addition to the travel accounts cited above, I've collected over twenty from Rainbow Bridge's first half century. Some may be found in James E. Babbitt's useful compilation, *Rainbow Trails: Early-Day Adventures in Rainbow Bridge Country* (Page, Ariz.: Glen Canyon Natural History Association, 1990). Also see the bibliography in Jett, "'Race' to 'Discover' Rainbow Natural Bridge." Two generalized (and generally satirical) descriptions of Anglo guides are Hoffman Birney, "Desert Dudes," *Saturday Evening Post* 202 (16 November 1929): 22–23, 217–18; and Wilbur Hall, "The Scenery Salters," *Sunset Magazine* 62 (January 1929): 11–13, 47–48.

62. "'Fax' Told about Upkeep of Road to Rainbow Lodge, Bridge," unidentified newspaper, 9 June 1939, fd. 19, Rainbow Bridge Collection, Special Collections, Cline Library, Northern Arizona University, Flagstaff; Barry M. Goldwater, "Long Vistas and Stone Arches," *Explorer's Journal* 66 (September 1988): 114–19, quotation from p. 116. In addition to my own perusal of the Rainbow Bridge register, I consulted Stephen C. Jett, *Tourism in the Navajo Country: Resources and Planning* (Window Rock, Ariz.: Navajo Tribal Museum, 1967), 103.

63. "Canyon Wonderland," box 2, fd. 3, Norman Nevills Papers, Special Collections, Marriott Library, University of Utah, Salt Lake City. Hal Rothman makes the transition from "heritage" to "recreational" tourism one of the themes of his *Devil's Bargains*.

64. Nevills, "Brief Biography of Capt. W. A. Nevills, W. E. Nevills, N. D. Nevills," box 1, fd. 1, Nevills Papers. Also see P. T. Reilly, "Norman Nevills: Whitewater Man of the West," *Utah Historical Quarterly* 55 (Spring 1987): 181–200; and Roy Webb, "'Never Was Anything More Heavenly': Nevills Expeditions on the San Juan River," *Blue Mountain Shadows* 12 (Summer 1993): 35–50.

65. *Salt Lake Tribune*, 20 July 1941, A-14; "Frontiers to Explore," *Elks Magazine* 22 (August 1943): 10–11, copy in Nevills Papers.

66. George F. Flavell, *The Log of the Panthon* (Boulder, Colo.: Pruett Publishing, 1987), 1–2; Julius F. Stone, *Canyon Country: The Romance of a Drop of Water and a Grain of Sand* (New York: G. P. Putnam's Sons, 1932); E. L. Kolb, *Through the Grand Canyon from Wyoming to Mexico* (New York: Macmillan, 1914); Gary Topping, "Charles Kelly's Glen Canyon Ventures and Adventures," *Utah Historical Quarterly* 55 (Spring 1987): 120–36.

67. "Down the Colorado with the Governor," *Deseret News*, 22 May 1926, 7. Information on Rust taken from his testimony in the Colorado River Case, 1929–31, microfilm copy at Utah State Historical Society Library; Roy Webb, *Call of the Colorado* (Moscow: University of Idaho Press, 1994), 126; and the Rust collection at the LDS Church Historical Department, Salt Lake City, Utah.

68. Webb, *Call of the Colorado*, 123. Also see Webb, "'Until Dissolved by Consent . . . ': The Western River Guides Association," *Utah Historical Quarterly* 60 (Summer 1992): 259–76. For a regional look at river running in the 1950s, see "Family Adventure . . . the River Run," *Sunset* 116 (April 1956): 57–65.

69. See David Lavender, *River Runners of the Grand Canyon* (Tucson: University of Arizona Press, 1985), 96–105.

70. "The Value of the 1940 Nevills Colorado River Expedition as a National Network Program," box 31, fd. 3, Nevills Papers.

71. For fuller treatment of the bridge, see Jared Farmer, "Undiscovered to Undiscoverable: Gregory Natural Bridge," *Utah Historical Quarterly* 63 (Spring 1995): 100–121. Information on the Explorers Club found in box 9, Nevills Papers.

72. "Canyon Voyage with Norman Nevills," 1948, box 2, fd. 3, Nevills Papers; Weldon Heald, "Loud Roars the San Juan," *Travel* 92 (May 1949): 29–31.

73. Joyce Rockwood Muench, "The Trip to the Rock That Goes Over: A Trip to Rainbow by Boat," *Arizona Highways* 25 (August 1949): 30–35. In fact, Greene wasn't first: John Wetherill and Pat Flattum motored (very slowly) upriver from Lee's Ferry to Forbidding Canyon in 1931. Harry Aleson made a complete reverse run of Glen Canyon in 1945. Most impressive of all, Bert Loper dragged and oared a boat the whole distance in 1908.

74. Otis R. Marston, "River Runners: Fast Water Navigation," *Utah Historical Quarterly* 28 (July 1960): 291–308, quotation from p. 308.

75. Gary Topping, "Harry Aleson and the Place No One Knew," *Utah Historical Quarterly* 52 (Spring 1984): 165–78, quotes on 167, 169. Also see Lavender, *River Runners*.

76. These quotations and facts come from Topping, *Glen Canyon*, 319–27. With his second wife, Elizabeth, Richard Sprang made some additional expeditions in the Glen; see Sprang, *Good-bye River*, and Barry Scholl, "Double Identity: The Two Lives of Dick Sprang," *Salt Lake City Magazine* 7 (May-June 1996): 43–45, 121.

77. Topping, *Glen Canyon*, 244–48.

78. Lee, interviewed by Roy Webb, 14 April 1984, transcript, Everett L. Cooley Oral History Collection, Special Collections, Marriott Library, University of Utah, Salt Lake City; Lee et al., "People on the River," *Journal of Arizona History* 17 (Spring 1976): 39–56, quotations from 54–55 (ellipses in the original).

79. Jim Stiles, "Glen Canyon Memories: Ken Sleight Remembers," in *The 1990 Utah Wilderness Calendar* (Salt Lake City: Golden Turtle Press), copy in author's possession. Also see Kenneth Sleight, interviewed by Everett L. Cooley, 6–7 November 1991, transcript, Everett L. Cooley Oral History Project, Special Collections, Marriott Library, University of Utah.

80. Kenneth Ross, "The San Juan–Colorado Trip," *American White Water* (February 1956): 14–16. Also see Georgie White Clark and Duane Newcomb, *Georgie Clark: Thirty Years of River Running* (San Francisco: Chronicle Books, 1977); and Richard E. Westwood, *Woman of the River: Georgie White Clark, White-Water Pioneer* (Logan: Utah State University Press, 1997). For an account of the original 1947 scout run, see Pearl Baker, *Trail on the Water* (Boulder, Colo.: Pruett Publishing Company, [ca. 1965]), 108–11.

81. Martin, *Story That Stands Like a Dam*, 173–74; Berger, *There Was a River*, 2; Aleson, advertisement, *Desert* 26 (April 1963): 34.

82. Abbey, *Desert Solitaire*, 154–55; 156–57. Abbey's original trip journal is on deposit at Special Collections, Main Library, University of Arizona, Tucson. A portion of it has been published in David Petersen, ed., *Confessions of a Barbarian: Selections from the Journals of Edward Abbey, 1951–1989* (Boston: Little, Brown and Company, 1994), 148–55.

83. Ann Ronald, *The New West of Edward Abbey* (Albuquerque: University of New Mexico Press, 1982), 76; Abbey, *Desert Solitaire*, 162–64, 152. For background, see James Bishop, Jr., *Epitaph for a Desert Anarchist: The Life and Legacy of Edward Abbey* (New York: Atheneum, 1994); and James R. Hepworth and Gregory McNamee, eds., *Resist Much, Obey Little: Remembering Ed Abbey*, rev. ed. (San Francisco: Sierra Club Books, 1996).

84. Porter, *Place No One Knew*, rev. ed., 7.

85. Reilly, interviewed by Gary Topping, 16 May 1986, transcript, box 1, Reilly Papers, Utah State Historical Society Library; Sprang, "Recorded Reminiscences of Hite.

86. Jack Goodman, "Big Boating Rush along the Colorado River," *New York Times*, 29 July 1962, sec. 10, 17.

87. Stewart L. Udall, "'Try the Vigorous Life,'" *This Week*, 12 February 1961, 10, 12, 14–15, copy in the Udall Papers, Special Collections, Main Library, University of Arizona, Tucson.

88. Ben Avery, "Governors Start River Run," *Arizona Republic* (Phoenix), 27 May 1962, A-18.

89. Jesse D. Jennings, "The Glen Canyon: A Multi-Discipline Project," *Utah Historical Quarterly* 33 (Winter 1965): 35–50, quotation from p. 36. The University of Utah published the official reports of the Salvage Project as part of its series "Anthropological Papers."

90. Jennings, *Accidental Archaeologist: Memoirs of Jesse D. Jennings* (Salt Lake City: University of Utah Press, 1994), 216.

91. Martin, *Story That Stands Like a Dam*, 140; *New Beginnings: The Story of Page, Arizona*, video, John Wesley Powell Memorial Museum, Page, Arizona, 1988.

92. "The End of the Rainbow Trail," *National Parks Magazine* 35 (March 1961): 8–10, quotation from p. 10.

93. Mike Korologos, "Canyon Wilds Sink beneath Big Lake," *Salt Lake Tribune*, 21 May 1963, B-5; Pat Capson, "Safari Afloat," *Desert* 29 (May 1966): 8–9, quotation from p. 8. Magazine coverage from Lake Powell's early years includes Charles L. Cadieux, "Exploring Lake Powell," *Yachting* 128 (November 1970): 72–73, 106, 108; Fred Clark, Jr., "Gunkholing the Glens," *Yachting* (August 1967): 48–50, 78–79; Floyd Dominy, "Yours to Discover," *Western Gateways* 5 (Spring 1965): 12–15, 22, 42–43; Walter Meayers Edwards, "Lake Powell: Waterway to Desert Wonders," *National Geographic* 132 (July 1967): 44–75; Dan Fales, "Lake Powell: A Spectacular Test Ground for Glastron's Vagabond," *Popular Mechanics* 131 (February 1969): 126–29, 224; A. Golay, "Lake Powell Idyl," *Western Gateways* 9 (March 1969): 48–53, 91–97; Randall Henderson, "Lake in the Redrock Canyons," *Westways* 56 (March 1964): 20–22; Joyce Rockwood Muench, "Fill'er Up: A New Lake Is Born," *Motor Boating* 133 (May 1964): 21–23, 110; Choral Pepper, "Lake Powell: Adventure Is Now!" *Desert* 30 (April 1967): 25–27; Jack Pepper, "Lake Powell Adventure," *Desert* 33 (May 1970): 14–17, 38–39; Pat Perrett, "A New 'Desert' for Cruising," *Outdoors* 6 (August 1964): 2–9; Elizabeth Ward, "America's Newest Water Playground," *Ford Times* 57 (October 1964): 17–21. Also see the January 1964 special issue of *Arizona Highways* and *Lake Powell Vacationland*, the yearly supplement to *Western Gateways*.

94. David Brower, "Glen Canyon: The Year of the Last Look," *Sierra Club Bulletin* 47 (June 1962): 7; "Wahweap Lodge & Marina," *Lake Powell Vacationland* 1 (1963): 12.

95. Jack Pepper, "A Lake Is Born," *Desert* 26 (July 1963): 20–24, quotation from p. 24. Jones, interviewed by Gary Topping, 24–25 March 1995, typescript, 31–32, Utah State Historical Society Library.

96. Ralph Gray, "From Sun-Clad Sea to Shining Mountains," *National Geographic* 125 (April 1964): 542–89, quotation from p. 564. Also see "Conversation With: Art Greene," *Western Gateways* 8 (Spring 1968): 37–51.

97. *Wonderland Newsletter*, July 1963, copy in box 29, fd. 17, Harry Aleson

Papers, Utah State Historical Society Library (ellipsis in the original); Sleight, "The Lesson of Glen Canyon Dam," 1988, copy in Russell Martin Papers, John Wesley Powell Museum, Page, Ariz. Also see Meloy, *Raven's Exile,* 85–97.

98. Choral Pepper, "Caves, Canyons and Caches," *Desert* 27 (September 1964): 16–19, 32, quotations from 16, 17.

99. Figures from "Arizona's Sagebrush Rebels," *The Lamp* 45 (Spring 1963): 10–15; Maxine Brown Phillips, "The Strange New Language of a Magic Land," *Denver Post Empire Magazine,* 14 March 1965, 6–9.

100. Buz Fawcett, "Lake Powell," *Sports Afield* (June 1966): 25–27, 78–82, quotation from p. 26; "Glen Canyon National Recreation Area," brochure, July 1964, C. Gregory Crampton Papers (unsorted), Special Collections, Marriott Library, University of Utah.

101. "Powell Visits Break Previous Records," *San Juan Record* (Monticello, Utah), 20 January 1966; A. N. Wecksler, "Lake Powell," *The Boating Industry* 30 (January 1967): 76–81, quotation from p. 77.

102. Young, "Utah's Land of Standing Rocks," 9–14, quotation from p. 14; Mike Korologos, "High and Dry," *Salt Lake Tribune,* 19 May 1963, D-8; Upper Colorado River Commission, *Colorado River Storage Project: Year of the First Harvest; A Progress Report, 1963* (Salt Lake City, 1963).

103. Ed Will, "Utah: A Slice of Raw Frontier," *Saga* (January 1967): 15, 59–60, quotation from p. 60.

104. William Cronon, "Landscapes of Abundance and Scarcity," in *The Oxford History of the American West,* ed. Clyde A. Milner II, Carol A. O'Connor, and Martha A. Sandweiss (New York: Oxford University Press, 1994), 633. Also see William Cronon, "Revisiting the Vanishing Frontier: The Legacy of Frederick Jackson Turner," *Western Historical Quarterly* 18 (April 1987): 157–76.

105. Again, it is William Cronon who has most persuasively argued for the deconstruction of the wilderness idea. Read "The Trouble with Wilderness," as well as Michael P. Cohen's thoughtful response, "Resistance to Wilderness," *Environmental History* 1 (January 1996): 33–42. Other pertinent articles include J. Baird Callicott, "The Wilderness Idea Revisited: The Sustainable Development Alternative," *The Environmental Professional* 13 (1991): 235–47; William M. Denevan, "The Pristine Myth: The Landscapes of the Americas in 1492," *Annals of the Association of American Geographers* 82 (1992): 369–85; Jared Farmer, "Field Notes: Glen Canyon and the Persistence of Wilderness," *Western Historical Quarterly* 27 (Summer 1996): 210–22; and Paul S. Sutter, "'A Blank Spot on the Map': Aldo Leopold, Wilderness, and U.S. Forest Service Policy, 1909–1924," *Western Historical Quarterly* 29 (Summer 1998): 187–214.

106. Louis Corbeau, "Lake Powell Is Being Filled," *Motor Boating* 112 (August 1963): 44–46.

107. Reed Madsen, "Utah's Paving Way to New Kind of Fun," *Deseret News,* 11 January 1966.

108. George S. Wells, "Lake Powell," *Travel* 129 (March 1968): 52–56, 66–67, quotation from p. 67.

109. Berger, *There Was a River,* 37, 39.

110. Philip Ferry, "Rainbow in the Canyon," *Pacific Discovery* 2 (September-October 1949): 14–19, quotation from p. 14.

111. Advertisement, *Desert* 24 (July 1961): 35.

112. Wetherill register, 21 September 1929, copy in box 250, fd. 13, Marston Papers.

113. Stegner, "San Juan and Glen Canyon," in *Sound of Mountain Water,* 120, originally published as a magazine article in 1947.

PART 3. BEAUTY MADE ACCESSIBLE

1. Joyce Rockwood Muench, "Lake Powell: America's Newest Playground," *Arizona Highways* 40 (January 1964): 16–37, quotation from p. 16.

2. Thelma Hall Towle, "Boat Trip to Rainbow Bridge," *Arizona Highways* 41 (July 1965): 2–11.

3. Thelma Bonny (Hall) Towle to Frank E. Masland, 4 August 1965, box 320, fd. 14, Otis Marston Papers, Huntington Library, San Marino, Calif.

4. John Wesley Powell, *Geographical and Geological Surveys West of the Mississippi,* 43rd Cong., 1st sess., 1874, H. Rept. 612, quoted in Donald Worster, *Rivers of Empire: Water, Aridity, and the Growth of the American West* (New York: Pantheon Books, 1985), 133–34.

5. John Wesley Powell, *A Report on the Lands of the Arid Region of the United States, with a More Detailed Account of the Lands of Utah* (1879; reprint, Boston: Harvard and Common Press, 1983).

6. William Smythe, *The Conquest of Arid America,* rev. ed. (New York: Macmillan Company, 1905), preliminary page. For a detailed look at the roots of reclamation, see Donald J. Pisani, *To Reclaim a Divided West: Water, Law, and Public Policy, 1848–1902* (Albuquerque: University of New Mexico Press, 1992).

7. Worster, *Rivers of Empire,* 178.

8. See Reisner, *Cadillac Desert,* 125–50.

9. The standard account is Norris Hundley, Jr., *Water and the West: The Colorado River Compact and the Politics of Water in the American West* (Berkeley: University of California Press, 1975). More user-friendly is Hundley's "The West against Itself: The Colorado River—An Institutional History," in Gary D. Weatherford and F. Lee Brown, eds., *New Courses for the Colorado River: Major Issues for the Next Century* (Albuquerque: University of New Mexico Press, 1986), 9–49.

10. Frank Waters, *The Colorado* (New York: Rinehart and Company, 1946), 337; Daniel McCool, *Command of the Water: Iron Triangles, Federal Water Development, and Indian Water* (Berkeley: University of California Press, 1987), Table 6.

11. See Mark W. T. Harvey, *A Symbol of Wilderness: Echo Park and the American Conservation Movement* (Albuquerque: University of New Mexico Press, 1994), 23–49. Also see John E. Christensen, "The Impact of World War II," in Richard D. Poll, ed., *Utah's History* (Logan: Utah State University Press, 1989).

12. U.S. Department of the Interior, Bureau of Reclamation, *The Colorado River, "A Natural Menace Becomes a National Resource": A Comprehensive Report on the Development of the Water Resources of the Colorado River Basin for Irrigation, Power Production, and Other Beneficial Uses in Arizona, California, Colorado, Nevada, New Mexico, Utah, and Wyoming* (Washington: Government Printing Office, March 1946), 25.

13. Michael C. Robinson, *Water for the West: The Bureau of Reclamation, 1902–1977* (Chicago: Public Works Historical Society, 1979), 77.

14. House Committee on Interior and Insular Affairs, *Hearings on H.R. 270, 2836, 3384, and 4488 on Colorado River Storage Project*, 84th Cong., 1st sess., 1955, 189.

15. Senate Committee on Interior and Insular Affairs, *Hearings on S. 500 on Colorado River Storage Project*, 84th Cong., 1st sess., 1955, 633; Harvey, *Symbol of Wilderness*, 90–91.

16. Bernard DeVoto, "Shall We Let Them Ruin Our National Parks?" *Saturday Evening Post* 223 (22 July 1950), 17–19, 42, quotation from p. 42. Also see Glenn Sandiford, "Bernard De Voto and His Forgotten Contribution to Echo Park," *Utah Historical Quarterly* 59 (Winter 1991): 72–86.

17. My account of the Echo Park debate draws heavily from Harvey, *Symbol of Wilderness*. Also see Jon M. Cosco, *Echo Park: Struggle for Preservation* (Boulder, Colo.: Johnson Books, 1995); Elmo Richardson, *Dams, Parks, and Politics: Resource Development and Preservation in the Truman-Eisenhower Era* (Lexington: University Press of Kentucky, 1973); Michael P. Cohen, *The History of the Sierra Club, 1892–1970* (San Francisco: Sierra Club Books, 1988), 143–86; and "Echo Park Controversy Resolved," *Living Wilderness* 20 (Winter-Spring 1955–56): 23–43.

18. Senate Committee on Interior and Insular Affairs, *Hearings on S. 1555 on Colorado River Storage Project*, 83d Cong., 2d sess., 1954, 568.

19. House Committee on Interior and Insular Affairs, *Hearings on H.R. 4449, 4443, and 4463 on Colorado River Storage Project*, 83d Cong., 2d sess., 1954, 267.

20. See R. Nash, *Wilderness and the American Mind*, 161–81; and Alfred Runte, *National Parks: The American Experience*, 2d ed. (Lincoln: University of Nebraska Press, 1987), 78–81, 89–91.

21. *Hearings on S. 500*, 708.

22. *Los Angeles Times*, 30 August 1953; *Hearings on S. 1555*, 498. Also see Roy Webb, *Riverman: The Story of Bus Hatch* (Rock Springs, Wyo.: Labyrinth Publishing, 1989).

23. *Hearings on H.R. 4449*, 853–55; *Hearings on S. 1555*, 679.

24. *Hearings on H.R. 4449*, 769.

25. Briant H. Stringham, Chairman, Colorado River Development Association, in *Hearings on S. 1555*, 193.

26. *Hearings on H.R. 270*, 1145–46; *Hearings on S. 1555*, 499–500.

27. Utah Committee on Industrial and Employment Planning and the Upper Colorado River Commission, "A Rugged 'No-Man's' Land or a Sportsman

Paradise?" pamphlet, ca. 1954, copy in Special Collections, Merrill Library, Utah State University, Logan; Upper Colorado River Commission, "Tomorrow's Playground for Millions of Americans," pamphlet, ca. 1955, Merrill Library.

28. *Hearings on H.R. 4449,* 304.

29. David Brower, in *Hearings on H.R. 4449,* 792–93.

30. Harvey, "Echo Park," 43–67, quotation from p. 58.

31. *Hearings on S. 1555,* 662–69.

32. William Thompson, "Glen Canyon, the Sublime," *National Parks* 29 (October–December 1955): 146–51; "Afield with Your Executive Secretary," ibid., 167–70.

33. For background, see Mark W. T. Harvey, "Defending the Park System: The Controversy over Rainbow Bridge," *New Mexico Historical Review* 73 (January 1998): 45–68; and Martin, *Story That Stands Like a Dam,* 215–46. On the court case, see Friends of the Earth, et al., v. Armstrong, *Federal Supplement* 360 (1973), 165–98; Friends of the Earth, et al., v. Armstrong, *Federal Reporter* 485, second series (1973); Felicity Hannay, "Note: In Memoriam: Rainbow Bridge National Monument," *Ecology Law Quarterly* 4, no. 2 (1974): 385–413; and John B. Draper, "The Rainbow Bridge Case and Reclamation Projects in Reserved Areas," *Natural Resources Journal* 14 (July 1974): 431–45.

34. Porter, *Place No One Knew;* Dellenbaugh quoted in Roy Webb, *If We Had a Boat: Green River Explorers, Adventurers, and Runners* (Salt Lake City: University of Utah Press, 1986), 161. Brower's files are found at the Bancroft Library, University of California, Berkeley.

35. John Graves, *Goodbye to a River* (New York: Alfred A. Knopf, 1960), 9.

36. Brower to prospective donators, February 1963, box 30, fd. 28, Sierra Club Members Papers, Bancroft Library. For Brower's perspective on Glen Canyon, see his memoir, *For Earth's Sake: The Life and Times of David Brower* (Salt Lake City: Gibbs Smith, 1990), 341–52.

37. For background on Dominy, see Reisner, *Cadillac Desert,* 222–63.

38. Dominy, "Open Spaces for All Americans," speech, 1 April 1965, box 32, Floyd Dominy Papers, American Heritage Center, University of Wyoming, Laramie; an excerpted version was printed in the *Sierra Club Bulletin* 50 (May 1965): 12–17, with ironic photographs as rebuttal.

39. Bureau of Reclamation, *"Natural Menace Becomes a National Resource,"* 88, 249; "Powell Plans to Exceed $16 Million," *Salt Lake Tribune,* 29 July 1965, B-1.

40. Dominy, "Open Spaces"; emphasis mine.

41. Ottis Peterson to Chief of Publications Branch, 14 December 1964, box 21, Dominy Papers; N. O. Wood, Jr., to Government Printing Office, 3 February 1965, box 21, Dominy Papers.

42. Correspondence located in box 21, Dominy Papers.

43. "Is the Bureau of Reclamation Guilty of Illegal Activities?" *Congressional Record,* 7 June 1965, 12190.

44. Moss to Dominy, 23 December 1964, 17 May 1965, box 21, Dominy Papers.

45. Rosin to Dominy, 4 June 1965, box 21, Dominy Papers.

46. Alfred G. Etter, "Jewels, Gold, and God—or Nearer My God to Thee," *Defenders of Wildlife News* (June 1965); reprinted in *Sierra Club Bulletin* 50 (September 1965): 9–10.

47. Alfred G. Etter, "Anno Dominy," *Defenders of Wildlife News* (January–February–March 1966), 59.

48. For an account of the controversy, see R. Nash, *Wilderness and the American Mind*, 227–37. Also see Byron E. Pearson, "Salvation for Grand Canyon: Congress, the Sierra Club, and the Dam Controversy of 1966–68," *Journal of the Southwest* 36 (Summer 1994): 159–75; and Robert Dean, "'Dam Building Still Had Some Magic Then': Stewart Udall, the Central Arizona Project, and the Evolution of the Pacific Southwest Water Plan, 1963–1968," *Pacific Historical Review* 66 (February 1997): 81–98.

49. Jean Duffy, "Glamour Going to Lake Powell," *Arizona Republic*, 21 November 1965; George S. Wells, "Lake Powell," *Travel* 129 (March 1968): 52–56, 66–67, quotation from p. 52; Knights interviewed by Russell Martin, 9 October 1985, Russell Martin Papers (unsorted), John Wesley Powell Museum, Page, Ariz.; Jerry Ruhlow, "Submerged Caves," *Los Angeles Herald-Examiner California Living*, 27 August 1967, 30, copy at Utah State Archives, Salt Lake City; Walter Meayers Edwards, "Lake Powell: Waterway to Desert Wonders," *National Geographic* 132 (July 1967): 44–75, quotation from p. 75; Al Ball, "Lake Powell, New Found Beauty," *Lake Powell Vacationland* [*Western Gateways*] 2 (1964 edition): 6–12, 22, 54, quotation from p. 8.

50. Staveley, *Broken Waters Sing*, 136–37.

51. Tone, letter, *Sierra Club Bulletin*, 51 (July–August 1966): 24; Sleight, "To All Citizens," letter, 7 July 1966, copy in Otis Marston Papers.

52. Phil Pennington, in *Glen Canyon* (Sierra Club, 1965), filmstrip, distributed on video by the Glen Canyon Institute, Salt Lake City, Utah.

53. McPhee, *Encounters with the Archdruid*, 200.

54. François Leydet, *Time and the River Flowing: Grand Canyon* (San Francisco: Sierra Club, 1964), 159; McPhee, *Encounters with the Archdruid*, 200–203.

55. Jett, "Last Trip down the Escalante," box 315, Otis Marston Papers; Dan Fales, "Lake Powell: A Spectacular Test Ground for Glastron's Vagabond," *Popular Mechanics* 131 (February 1969): 126–29, 224; Barnes, *Canyon Country Arches and Bridges*, 404–5; Joseph Bauman, "Lake Powell: It's Full and Has It Changed," *Deseret News*, 28 June 1980. Also see Farmer, "Undiscovered to Undiscoverable," and James Cogan, "The Drowning of Coyote Gulch," *Sierra* 66 (September-October 1981): 24–27.

56. Jack Hobbs, "Powell's New Popularity," *Utah Holiday* 6 (June 1977): 78–79.

57. Chris Davis, "Wild West Water Skiing," *Motor Boating and Sailing* 159 (February 1987): 52–57, 120, 122, quotation from p. 120.

58. Michael Verdon, "Canyon Cruising," *Motor Boating & Sailing* 176 (September 1995): 43–44, 84–89, quotation from p. 84; Dick Hodgson, *An Explorer's Guide to Lake Powell Country* (Sioux Center, Iowa: self-published, 1993).

59. Rob Schultheis, "The Lake in the Desert," *Outside* (June 1984): 38–44, 69–71, quotes on 43, 40.

60. Bob Hirsch, "The Different Lake Powell," *Phoenix* (December 1978).

61. Glen Canyon Dam dedication program, 22 September 1966, copy in box 147, fd. 3, Stewart Udall Papers, Special Collections, Main Library, University of Arizona, Tucson.

62. Lee Benson, "Dangling Rope a Watery Oasis," *Deseret News*, 20 August 1991, D-1.

63. Ray Grass, "Houseboats Offer Comfort, Convenience," *Deseret News*, 15 June 1995, D-1.

64. "Conversation With: Frank Wright," *Western Gateways* 7 (Spring 1967): 37–43.

65. National Park Service, Rocky Mountain Regional Office, *The Carrying Capacity of Lake Powell: A Management Analysis of Capacity for Boater Recreation*, report, November 1987, 39.

66. "Glen Canyon to Attract Two Million," *Salt Lake Tribune*, 26 May 1962, B-3.

67. Zane Grey, *Tales of the Lonely Trails* (New York: Harper and Brothers, 1922), 17.

68. For an overview, see "Unexpected Popularity Gives Powell Problems," *Deseret News*, 22 September 1994, D-1.

69. "Del Webb Will Sell Lake Powell Marinas," *Deseret News*, 13 September 1988, B-7.

70. For background on Art Greene's life, I relied on Stan Jones, "Lake Powell Line," *Arizona Waterways*, November 1978, 12, 16, 18, also found in *Stan Jones' Ramblings by Boat and Boot in Lake Powell Country* (Page, Ariz.: Sun Country Publications, 1998), 160–66.

71. Greene to Vaud E. Larson, March 1965, box 20, Dominy Papers. Larson forwarded the letter to his boss, Floyd Dominy, who liked it so much that he often quoted from it in his speeches and correspondence.

72. C. William Harrison, "A Voyage to a Rocky Rainbow," *Desert* 42 (October 1979): 12–15, quotation from p. 15.

73. Ray Watton interviewed by Russell Martin, 23 January 1986, Russell Martin Papers, John Wesley Powell Museum, Page, Ariz.

74. Abbey to Frank Moss, 26 March 1972, box 445, Frank Moss Papers, Special Collections, Marriott Library, University of Utah, Salt Lake City. The Rainbow Bridge register is located in archival storage at Glen Canyon National Recreation Area headquarters, Page, Ariz.

75. Jim Carrier, *Down the Colorado: Travels on a Western Waterway* (Boulder, Colo.: Roberts Rinehart, 1989), 69; Deborah Frazier, "Sacred Span Lures Divers," *Rocky Mountain News*, 11 September 1988, 37.

76. Badoni v. Higginson, *Federal Supplement* 455 (1977), 641–50, quotation from p. 645.

77. Badoni v. Higginson, *Federal Reporter* 638, 2d series (1980), 172–81, quotation from p. 179.

78. Luckert, *Navajo Mountain*, 57.

79. "12 Points," copy in author's possession. I relied on the *Salt Lake Tribune*'s coverage of the protest/ceremony.

80. Christopher Smith and Elizabeth Manning, "The Sacred and the Profane Collide in the West," *High Country News*, 26 May 1997, quotations from pp. 1 and 11.

81. U.S. Department of the Interior, National Park Service, Rocky Mountain Regional Office, *Rainbow Bridge National Monument General Management Plan, Development Concept Plan, and Interpretive Prospectus*, June 1993, Appendix B, 11.

82. Stegner, "Glen Canyon Submersus," in *Sound of Mountain Water*, 126, 128, 132–33; originally published as "Lake Powell," *Holiday* (May 1966).

83. Dominy to Stegner, 20 April 1966, box 19, fd. 23, Sierra Club Members Papers, Bancroft Library, University of California, Berkeley.

84. Buck Tilton, "The Silence of the Lands," *Backpacker* 21 (August 1993): 56–65, 94; National Park Service, *Carrying Capacity of Lake Powell*.

85. *Lake Powell: Jewel of the Colorado* (Washington, D.C.: Government Printing Office, 1965), 16; Madaline Burr, "Lake Powell Experiences: Bare Skin, Boats & Booze" (1992), box 77, fd. 10, Folklore Collection, Special Collections, Marriott Library, University of Utah; Scott Thybony, *Canyon Country Parklands: Treasures of the Great Plateau* (Washington, D.C.: National Geographic Society, 1993), 114.

86. Kim Richardson, "The Quest for the Endless Ski," 1993, essay in the author's possession; Stan Jones, interviewed by the author, 3 August 1995.

87. Jerry Spangler, "Lake Powell Visitors to Get an Education," *Deseret News*, 14 October 1991, B–1.

88. Vince Horiuchi and Jeannie Hunt, "Drinkers, Fighters, Fornicators: Powell Officers Vow to Take Beach Back," *Deseret News*, 5 June 1992, A-1.

89. See Brian Maffly, "Rangers to Crack Down on Bullfrog Booze Bash," *Salt Lake Tribune*, 31 March 1995, B-1.

90. Debra Shore, "Badlands," *Outside* 19 (July 1994): 56–71, quotation from p. 61.

91. See Brian Maffly, "Beach Bash at Lake Powell Draws a Platoon of Party Troopers," *Salt Lake Tribune*, 28 May 1995, B-1.

92. "Action Curbs Lake Waste," *Salt Lake Tribune*, 27 July 1969, C-5; National Park Service, "Lake Powell Pure," flyer, ca. 1995, copy in possession of author.

93. Reilly, "Glen Canyon Cruise, August 3–11, 1964," typescript, box 1, fd. 10, P. T. Reilly Papers, Utah State Historical Society Library.

94. Ralph Blumenthal, "5-Year-Old Lake at Glen Canyon Already Littered," *New York Times*, 10 July 1968, 18; Dave Conley, "Lake Powell: Paradise or Paradise Lost," *Deseret News*, 21 August 1983, T-1, 6.

95. Tom Kuhn, "Deep Waters," *Arizona Highways* 66 (April 1990): 28–33.

96. Joseph Bauman, "Toxic Junk Almost Led to Closure of Resort," *Deseret News*, 22 December 1990, A-1.

97. "2 Firms Fined for Using Lake Powell as Landfill," *Deseret News*, 13 May 1993.

98. Sabra Chartrand, "Houseboating through a Realm of Rock," *New York Times*, 22 May 1994, sec. 5, 29, 31.

99. Kolb, *Through the Grand Canyon*, 15.

100. See William F. Sigler and John W. Sigler, *Fishes of Utah: A Natural History* (Salt Lake City: University of Utah Press, 1996), 109–14. Information on squawfish reproductive cycle drawn from conversations with Lin Alder.

101. Greene, interview notes by Russell Martin, 9 January 1986, Russell Martin Papers.

102. Jones, interviewed by Gary Topping, 24–25 March 1995, transcript, Utah State Historical Society Library, 32. For an overview of regional natural history, see Angus Woodbury et al., *Ecological Studies of the Flora and Fauna in Glen Canyon*, University of Utah Anthropological Papers 40 (Salt Lake City: University of Utah Press, 1959).

103. Shelton, "Glen Canyon on the Colorado," in *The Forgotten Language: Contemporary Poets and Nature*, ed. Christopher Merrill (Salt Lake City: Gibbs Smith, 1991), 132–35; Tom Parrett, "Great Walls of Utah," *Motor Boating and Sailing* 145 (February 1980): 68–71, 179–82, quotation from p. 182.

104. Debate at the University of Utah, 9 October 1995; quotations are from the author's notes.

105. David Brower, "Let the River Run Through It," *Sierra* 82 (March/April 1997): 42–43, 64. For a contrasting view of the utility of the Colorado River Compact, see George Sibley, "A Tale of Two Rivers: The Desert Empire and the Mountain," *High Country News*, 10 November 1997.

106. Brent Israelsen, "St. George Seeking Lake Powell Pipeline," *Salt Lake Tribune*, 14 November 1997, B-1, 5.

107. Lee Siegel, "Flood Master: Raze Glen Canyon Dam," *Salt Lake Tribune*, 20 December 1996, B-1, 7.

108. Jason Zengerle, "Water over the Dam," *The New Republic*, 24 November 1997, 20–22. On the downstream effects of the dam, see Steven W. Carothers and Bryan T. Brown, *The Colorado River through Grand Canyon: Natural History and Human Change* (Tucson: University of Arizona Press, 1991); and U.S. Department of Interior, Bureau of Reclamation, *Operation of Glen Canyon Dam*, final environmental impact statement, March 1995.

109. Greg Hanscom, "Reclaiming a Lost Canyon," *High Country News*, 10 November 1997, 11; James Brooke, "In the Balance, the Future of a Lake," *New York Times*, 22 September 1997, A-10.

110. Siegel, "Flood Master"; Ray Boren, "Lake Powell Fight Makes Waves," *Deseret News*, 20 September 1997.

111. Matthew Brown, "To Regain Glen Canyon, Sierra Club Wants to Pull Plug on Lake Powell," *Salt Lake Tribune*, 30 December 1996, D-1; V. Dion Haynes, "Sierra Club: Draining Lake Powell Would Save Ecosystem," *Salt Lake Tribune*, 6 July 1997, A-3; "10 Really Dumb Ideas," *Deseret News*, 23 September 1997.

Also see House Committee on Resources, *Joint Hearing on the Sierra Club's Proposal to Drain Lake Powell or Reduce Its Water Storage Capability,* 105th Cong., 1st sess., 23 September 1997.

112. Tom Wharton, "Sierra Club: Let's Drain Lake Powell," *Salt Lake Tribune,* 31 October 1996, B-1, 3.

113. Paul Fisher, letter, *Deseret News,* 6 October 1997.

114. Steve Netherby, "Houseboat Camping," *Field & Stream* 89 (May 1984): 103, 114–18, quotation from p. 118.

115. "Timely Tips Can Enhance 'Ultimate Family Vacation,'" *Deseret News,* 16 August 1992, S-7.

AFTERWORD

1. Gary Ladd, *Lake Powell: A Photographic Essay of Glen Canyon National Recreation Area* (Santa Barbara, Calif.: Companion Press, 1994), 12.

2. Joan Staveley, interviewed by the author, 1 August 1995.

3. Arches National Park visitation figures provided by Park Service staff, personal communication to author.

4. Page Stegner, "Red Ledge Province," *Sierra* 79 (March/April 1994): 92–100, 144–46, quotation from p. 97–98.

5. Kenneth Brown, *Four Corners: History, Land, and People of the Desert Southwest* (New York: HarperCollins, 1995), 349. For background on Moab and tourism, see Raye C. Ringholz, *Little Town Blues: Voices from the Changing West* (Salt Lake City: Gibbs Smith, 1992); and Timothy Egan, "Boon or Bane?: Tourism Pays, But It's Costly to the Land and Way of Life," *Deseret News,* 27 November 1994, B-1. Also see the back issues of Moab's independent newspaper, *The Canyon Country Zephyr.*

6. James T. Yenckel, "Arches Unrivaled: Five Little-Known Parklands in Utah's Canyon Country," *Washington Post,* 17 July 1994, E-1, 9–10; Rob White, "Sacred Places: The West's New, Booming Extractive Industry," *High Country News,* 7 March 1994, 16. Also see Christopher Smith, "I Came, I Saw, I Wrote a Guidebook," *High Country News,* 4 September 1995, 1, 8–11; and Scott Norris, ed., *Discovered Country: Tourism and Survival in the American West* (Albuquerque: Stone Ladder Press, 1994). For historical context, see Richard White, "Discovering Nature in North America," *Journal of American History* 79 (December 1992): 874–91.

7. Rosalind Johnson, et al., "People on the River," *The Journal of Arizona History* 17 (Spring 1976): 39–56, quotation from p. 47.

8. Jean Starobinski, "The Idea of Nostalgia," *Diogenes* 54 (Summer 1966): 81–103. Also see David Lowenthal, *The Past Is a Foreign Country* (Cambridge: Cambridge University Press, 1985), 8–13.

9. Renato Rosaldo, *Culture and Truth: The Remaking of Social Analysis* (Boston: Beacon Press, 1989), 69–70.

10. J. B. Jackson, "The Four Corners Country," *Landscape* 10 (Fall 1960): 20–26, quotation from p. 20.

11. Wallace Stegner, ed., *This Is Dinosaur: Echo Park Country and Its Magic Rivers* (New York: Alfred A. Knopf, 1955), 17, italics in original.

12. Terry Tempest Williams, *Coyote's Canyon* (Salt Lake City: Gibbs Smith, 1989), 19; T. H. Watkins, *Stone Time: Southern Utah: A Portrait and a Meditation* (Santa Fe: Clear Light Publishers, 1994); Gary Paul Nabhan and Caroline Wilson, *Canyons of Color: Utah's Slickrock Wildlands* (New York: HarperCollinsWest, 1995), 20; Edward Abbey, *The Journey Home* (New York: E. P. Dutton, 1977), 88.

13. Kittredge, *Who Owns the West?*, 35.

14. Unless otherwise noted, these and the following quotations come from W. L. Rusho, *Everett Ruess: A Vagabond for Beauty* (Salt Lake City: Gibbs Smith, 1983). For more of Ruess's writings, see W. L. Rusho, ed., *Wilderness Journals of Everett Ruess* (Salt Lake City: Gibbs Smith, 1998).

15. Mark A. Taylor, *Sandstone Sunsets: In Search of Everett Ruess* (Salt Lake City: Gibbs Smith, 1997), 46.

16. John U. Terrell, "Indians Furnish Clue to Lost Artist's Trail," *Salt Lake Tribune*, 27 August 1935.

17. John U. Terrell, "Desert Folk Believe Ruess Killer Victim," *Salt Lake Tribune*, 28 August 1935.

18. Stella and Christopher Ruess to D. B. McGue, 2 February 1938, Ruess Family Papers, Utah State Historical Society Library, Salt Lake City.

19. John P. O'Grady, *Pilgrims to the Wild: Everett Ruess, Henry David Thoreau, John Muir, Clarence King, Mary Austin* (Salt Lake City: University of Utah Press, 1993), 1. Interpretations of Ruess's life can be found in Bruce Berger, *The Telling Distance: Conversations with the American Desert* (Portland: Breitenbush Books, 1990), 9–24; Geary, *Proper Edge of the Sky*, 150–55; Jon Krakauer, *Into the Wild* (New York: Villard, 1996), 88–97; N. Scott Momaday, "Everett Ruess: The Dark Trail into Myth," *American West* 24 (April 1987): 67–70; Wallace Stegner, *Mormon Country* (New York: Duell, Sloan and Pearce, 1942), 319–30; and Scott Thybony, *Burntwater* (Tucson: University of Arizona Press, 1997): 45–66.

AN OUTLINE HISTORY OF GLEN CANYON
BEFORE THE DAM

1. Jesse D. Jennings, *Glen Canyon: A Summary*, University of Utah Anthropological Papers 81 (Salt Lake City: University of Utah Press, 1966), 63. Also see the recent follow-up to Jennings's summary: Phil R. Geib, *Glen Canyon Revisited*, University of Utah Anthropological Papers 119 (Salt Lake City: University of Utah Press, 1996).

2. David Roberts, *In Search of the Old Ones: Exploring the Anasazi World of the Southwest* (New York: Simon & Schuster, 1996), 213.

3. Ted J. Warner, ed., *The Domínguez-Escalante Journal: Their Expedition*

through Colorado, Utah, Arizona, and New Mexico in 1776 (1976; reprint, Salt Lake City: University of Utah Press, 1995), 121.

4. Topping, *Glen Canyon*, 67.

5. Charles Peterson, *Look to the Mountains: Southeastern Utah and the La Sal National Forest* (Provo, Utah: Brigham Young University Press, 1975), 79.

6. Jennings, *Glen Canyon*, 42.

7. See Dwight L. Smith and C. Gregory Crampton, eds., *The Colorado River Survey: Robert B. Stanton and the Denver, Colorado Canyon & Pacific Railroad* (Salt Lake City: Howe Brothers, 1987).

8. See C. Gregory Crampton and Dwight L. Smith, eds., *The Hoskanini Papers: Mining in Glen Canyon, 1897–1902, by Robert B. Stanton*, University of Utah Anthropological Papers 54 (Salt Lake City: University of Utah Press, 1961).

9. See W. L. Rusho, *Lee's Ferry: Desert River Crossing*, 3d ed. (St. George, Utah: Tower Productions, 1998).

10. On river runners, see Webb, *Call of the Colorado*.

11. C. Gregory Crampton, "History in Glen Canyon," *Reclamation Era* 45 (May 1959): 41–44, 52, quote on 52. For more detailed historical overviews, see Crampton, *Outline History of the Glen Canyon Region, 1776–1922*, University of Utah Anthropological Papers 42 (Salt Lake City: University of Utah Press, 1959); and Crampton, *Ghosts of Glen Canyon*. For background on the history portion of the salvage project, see Topping, *Glen Canyon*, 340–44; Martin, *Story that Stands Like a Dam*, 103–31; and Crampton interviewed by Jay Haymond, 15 November 1994, transcript at Utah State Historical Society Library. Crampton's sourcebooks are *Historical Sites in Cataract and Narrow Canyons, and in Glen Canyon to California Bar*, University of Utah Anthropological Papers 72 (Salt Lake City: University of Utah Press, 1964); *Historical Sites in Glen Canyon, Mouth of Hansen Creek to Mouth of the San Juan River*, University of Utah Anthropological Papers 61 (Salt Lake City: University of Utah Press, 1962); *Historical Sites in Glen Canyon, Mouth of San Juan River to Lee's Ferry*, University of Utah Anthropological Papers 46 (Salt Lake City: University of Utah Press, 1960); and *The San Juan Canyon Historical Sites*, University of Utah Anthropological Papers 70 (Salt Lake City: University of Utah Press, 1964). Many of the details in my own outline history are drawn from these sourcebooks. Also see Jared Farmer, "Remembering Paradise: Histories of Glen Canyon" (master's thesis, University of Montana, 1998).

SUGGESTIONS FOR FURTHER READING

An excellent bibliography on Glen Canyon can be found in Gary Topping, *Glen Canyon and the San Juan Country* (Moscow: University of Idaho Press, 1997). By comparison, the following reading list is wide and shallow: though it covers more than the canyon, it contains only the most salient (and accessible) books and monographs. Titles appear once, though some would obviously fit under more than one heading. For periodical and archival material, please consult the preceding notes. I'll mention, however, that the biweekly newspaper *High Country News* (published in Paonia, Colorado) is essential for understanding contemporary land-use issues in the interior West.

THE COLORADO PLATEAU

Baars, Donald L. *The Colorado Plateau: A Geologic History*. Rev. ed. Albuquerque: University of New Mexico Press, 1983.

Brown, Kenneth A. *Four Corners: History, Land, and People of the Desert Southwest*. New York: HarperCollins, 1995.

Gómez, Arthur R. *Quest for the Golden Circle: The Four Corners and the Metropolitan West*. Albuquerque: University of New Mexico Press, 1994.

THE CANYON COUNTRY

Abbey, Edward. *Desert Solitaire: A Season in the Wilderness*. New York: McGraw-Hill, 1968.

Abbey, Edward, and Philip Hyde. *Slickrock: Endangered Canyons of the Southwest*. New York: Sierra Club/Charles Scribner's Sons, 1971.

Bauman, Joseph M., Jr. *Stone House Lands: The San Rafael Reef*. Salt Lake City: University of Utah Press, 1987.

Crampton, C. Gregory. *Standing Up Country: The Canyon Lands of Utah and Arizona*. New York: Alfred A. Knopf, 1964.

Frost, Kent. *My Canyonlands*. New York: Abelard-Schuman, 1971.

Gregory, Herbert E. *The San Juan Country: A Geographic and Geologic Reconnaissance of Southeastern Utah*. U.S. Geological Survey Professional Paper 188. Washington, D.C.: Government Printing Office, 1938.

Gregory, Herbert E., and Raymond C. Moore. *The Kaiparowits Region: A Geographic and Geological Reconnaissance*. U.S. Geological Survey Professional Paper 164. Washington, D.C.: Government Printing Office, 1931.

Negri, Richard F., ed. *Tales of Canyonlands Cowboys*. Logan: Utah State University Press, 1997.

Roylance, Ward J. *The Enchanted Wilderness: A Red Rock Odyssey*. Torrey, Utah: By the author, 1986.

Rusho, W. L. *Everett Ruess: A Vagabond for Beauty*. Salt Lake City: Gibbs Smith, 1983.

Zwinger, Ann. *Wind in the Rock: The Canyonlands of Southeastern Utah*. Tucson: University of Arizona Press, 1986.

GLEN CANYON AND LAKE POWELL

Abbey, Edward. *The Monkey Wrench Gang*. Philadelphia: J. B. Lippincott, 1975.

Berger, Bruce. *There Was a River*. Tucson: University of Arizona Press, 1994.

Crampton, C. Gregory. *Ghosts of Glen Canyon: History beneath Lake Powell*. Rev. ed. St. George, Utah: Publishers Place, 1994.

Inskip, Eleanor, ed. *The Colorado River through Glen Canyon before Lake Powell: Historic Photo Journal, 1872 to 1964*. Moab, Utah: Inskip Ink, 1995.

Jennings, Jesse D. *Glen Canyon: A Summary*. University of Utah Anthropological Papers 81. Salt Lake City: University of Utah Press, 1966.

Jones, Stan. *Stan Jones' Ramblings by Boat and Boot in Lake Powell Country*. Page, Ariz: Sun Country Publications, 1998.

Lee, Katie. *All My Rivers Are Gone: A Journey of Discovery through Glen Canyon*. Boulder, Colo.: Johnson Books, 1998.

Martin, Russell. *A Story that Stands Like a Dam: Glen Canyon and the Struggle for the Soul of the West*. New York: Henry Holt and Company, 1989.

McPhee, John. *Encounters with the Archdruid*. New York: Farrar, Straus and Giroux, 1971.

Porter, Eliot. *The Place No One Knew: Glen Canyon on the Colorado*. San Francisco: Sierra Club, 1963.

Potter, Loren D., and Charles L. Drake. *Lake Powell: Virgin Flow to Dynamo*. Albuquerque: University of New Mexico Press, 1989.

Rusho, W. L., with C. Gregory Crampton. *Lee's Ferry: Desert River Crossing*. 3d ed. St. George, Utah: Tower Productions, 1998.

Sprang, Elizabeth. *Good-by River*. 1979. Reprint, Las Cruces, N.Mex.: Kiva Press, 1992.

Stegner, Wallace. *The Sound of Mountain Water*. Garden City, New York: Doubleday and Company, 1969.

U.S. Bureau of Reclamation. *Lake Powell: Jewel of the Colorado*. Washington, D.C.: Government Printing Office, 1965.

RAINBOW BRIDGE

Babbitt, James E., comp. *Rainbow Trails: Early-Day Adventures in Rainbow Bridge Country*. Page, Ariz.: Glen Canyon Natural History Association, 1990.

Bernheimer, Charles L. *Rainbow Bridge: Circling Navajo Mountain and Explorations in the "Bad Lands" of Southern Utah and Northern Arizona*. New York: Doubleday, Page and Co., 1924.

Gillmor, Frances, and Louisa Wade Wetherill. *Traders to the Navajo: The Story of the Wetherills of Kayenta*. 1934. Reprint, Albuquerque: University of New Mexico Press, 1953.

Kluckhorn, Clyde. *To the Foot of the Rainbow: A Tale of Twenty-Five Hundred Miles of Wandering on Horseback through the Southwest Enchanted Land*. 1927 Reprint. Albuquerque: University of New Mexico Press, 1992.

Luckert, Karl W. *Navajo Mountain and Rainbow Bridge Religion*. Flagstaff: Museum of Northern Arizona, 1977.

INDIANS AND MORMONS

Arrington, Leonard J., and Davis Bitton. *The Mormon Experience*. New York: Alfred A. Knopf, 1979.

Geary, Edward A. *The Proper Edge of the Sky: The High Plateau Country of Utah*. Salt Lake City: University of Utah Press, 1992.

Kelley, Klara Bonsack, and Harris Francis. *Navajo Sacred Places*. Bloomington: Indiana University Press, 1994.

McPherson, Robert S. *A History of San Juan County: In the Palm of Time*. Salt Lake City: Utah State Historical Society, 1995.

————. *Sacred Land, Sacred View: Navajo Perceptions of the Four Corners Region*. Provo, Utah: Brigham Young University Charles Redd Center for Western Studies, 1992.

Miller, David E. *Hole in the Rock: An Epic in the Colonization of the Great American West*. 2d ed. Salt Lake City: University of Utah Press, 1966.

Roberts, David. *In Search of the Old Ones: Exploring the Anasazi World of the Southwest*. New York: Simon and Schuster, 1996.

Stegner, Wallace. *Mormon Country*. New York: Duell, Sloan and Pearce, 1942.

Trimble, Stephen. *The People: Indians of the American Southwest*. Santa Fe: School of American Research Press, 1993.

PARKS AND WILDERNESS

Cronon, William, ed. *Uncommon Ground: Toward Reinventing Nature*. New York: W. W. Norton, 1995.

Harvey, Mark W. T. *A Symbol of Wilderness: Echo Park and the American Conservation Movement*. Albuquerque: University of New Mexico Press, 1994.

Nash, Roderick. *Wilderness and the American Mind.* 3d ed. New Haven: Yale University Press, 1982.

Rothman, Hal K. *Preserving Different Pasts: The American National Monuments.* Urbana: University of Illinois Press, 1989.

Runte, Alfred. *National Parks: The American Experience.* 3d ed. Lincoln: University of Nebraska Press, 1997.

Sax, Joseph L. *Mountains Without Handrails: Reflections on the National Parks.* Ann Arbor: University of Michigan Press, 1980.

Sellars, Richard West. *Preserving Nature in the National Parks: A History.* New Haven: Yale University Press, 1997.

Stegner, Wallace, ed. *This Is Dinosaur: Echo Park Country and Its Magic Rivers.* New York: Alfred A. Knopf, 1955.

Utah Wilderness Coalition. *Wilderness at the Edge: A Citizen Proposal to Protect Utah's Canyons and Deserts.* Salt Lake City: By the author, 1990.

Zaslowsky, Dyan, and T. H. Watkins. *These American Lands: Parks, Wilderness, and the Public Lands.* Rev. ed. Washington, D.C.: Island Press, 1994.

TOURISM

Athearn, Robert G. *The Mythic West in Twentieth-Century America.* Lawrence: Unversity Press of Kansas, 1986.

Hyde, Anne Farrar. *An American Vision: Far Western Landscape and National Culture, 1820–1920.* New York: New York University Press, 1990.

Norris, Scott, ed. *Discovered Country: Tourism and Survival in the American West.* Albuquerque: Stone Ladder Press, 1994.

Pomeroy, Earl. *In Search of the Golden West: The Tourist in Western America.* New York: Alfred A. Knopf, 1957.

Rothman, Hal K. *Devil's Bargains: Tourism in the Twentieth-Century American West.* Lawrence: University Press of Kansas, 1998.

Woodbury, Angus M. *A History of Southern Utah and Its National Parks.* 1944. Reprint, Salt Lake City: Utah State Historical Society, 1950.

RIVERS AND DAMS

Carothers, Steven W., and Bryan T. Brown. *The Colorado River through Grand Canyon.* Tucson: University of Arizona Press, 1991.

Collier, Michael, Robert H. Webb, and John C. Schmidt. *Dams and Rivers: A Primer on the Downstream Effects of Dams.* Tucson: U.S. Geological Survey, 1996.

Fradkin, Philip L. *A River No More: The Colorado River and the West.* Rev. ed. Berkeley: University of California Press, 1995.

High Country News. *Western Water Made Simple.* Washington, D.C.: Island Press, 1987.

Meloy, Ellen. *Raven's Exile: A Season on the Green River*. New York: Henry Holt and Company, 1994.

Palmer, Tim. *Endangered Rivers and the Conservation Movement*. Berkeley: University of California Press, 1986.

Powell, John Wesley. *The Exploration of the Colorado River and Its Canyons*. 1895. Reprint, New York: Dover Publications, 1961.

Reisner, Marc. *Cadillac Desert: The American West and Its Disappearing Water*. New York: Penguin Books, 1986.

Watkins, T. H., et al. *The Grand Colorado: The Story of a River and Its Canyons*. Palo Alto, Calif.: American West Publishing Company, 1969.

Weatherford, Gary D. and F. Lee Brown, eds. *New Courses for the Colorado River: Major Issues for the Next Century*. Albuquerque: University of New Mexico Press, 1986.

Webb, Roy. *Call of the Colorado*. Moscow: University of Idaho Press, 1994.

White, Richard. *The Organic Machine: The Remaking of the Columbia River*. New York: Hill and Wang, 1995

Worster, Donald. *Rivers of Empire: Water, Aridity, and the Growth of the American West*. New York: Pantheon Books, 1985.

THE CHANGING WEST

Abbott, Carl. *The Metropolitan Frontier: Cities in the Modern American West*. Tucson: University of Arizona Press, 1993.

Kittredge, William. *Hole in the Sky: A Memoir*. New York: Alfred A. Knopf, 1992.
————. *Who Owns the West?* San Francisco: Mercury House, 1996.

Klett, Mark. *Revealing Territory: Photographs of the Southwest*. Albuquerque: University of New Mexico Press, 1992.

Power, Thomas M. *Lost Landscapes and Failed Economies: The Search for a Value of Place*. Washington, D.C.: Island Press, 1996.

Riebsame, William E., et al., eds. *Atlas of the New West: Portrait of a Changing Region*. New York: W. W. Norton, 1997.

ILLUSTRATION CREDITS

Philip Hyde
The Colorado River at Klondike Bar, Glen Canyon, 1962. Used by permission.

Mark Klett
"Campsite reached by boat through watery canyons, Lake Powell, 8/20/83."
Used by permission.
"Campsite No. 2 at the end of Desolation Canyon, Lake Powell, 5/26/88."
Used by permission.

National Archives
The first photograph of Rainbow Bridge, 1909.

U.S. Department of the Interior, Bureau of Reclamation
Glen Canyon dam site before blasting began, 1956.
Workers place concrete on two of the blocks composing Glen Canyon Dam.
Glen Canyon Dam.
View of Hole in the Rock, 1967. Note Lake Powell at bottom.
Ends of the earth, 1956.
Arth Chaffin and Woody Edgell on the Hite ferry's last official day, 1964.
Tourists read the historical marker at Rainbow Bridge, 1967.
Kane Creek road under construction, 1957.
Mouth of Bridge Canyon on the way to Rainbow Bridge, Lake Powell, 1965.
Gregory Natural Bridge. Note human figure for scale.
Gregory Natural Bridge on the way under, 1965.
The easy, waterborne access to Rainbow Bridge, 1983.
Junction of San Juan (left) and Colorado rivers in Glen Canyon, 1963.
Lake Powell visitors at Everett Ruess's place of disappearance, 1967.

Utah State Historical Society
Welcome and warning for motorists, ca. 1940. Used by permission, all rights
reserved.
River runners in Glen Canyon, ca. 1950. Used by permission, all rights
reserved.

INDEX

description of, xvii–xviii; impact of tourism on, xxi, xxiv, 192–95, 198–99; maps of, xix, 124–25; names for, xviii–xx; population of, xviii, 198; summary history of, xxi
Canyon Country Parkway, 40, 44
Canyonlands National Park, 28, 31–33
Canyon Surveys, 100–101, 109
Canyon Tours, 163
Capitol Reef National Monument, 17–18, 20–21, 57
Capitol Reef National Park, xxiv, 4, 41–42, 44
carnotite, 23
Cataract Canyon, 33, 216, 219
Cathedral in the Desert, 155, 192
Central Arizona Project, 147, 150, 153
Chaffin, Arthur, 49–54, 58, 221; photograph of, 54
Chapman, Oscar, 135–36
Civilian Conservation Corps, 46
Clinton, Bill, xvi, 67
Clyde, George, 32
Collier, John, 85
Colorado Plateau, 37; description of, xviii; uranium boom on, 23–26
Colorado River, 11, 132–33, 197, 216; photographs of, 103, 193
Colorado River Compact, 132–33, 143, 182
Colorado River Storage Project: brief description of, xi; debate over, 102, 137–44; origins of, 134–36; and Rainbow Bridge National Monument, 144–45, 169; and recreation, 140, 147–48. See also Echo Park Dam
Commercial Club of Salt Lake, 12, 15
conservation movement, xiii–xiv; and Echo Park Dam, 134–38, 140–42, 144; and Glen Canyon, 144–46; and proposed dams in Grand Canyon, 149, 152–53; and Rainbow Bridge National Monument, 143–45. See also Brower, David; names of individual

conservation groups; wilderness
Corps of Engineers, xiv, 136–37
Crampton, C. Gregory, 222
Crossing of the Fathers, 216–17
Cummings, Byron, 66, 68–70

dams: heyday of, xiv; reevaluation of, xiv–xvi, 184–85, 200–201
Dandy Crossing, 49, 218
Dangling Rope Marina, 160
Davis, Arthur Powell, 132
Davis Gulch, 208, 209–10; photograph of, 208
Defiance House, 101
Del E. Webb (corp.), 163, 166, 177
Dellenbaugh, Frederick, 12, 145, 221
Denver & Rio Grande Railroad, 73
Denver, Colorado Canyon & Pacific Railroad, 219–20
Dern, George, 96
Deseret News, 39, 98
desert, attitudes about, 81–82
Desert Magazine, 29–30, 114
Desert Solitaire (Edward Abbey), xx, xxiv, 105–6, 194
Despain, Roy, 141
De Voto, Bernard, 136
Dinosaur National Monument, xiii–xiv, 102, 135–42, 144, 146
discovery, 72, 194–95
Domínguez-Escalante expedition, 215–16, 221
Dominy, Floyd, 147–52, 155, 158, 162, 171–72, 182, 248n. 71
Douglass, William, 66–70
Drury, Newton, 135–36
Dutton, Clarence, 11–12, 46
Earth First!, xii, 2
Echo Camp, 90, 239n. 57
Echo Park, 135, 140–41
Echo Park Dam, 134–38, 140–42, 144
Edgell, Woody, 53, 108; photograph of, 54
Eggert, Charles, 140
Eisenhower, Dwight, 137

Escalante National Monument (proposed), 19–20
Escalante River, 38–39, 98, 154–55, 158, 171–72, 192, 213, 218
Escalante (Utah), 39–40, 44, 88, 198, 205–7, 218
fish, 158, 178–79
Flagstaff (Ariz.), 34
Flaming Gorge Dam, xvi, 115, 145, 184, 200–201
Flavell, George, 96
Forbidding Canyon, xvii, 94, 98, 107–9, 117, 120, 126, 160; photograph of, 127
Forgotten Canyon, 100–101
Fred Harvey Company, 82
Friends of Glen Canyon, 102
frontier thesis, 64–65, 116–17
Frost, Fern, 30–31
Frost, Kent, 30–31

Galloway, Nat, 96
Garfield County (Utah), 36, 40–44, 47–48, 51
Garn, Jake, 42
General Land Office, 66–67
Geological Survey (U.S.), 24, 64, 92, 221
Gilbert, Grove Karl, 64
Glen Canyon: animal life of, 101, 178–80; archaeological remains in, 101, 109, 172–73, 176, 213–14; Boy Scouts in, 103–4, 162, 167; early travel in, 95–96; late-term travel in, 104–9; mining in, 48–49, 218–21; naming of, xvi; photographs of, xiii, xxvii, 103, 193; river guides of, 96–104; salvage project in, 109–10, 114, 222
Glen Canyon Bridge, 34
Glen Canyon Dam, xiv, 134; construction of, 34–36, 104, 110–11; environmental impact of, xii, 153, 178–80, 184; hatred for, xii–xiii, 171, 180, 187; "high" vs. "low," 142–43; photographs of, xv, xxii
Glen Canyon damsite, photograph of, xiii

Glen Canyon Environmental Studies, 184
Glen Canyon Institute, 185
Glen Canyon National Recreation Area, xi, 39, 111; concessionaires at, 160, 162–64; early history of, 33, 35; and Escalante River policy, 172; law enforcement at, 174–75; and Rainbow Bridge policy, 162, 170; visitation to, 118, 162, 172. *See also* Lake Powell
Golden Circle, 18, 34, 37–40, 55
Goldwater, Barry, xxvi, 94
Goulding, Harry, 163
Grand Canyon, 87–88, 97, 200, 216–17; artificial flood in, xvi; effect of Glen Canyon Dam on, xii, 153, 184; proposed dams in, 147–50, 152–53
Grand County (Utah), 4; development of tourism in, 28, 30, 33, 48; uranium boom in, 25–26, 28
Grand Staircase–Escalante National Monument, 67
Grant, Ulysses, III, 136
Greene, Art, 99, 109, 112–13, 163–65
Green River, 135, 139, 178, 197, 200–201
Green River (Utah), 49, 216, 220
Gregory, Herbert, 64, 85, 88, 98
Gregory Natural Bridge, 98, 155–58, 165; photographs of, 156–57
Grey, Zane, 72–75, 77–78, 88–89, 119, 162, 201–2, 221

Hall, Ansel, 85–86, 98
Halls Crossing Marina, 115
Hamblin, Jacob, 217
Hanksville (Utah), 49–50
Hansen, James, 186
Happy Jack Mine, 38, 51–52
Hashkeneinii, 68–69, 218
Hatch, Bus, 97, 139
Hell's Backbone, 46
Henderson, Randall, 29–30
Henry Mountains, 28, 41, 54, 64, 217, 220

ABOUT THE AUTHOR

Jared Farmer was born and raised in Provo, Utah, at the base of Mt. Timpanogos. A graduate of Utah State University and the University of Montana, he has published in the *Western Historical Quarterly*, the *Utah Historical Quarterly*, and the *Journal of the Southwest*. When not in the archives, he loves to play frisbee by alpenglow. His Zion stands with hills surrounded.